Developing Android Applications with Adobe AIR

Véronique Brossier

Beijing · Cambridge · Farnham · Köln · Sebastopol · Tokyo

Developing Android Applications with Adobe AIR

by Véronique Brossier

Copyright © 2011 Véronique Brossier. All rights reserved.
Printed in the United States of America.

Published by O'Reilly Media, Inc., 1005 Gravenstein Highway North, Sebastopol, CA 95472.

O'Reilly books may be purchased for educational, business, or sales promotional use. Online editions are also available for most titles (*http://my.safaribooksonline.com*). For more information, contact our corporate/institutional sales department: (800) 998-9938 or *corporate@oreilly.com*.

Editor:	Mary Treseler	**Indexer:**	John Bickelhaupt
Production Editor:	Kristen Borg	**Cover Designer:**	Karen Montgomery
Copyeditor:	Audrey Doyle	**Interior Designer:**	David Futato
Proofreader:	Kristen Borg	**Illustrator:**	Robert Romano

Printing History:

May 2011:	First Edition.

ISBN: 978-1-449-39482-0

[LSI]

1303315416

A mon père.

A ma mère.

Adobe
Developer
Library

Adobe Developer Library, a copublishing partnership between O'Reilly Media Inc., and Adobe Systems, Inc., is the authoritative resource for developers using Adobe technologies. These comprehensive resources offer learning solutions to help developers create cutting-edge interactive web applications that can reach virtually anyone on any platform.

With top-quality books and innovative online resources covering the latest tools for rich-Internet application development, the *Adobe Developer Library* delivers expert training straight from the source. Topics include ActionScript, Adobe Flex®, Adobe Flash®, and Adobe Acrobat®.

Get the latest news about books, online resources, and more at *http://adobedeveloper library.com*.

Table of Contents

Foreword

Building engaging experiences for stand-alone applications is much harder than it should be. With Adobe AIR, we give developers and designers a tool to turn their ideas into applications quickly and easily. As new mobile platforms emerged, we have extended the reach of our customers by bringing AIR to those platforms. Véronique's book is a great introduction to everything you need to know to use AIR to build some awesome applications, taking advantage of some of the new capabilities available on mobile platforms, like geolocation, touch, and other sensors. Now get coding!

—Arno Gourdol, Director of Engineering, Flash Runtime Foundation

Preface

If you can't explain it simply, you don't understand it
well enough.

—Albert Einstein

The proliferation of the cellular phone has revolutionized the way we connect to the world and communicate with one another. It is the foundation of a mobile lifestyle.

Although the evolution of cell phone technology is progressing thanks to hardware manufacturers and platform engineers, the unveiling of its potential is in the hands of application creators.

Toward that end, Google and the Open Handset Alliance have developed Android, an operating system that runs on many mobile devices. Adobe and the Open Screen Project offer AIR as a development tool for various mobile systems. Both efforts bring some uniformity to this fragmented world.

This book is about developing for the Android platform using Adobe AIR. My goal is to provide in-depth information on the various topics specific to mobile development. My wish is that this book will help you create quality applications.

Audience

This book is for developers. It aims to attract enthusiast coders who are curious about both the technology and the user experience. I try to provide as much background information as possible on all topics, and not just an ActionScript reference guide.

Today is still the beginning of the mobile era, and any one of you is a potential innovator. Your contribution can influence the future of mobile technology.

Assumptions This Book Makes

This book assumes you already have basic to intermediate experience with the Action-Script 3 language. For example, you should know how to create an event listener, understand different data types, and know what a class is. If you need to learn the fundamentals of the language or get a refresher, I recommend *Essential ActionScript 3.0* by Colin Moock (O'Reilly).

I introduce each topic from the ground up. I also provide code samples in snippets so that you can absorb the concept in small steps. Finally, I use pure ActionScript only, and few third-party libraries.

Contents of This Book

This book is divided into four sections:

Chapters 1 through 5 go over the technology, the environment, and the fundamentals of creating and publishing an AIR application.

Chapters 6 through 14 cover functionality-specific topics like multitouch technology, using the accelerometer, using the native camera, geolocation, audio, video, and more.

Chapters 15 through 17 cover some more advanced topics, propose an architecture to manage multiple views, and offer the code for a full application.

Chapters 18 and 19 provide suggestions on best practices for asset management and development.

In addition, this book has a companion website (*http://oreilly.com/catalog/ 9781449394820*) from which you can download code samples that you can compile and install on your mobile device.

Conventions Used in This Book

The following typographical conventions are used in this book:

Italic
> Indicates filenames, file extensions, directory paths, URLs, email addresses, and new terms where they are defined

`Constant width`
> Indicates language and script elements, such as class names, types, namespaces, attributes, methods, variables, keywords, functions, modules, commands, properties, parameters, values, objects, events, XML and HTML tags, and similar elements

`Constant width bold`
> Indicates commands or text to be typed by the user

`Constant width italic`
> Indicates text that should be replaced with user-supplied values

This icon signifies a tip, suggestion, or general note.

 This icon indicates a warning or caution.

Note that I prefer placing curly braces on the same line of code, as I feel this makes the code easier to read in print form and does not use space unnecessarily. I also did away with the convention of private variables with an underscore for the same reason.

I introduce a new API or class in small code segments to illustrate an explanation.

Using Code Examples

This book is here to help you get your job done. In general, you may use the code in this book in your programs and documentation. You do not need to contact us for permission unless you're reproducing a significant portion of the code. For example, writing a program that uses several chunks of code from this book does not require permission. Selling or distributing a CD-ROM of examples from this book does require permission. Answering a question by citing this book and quoting example code does not require permission. Incorporating a significant amount of example code from this book into your product's documentation does require permission.

We appreciate, but do not require, attribution. An attribution usually includes the title, author, publisher, and ISBN. For example: "*Developing Android Applications with Adobe AIR* by Véronique Brossier. Copyright 2011 Véronique Brossier, 978-1-44939-482-0."

If you feel your use of code examples falls outside fair use or the permission given here, feel free to contact us at *permissions@oreilly.com*.

We'd Like to Hear from You

Please address comments and questions concerning this book to the publisher:

O'Reilly Media, Inc.
1005 Gravenstein Highway North
Sebastopol, CA 95472
(800) 998-9938 (in the United States or Canada)
(707) 829-0515 (international or local)
(707) 829-0104 (fax)

We have a web page for this book, where we list errata, examples, and any additional information. You can access this page at:

http://www.oreilly.com/catalog/9781449394820

To comment or ask technical questions about this book, send email to:

bookquestions@oreilly.com

For more information about our books, courses, conferences, and news, see our website at *http://www.oreilly.com*.

Find us on Facebook: *http://facebook.com/oreilly*

Follow us on Twitter: *http://twitter.com/oreillymedia*

Watch us on YouTube: *http://www.youtube.com/oreillymedia*

Safari® Books Online

Safari Books Online is an on-demand digital library that lets you easily search over 7,500 technology and creative reference books and videos to find the answers you need quickly.

With a subscription, you can read any page and watch any video from our library online. Read books on your cell phone and mobile devices. Access new titles before they are available for print, get exclusive access to manuscripts in development, and post feedback for the authors. Copy and paste code samples, organize your favorites, download chapters, bookmark key sections, create notes, print out pages, and benefit from tons of other time-saving features.

O'Reilly Media has uploaded this book to the Safari Books Online service. To have full digital access to this book and others on similar topics from O'Reilly and other publishers, sign up for free at *http://my.safaribooksonline.com*.

Acknowledgments

Thank you to Arno Gourdol, Director of Engineering, Flash Runtime Foundation, and to the AIR team for their hard work and responsiveness during the prerelease of this product (in particular, Mohit Arora, Syed Mohd Mehadi, Romil Mittal, and Ashutosh Jagdish Sharma). I would like to express my appreciation to Joe Ward, who did a stellar job of providing answers and documentation on all aspects of the technology.

I would like to acknowledge all my fellow developers on the AIR for Android prerelease list, in particular, Jyunpei Furukawa and Pascal Sahuc.

Thanks to O'Reilly editor Mary Treseler, copyeditor Audrey Doyle, production editor Kristen Borg, and illustrator Robert Romano. Thank you to the O'Reilly technical reviewers: Tom Barker, Rich Tretola, Matthew David, Chris Griffith, and a special thank to Kevin Bahadoor.

In addition to the O'Reilly technical editors, I asked friends and professional acquaintances to review parts of this book. They each read a single chapter based on their expertise; several generous souls reviewed more than one.

Thank you to Francois Balmelle, David Cameron, Danny Durra, Renaun Erickson, Judah Frangipane, Ben Garney, Colin Holgate, Alexandre Houdent, Kevin Hoyt, Lisa Larson-Kelley, Elliot Mebane, Doug McCune, André Michelle, Keith Peters, Brian Rinaldi, Michael Thornburgh, and Edwin Van Rijkom.

Thank you to Grant Garrett for letting me use the Influxis services to test my video applications, to Jonathan Bryski for the walk cycle drawing, and to Pier Borra at MTVNetworks for the sabbatical to jumpstart the writing process.

Merci to Thibault Imbert for his contagious enthusiasm when I first considered writing a book. Thank you to Rich Shupe for sharing his experience as an author and his great sense of humor.

I would like to express my gratitude to Mike Chambers and Colin Moock for helping me at some point along the way in an industry where being a woman often means being invisible.

Thank you to Satyen Mehta, my partner, for his patience and great support (he addresses me as The Jacqueline Cousteau of Flash), and for cooking me many delicious meals while I was writing.

CMB's gentle presence and entertaining behavior released a lot of my stress while I was working at night. I am sorry that a *Mesocricetus auratus* didn't make the cover of this book.

CHAPTER 1

AIR

Intelligence is the faculty of making artificial objects,
especially tools to make tools.

—Henri Bergson

Adobe Integrated Runtime (AIR), initially code-named Apollo, was created in 2007 as an environment for building Rich Internet Applications (RIAs) running outside the browser while benefiting from desktop features. With AIR, developers can write desktop software using ActionScript, HTML, or JavaScript for the Windows, Macintosh, and Linux platforms. Each application is installed as a standalone client application; its proper execution requires that the AIR runtime be installed in the environment. Figure 1-1 shows the Apollo and AIR logos.

Figure 1-1. Apollo and AIR logos

AIR version 2.5 focused on mobile development and introduced new features such as geolocation capability, accelerometer capability, and multitouch inputs. AIR is targeted at smartphones as well as tablet computers and netbooks.

AIR 2.5 and later supports the Android platform. Android is an operating system based on the open source Linux platform. It was initially developed by Google, and was further expanded by the Open Handset Alliance for use with mobile devices. Android runs applications developed using the Java programming language and packaged as an Android Package (APK) file.

Adobe adapted AIR as a tool for ActionScript programmers to make Android applications. HTML/Ajax mobile development is not available for AIR for Android.

The purpose of this book is to teach you everything you need to know—and more—to develop AIR applications for the Android platform.

Beyond Android, the Adobe Open Screen Project has brought AIR to RIM for BlackBerry, and is committed to bringing it to other partners in the future. For more information on the Open Screen Project, go to *http://www.openscreenproject.org/*.

The premise of this effort is to offer a uniform tool for a fragmented mobile world. One could hope that AIR will be to mobile development what Flash Player is to the Internet. It enables ease of development and distribution of applications across platforms and browsers.

Installing the Adobe Development Tools

The Adobe development tools come in several forms: Flash Professional CS5.5 and Flash Builder 4.5. They support Android OS 2.2 (named Froyo) and later, as well as devices with an ARMv7 or higher processor. AIR for Android does not work with earlier versions of the Android system.

Flash Professional CS5.5

The latest version of Flash Professional comes with the AIR for Android extension bundled. No separate download or additional installation is needed. When you launch CS5.5 and select File→New, you will see an AIR for Android option under the General tab or an AIR for Android category under Templates.

Flash Builder 4.5

Burrito is the code name for the new version of Flash Builder, in public beta at the time of this writing. You can download Burrito from the Adobe Labs website at *http://labs .adobe.com/technologies/flashbuilder_burrito/*.

Burrito has templates for Flex Mobile and ActionScript Mobile projects.

Both products, Flash Professional and Flash Builder, include the AIR SDK and tools to automate deployment to devices. We will build our first AIR for Android application in Chapter 2.

Installing the AIR Runtime on an Android Device

The AIR runtime stores the native AS classes which an Android application can reference. It is invoked by your application when it launches. It only needs to be installed on the device once and is shared by all AIR applications.

The AIR runtime is the C/C++ implementation of the Flash engine, rendering engine, and virtual machine.

The AIR runtime comes installed on some new Android devices, but not all. As with all applications installed on an Android device, the AIR runtime is packaged as an APK file. If you do not have Adobe AIR yet, search for it in the Android Market application on your device, download it, and install it. You will need it in the next chapter.

Future AIR updates will also be deployed via the Android Market to adapt to Android evolution. For instance, the AIR 2.6 runtime became available in February 2011 to run on Android 2.2 (Froyo), Android 2.3 (Gingerbread), and Android 3.0 (Honeycomb). It provides new features and performance improvements.

Using AIR on Android creates an additional layer on top of the platform, and communicates with it. You do not need to know the inner workings of this process, but being familiar with the Android system may be helpful. Chapter 3 will go over some of that.

What Is in the AIR SDK

The AIR SDK is the set of tools used to package and deploy your AIR application. It comes bundled in the tools, so no additional installation is needed. The tools take care of accessing these files without any development on your part.

The AIR SDK consists of the following:

AIR Developer Tool (ADT)
> ADT is a multipurpose tool written in Java. It requires Java 1.5 or later, and is used to package the AIR application for Android devices. It creates a different package based on the target defined: *apk* for distribution, *apk-emulator* for the emulator, or *apk-debug* to debug locally or on the device. ADT creates the self-signed digital code certificate used to sign the application with an option to expand the validity period to conform to Android specifications. It installs, uninstalls, and launches the application on the Android device.
>
> The ADT tool is called *adt* or *adt.bat* and is located in the *bin* folder. *adt.jar* is the executable file called by *adt* or *adt.bat* and is located in the *lib* folder.

AIR Debug Launcher (ADL)
> ADL is used to test your AIR application during development without packaging it. It uses the runtime included in the SDK, and prints trace statements and runtime errors. It is also used to start a Flash Debugger (FDB) session.
>
> The ADL tool is called *adl* or *adl.exe* and is located in the *bin* folder.

AIR runtime

    The AIR runtime is used to launch and test your application during the development and debugging process, before you install the application on the device. It contains the emulator and device versions for both desktop and Android devices.

    The AIR runtime is called *Runtime.apk* and is located in the *runtimes* folder.

Frameworks

    The *Frameworks* directory includes all the AIR core libraries.

Adobe recently made available some documentation on using the command-line tool for ADT. We will cover these commands in Chapter 3. If you need an explanation or a refresher on using the command-line tool, please refer to "Using the Command-Line Tool" on page 27 in Chapter 3.

New ActionScript Libraries

Many libraries were added to AIR 2.5 with a specific focus on mobile development. We will cover all of them in detail in the chapters to come. Here is a list of the new functionality and APIs, and the chapters in which they are discussed:

Chapter 2, *Call Me, Text Me*

- AIR application debugging on Android
- Simulation on the desktop
- URI schemes to invoke native Android applications

Chapter 4, *Permissions, Certificates, and Installation*

- Application icons
- Certificate validity
- Application permissions
- Application versioning

Chapter 5, *Evaluating Device Capabilities and Handling Multiple Devices*

- Screen orientation API
- System idle detection and overwrite
- New soft keys to register for keyboard events on the Android device
- Virtual keyboard

Chapter 7, *Multitouch Technology*

- Gestures
- Multitouch capability

Chapter 8, *Accelerometer*

- Accelerometer

Chapter 9, *Camera*

- Access to the device's camera application
- Access to the device's media library

Chapter 10, *Geolocation*

- Geolocation

Chapter 11, *Microphone and Audio*

- Access to the device's microphone

Chapter 12, *Video*

- Camera video capture

Chapter 13, *StageWebView*

- StageWebView, used to render HTML content inside mobile AIR applications
- NetworkInfo

Chapter 14, *Hardware Acceleration*

- OpenGL ES 2 and hardware acceleration

Functionalities Not Yet Supported

Some features are not yet supported in AIR at the time of this writing, while others may not be planned as part of future releases. For instance, some APIs and features that are missing from AIR include those for activating the phone's vibrate function via AIR, accessing the native Android contact list, creating Android intents, messaging to the status/notification bar, enabling one AIR application to open another, and creating widgets.

If you would like a specific feature added to AIR, send a request to Adobe at *https:// www.adobe.com/cfusion/mmform/index.cfm?name=wishform*.

AIR on the Desktop Versus AIR on Android

If you want to convert an existing AIR desktop application to Android, you must make a few changes:

- If you are using Flash Builder, the `WindowedApplication` application MXML tag needs to be changed to `ViewNavigatorApplication`. `WindowedApplication` assumes there is a `NativeWindow`, which is not the case on Android.
- In the `Application` descriptor, the namespace must be 2.6 or later and the `visible` tag must be set to `true`.
- The AIR SDK packaging command must use `apk` as the target.

The following desktop functionalities are not supported on Android:

ActionScript 2, ContextMenu, DatagramSocket, Dockicon, EncryptedLocalStore, HTMLoader, LocalConnection, NativeMenu, NativeWindow, PrintJob, Secure-Socket, ServerSocket, StorageVolumeInfo, SystemTrayIcon, Updater, XMLSigna-tureValidator

Mobile Flash Player 10.1 Versus AIR 2.6 on Android

The Flash Player, version 10.1, first became available in Android 2.2 in June 2010. It runs within the device's native browser. Developing applications for the mobile browser is beyond the scope of this book. However, understanding the similarities and differences between the two environments is important, especially if mobile development is new to you.

- Both types of applications are cross-platform rich media applications. They both use the ActionScript language, but AIR for Android only supports ActionScript 3.
- Both benefit from recent performance and optimization improvements, such as hardware acceleration for graphics and video, bitmap manipulation, battery and CPU optimization, better memory utilization, and scripting optimization.
- Applications running in the Flash Player browser plug-in are typically located on a website and do not require installation. They rely on the Flash plug-in. AIR applications require packaging, certificates, and installation on the device. They rely on the AIR runtime.
- Flash Player is subject to the browser sandbox and its restricted environment. The browser security is high because applications may come from many unknown websites. Persistent data is stored in the Flash Local Shared Object, but there is no access to the filesystem. AIR applications function as native applications and have access to local storage and system files. Persistent data may be stored in a local database. The user is informed upon installation of what data the application has access to via a list of permissions.
- AIR has additional functionality unique to mobile devices, such as geolocation, accelerometer capability, and access to the camera.

We will build our first application in the next chapter.

CHAPTER 2

Call Me, Text Me

What we have to learn to do, we learn by doing.

—Aristotle

In this chapter we will build an application to make a phone call, send a text message, and send an email. The first two tasks can only be done from a mobile phone. We will go through the process of creating the AIR application, packaging it as an Android application, and installing it on an Android device. We will then test it and debug it.

If you skipped Chapter 1, go back and follow the instructions to install the AIR runtime on your device from the Android Market.

Development, packaging, and debugging can all be done using Flash Professional CS5.5 or Flash Builder 4.5 (code named Burrito), available in the Adobe labs at the time of this writing. All tools come bundled with the Android Debug Bridge (ADB) used to run and install applications on an Android device.

 For the rest of the book, we will refer to Flash Professional CS5.5 as just Flash Professional. In addition, we will refer to Flash Builder 4.5 as just Flash Builder.

If you prefer to use other Adobe tools or third-party applications, we will cover some options in the section "Other Tools" on page 16.

Let's get started.

Setting Up Your Device

To set up your Android device, first select Settings→Applications→Development→USB debugging to initiate development mode on your device. On some devices, such as the Samsung Galaxy Tab, you need to set this first before plugging the device into your development computer; otherwise, the selection is grayed out. When your device is in debug mode, a bug-looking icon appears in the upper-left corner.

Select Settings→Applications→Development→Stay awake to prevent the screen from going to sleep while you are working and testing.

Plug your device into the USB port of your development computer. When your device is connected via USB, a fork-shaped icon appears in the upper-left corner. Figure 2-1 shows the bug and fork icons in the upper-left corner of the screen.

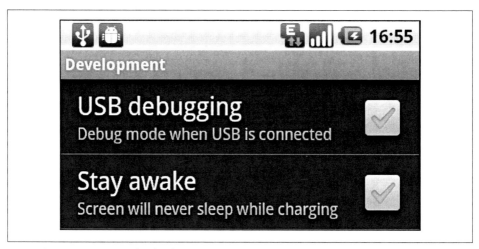

Figure 2-1. Device settings for development

Creating a Project

This section will take you through the process of creating the project step by step.

Using Flash Professional

Launch Flash Professional, create an AIR for Android template, and call it *first.fla*. The movie has a frame rate of 24 fps and a stage size of 480 by 800 pixels. At first, this dimension may seem large for a small device. Chapter 5, which covers screen resolution, will clarify this point.

Create the movie's document class by opening the Properties panel and clicking on the pencil icon to the right of the Class field. Leave the default selection at Flash Professional and enter the class name **Main**.

Using Flash Builder

When using Flash Builder, two mobile options are offered. Go to File→New→Flex Mobile Project or File→New→ActionScript Mobile Project. Use Flex Mobile if you want to use the Flex framework. Use ActionScript Mobile for pure ActionScript only. For our application, choose the latter. Give it a project name of **first**. Leave the setting as the default SDK, and click Next.

Creating the Application Descriptor

The application descriptor is an external XML file that is bundled with your *.swf* file during packaging. The application descriptor file is generated automatically, but you can modify the default settings.

The application descriptor contains the application's settings, such as its screen orientation. It also includes selected permissions. Permissions are set for some specific device functionality, such as GPS. We will review the application descriptor document in detail in Chapter 4.

Using Flash Professional

To edit the application descriptor in Flash Professional, follow these steps:

1. From the IDE, go to File→AIR Android settings.
2. Under the General tab, keep Portrait selected under Aspect Ratio, and then select "Full screen".
3. Under the Permissions tab, select Internet.
4. Click OK.

Using Flash Builder

To edit the application descriptor in Flash Builder, follow these steps:

1. Under Mobile Settings→Target platforms, select Google Android.
2. Under Permissions, select Internet.
3. Under Application Settings, select Full Screen and deselect "Automatically reorient".
4. Select Next.

5. Change the Main application file to *Main.as*.

6. Click Finish.

Writing the Code

For this exercise, we will draw three clickable sprites: one to make a phone call, one to send a text message, and one to send an email. Figure 2-2 shows our application and three native applications launched upon interactivity.

Figure 2-2. Left to right: our application with three buttons—one for calling, one for texting, and one for emailing—and the native applications launched based on the various choices

An AIR application cannot call, send a text message, or send an email directly, but it can invoke the native applications dedicated to these tasks and pass arguments such as the phone number or email address.

> The URI scheme is a way to include small data items inline. AIR passes the argument to the Android system according to the official `tel`, `sms`, and `email` URI schemes. If the argument contains invalid characters or spaces, the command will be ignored. Valid characters are digits, dots, and the plus sign (+). Android currently does not support multiple numbers or a body argument for a text message, but it does support multiple emails and a body argument for an email.
>
> If more than one application has a custom URI, the choices are represented in a menu. This is the case with `mailto`, as demonstrated in Figure 2-2, with both native email and Gmail applications.

Note that a mouse event works on a multitouch device as though it were a single-touch device.

Using Flash Professional

If you are using Flash Professional, add the following code to the Document class named Main, created earlier:

```
package  {
    import flash.display.Sprite;
    import flash.events.MouseEvent;
    import flash.net.URLRequest;
    import flash.net.navigateToURL;

    public class Main extends Sprite {

        public function Main() {
            // create the three sprites and their listeners
            var callButton:Sprite = createSprite(0xFF3300, 140, 150);
            callButton.addEventListener(MouseEvent.CLICK, callMe);
            addChild(callButton);

            var textButton:Sprite = createSprite(0x0099FF, 140, 350);
            textButton.addEventListener(MouseEvent.CLICK, textMe);
            addChild(textButton);

            var mailButton:Sprite = createSprite(0x00FF11, 140, 550);
            mailButton.addEventListener(MouseEvent.CLICK, mailMe);
            addChild(mailButton);
        }

        function createSprite(hue:int, xPos:int, yPos:int):Sprite {
            var temp:Sprite = new Sprite();
            temp.graphics.beginFill(hue, 1);
            temp.graphics.drawRect(0, 0, 200, 100);
            temp.graphics.endFill();
            temp.x = xPos;
            temp.y = yPos;
            return temp;
        }

        function callMe(event:MouseEvent):void {
            trace("calling");
            navigateToURL(new URLRequest('tel:18005551212'));
        }

        function textMe(event:MouseEvent):void {
            trace("texting");
            navigateToURL(new URLRequest('sms:18005551212'));
        }

        function mailMe(event:MouseEvent):void {
            trace("emailing");
            navigateToURL(new URLRequest
            ('mailto:veronique@somewhere.com?subject=Hello&body=World'));
        }
    }
}
```

Select Control→Test Movie→Test to compile the application. You should always run your code on the desktop before installing it on a device in case you have syntax errors.

Using Flash Builder

The code is the same.

Select the small black arrow to the right of the Run button, and then select Run Configurations. Under Mobile Application, select Main if it is not selected. The "Target platform" should be Google Android. Under "Launch method", select "On desktop" and choose your device from the pull-down menu. Click Run to compile and create the mobile application. If you don't see your device listed, you can add it manually.

 For Windows users, if you see the name of your device in the list, it indicates that the necessary drivers are preinstalled. Otherwise, make sure to install them.

Packaging Your Application As an APK File and Installing It on the Device

Let's go over the process of packaging and installing your application on the device.

Using Flash Professional

To package the application as an APK file in Flash Professional and install it on the Android device, follow these steps:

1. Go to File→AIR Android settings.
2. Under the Deployment tab, do the following:
    a. For the Certificate, select your AIR code-signing certificate if you already have one. To create a temporary one, click Create and fill out the form. At this stage, the only important field to remember is the password because you will need to enter it again shortly. We will discuss what a certificate is in Chapter 4.
    b. For the Android deployment type, choose "Device release".
    c. Under the "After publishing" section, select both "Install application on the connected Android device" and "Launch application on the connected Android device".
3. Select File→Publish. At this point, an APK file is created, which you can see on your computer. The APK file is installed on your device, and the device launches the application.

Using Flash Builder

To package the application as an APK file in Flash Builder and install it on the Android device, follow these steps:

1. Right-click on your project folder and select Properties.

2. Select ActionScript Build Packaging→Google Android→Digital Signature→Certificate. Select your AIR code-signing certificate if you already have one. To create a temporary one, click Create and fill out the form. At this stage, the only important field to remember is the password because you will need to enter it again shortly. Click OK.

3. Go back to Run Configurations. Under the launch method, select "On device" and then click Run. At this point, an APK file is created, which you can see in your project. The APK file is installed on your device, and the device launches the application.

 If this is the first time you are launching an AIR application on your device, the Adobe AIR license agreement will appear. You only need to agree to the terms once.

If you are familiar with developing AIR applications on the desktop, you may have noticed a difference here. The warning dialog does not appear on the device upon installation. Instead, Android displays the list of permissions your application subscribed to.

Testing and Debugging

The Adobe remote debugging session uses either USB (recommended) or WiFi, hence our Internet permission setup earlier.

For networking, turn on WiFi on the device and connect it to the same wireless network as your development computer under Settings→Wireless & Networks→Wi-Fi. If you are on Windows, make sure you disable your firewall (port 7935 must be open).

Using Flash Professional

To test and debug in Flash Professional, follow these steps:

1. Select File→AIR Android settings.

2. Under the Deployment tab, for "Android deployment type", choose Debug (see Figure 2-3).

3. Start a debug session by selecting Debug→Begin Remote Debug Session→ActionScript 3.0. Launch the application on the device.

If you are debugging using WiFi, when you are prompted for a hostname or IP address, enter it. On Windows, you can obtain this information by typing **ipconfig** at the command prompt. On the Mac, click on the WiFi icon and select Open Network Preferences; if you are using the Terminal window, type **ifconfig** and look for the address at the beginning of the line starting with "inet".

When the session starts, you should see "Waiting for Player to connect..."

Now launch your application. You should see "Remote Flash Player: app:/first.swf".

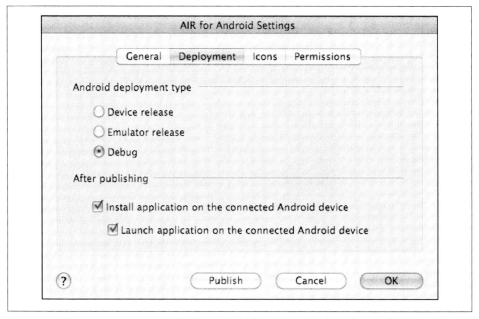

Figure 2-3. The Deployment tab of AIR for Android Settings on Flash Professional

Using Flash Builder

To test and debug in Flash Builder, click the Debug button at the top of the screen. When you click on the button you should see the trace statements in your Console window (see Figure 2-4).

In addition to traces in the output window, you get breakpoint control, the ability to step through code, and variable monitoring.

 There is a known issue with debugging not working the first time after installation on the device. Force-stop your application on the device and launch it again. This bug should be fixed in a future release.

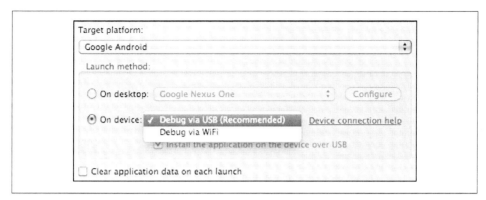

Figure 2-4. The Debug Settings option in Flash Builder

Mobile Utility Applications

Several mobile utility applications are available for AIR developers.

Launchpad

As its name indicates, this Adobe Labs beta tool gives Flex developers a head start in creating AIR desktop and mobile applications. Launchpad is an AIR application that generates a complete Flex project that is ready to import to Flash Builder.

The process consists of four steps. The Settings option is for the application descriptor and permissions. The Configuration option is for setting up listeners of various events, such as the application moving to the background. The Samples option is for importing sample code for the APIs, such as Geolocation or Microphone. The Generate option creates a ZIP file at the location of your choice, ready to be imported. Sample icons and assets are automatically included based on your selection.

For more information on Launchpad, go to *http://labs.adobe.com/technologies/air launchpad/*.

Device Central CS5

Adobe Device Central is not available for AIR development. At the time of this writing, it is targeted at Flash Player development only. It provides useful tools such as accelerometer simulation that can otherwise only be tested on the device. ADL provides some, albeit more limited, functionality. It can simulate soft keys and device rotation.

Package Assistant Pro

Serge Jespers, from Adobe, wrote an AIR application that facilitates the packaging of AIR applications for Android. You can download the Mac OS X and Windows versions from *http://www.webkitchen.be/package-assistant-pro/*. Note that you need the *.swf* file, the application descriptor file, and the code-signing certificate.

The packager preferences store the location of the AIR SDK *adt.jar* (located in *AIRsdk/ lib/*) and your code-signing certificate. The packaging process consists of a few easy steps, all accomplished via a user interface. Browse to select the required files, enter your certificate password, and choose a name for the APK file. You can choose to compile a device release or a debug version.

This tool is convenient if you use one of the tools we will discuss next, and is a nice GUI alternative to using the command-line tool.

De MonsterDebugger

De MonsterDebugger is an open source debugger for Flash, Flex, and AIR. Version 3.0 provides the ability to debug applications running on your device and send the output straight to an AIR desktop application. It lets you manipulate values, execute methods, and browse the display list. For more information, go to *http://demonsterdebugger.com/*.

Installing AIR on an Android Device via a Server

To install an AIR application via a server, on the Android device select Settings→Applications→Unknown Sources on the Android device.

Your server MIME type needs to be edited. The MIME media type for *.apk* is *application/vnd.android/package-archive*.

Upload the APK package to your web server. Open the native web browser on the device and enter the package URL. The device will download and install the application automatically. This may be useful if you want to make the application available to several members of a development team for testing purposes.

Other Tools

Developing AIR for Android is not limited to the tools mentioned so far. You can use a range of other products, but you need to manually install the SDKs and use the command-line tool. Please refer to the links provided for more information on how to use them.

The Android SDK provides great mobile tooling, which we will cover in Chapter 3. It is particularly valuable if you want to learn more about native processes while you are testing your application.

The Android SDK is used to install the application on the device. Refer to Chapter 3 for further instructions.

The AIR 2.6 SDK is used to package and deploy AIR applications for Android. For more information, go to *http://www.adobe.com/products/air/sdk/*.

In all of the following development environments, you need to "overlay" the AIR SDK. Links are provided for instructions:

- The free Flex and AIR SDK uses the Flex amxmlc compiler and AIR command-line tools. See *http://opensource.adobe.com/wiki/display/site/Home*.
- Power Flasher sells FDT, a development environment for ActionScript 3 and MXML, and offers the open source SOSmax, a socket output utility for debugging. See *http://fdt.powerflasher.com/docs/Community_Resources#Multiscreen:_Targeting_Mobile_Devices*.
- Flash Develop is an open source code editor for Windows. See *http://www.flashdevelop.org/community/viewtopic.php?f=9&t=8079&p=37453&hilit=AIR#p37453*.
- JetBrains sells IntelliJ IDEA, a cross-platform editor particularly favored by Java developers. See *http://www.jetbrains.com/idea/whatsnew/index.html*.

When you use a tool other than Flash Professional or Flash Builder, you need to manually create the application descriptor. It is not generated automatically, and it must be packaged along with your application. Here is the code for creating the application descriptor:

```
<application xmlns="http://ns.adobe.com/air/application/2.6">
<?xml version="1.0" encoding="utf-8" standalone="no"?>
<application xmlns="http://ns.adobe.com/air/application/2.6">
    <id>first</id>
    <filename>first</filename>
    <versionNumber>1.0.0</versionNumber>
    <initialWindow>
        <content>first.swf</content>
        <visible>true</visible>
        <fullScreen>true</fullScreen>
    </initialWindow>
    <supportedProfiles>mobileDevice</supportedProfiles>
<android>
    <manifestAdditions><![CDATA[
    <manifest android:installLocation="auto">
        <uses-permission android:name="android.permission.INTERNET"/>
    </manifest>
]]></manifestAdditions>
  </android>
</application>
```

You need a code-signing certificate. If you do not have one, you can create a self-signed certificate with the AIR ADT `-certificate` command. The instructions are available online at *http://help.adobe.com/en_US/air/build/WS5b3ccc516d4fbf351e63e3d118666ade46-7f74.html*.

To package the AIR application as an APK file, run the AIR Developer Tool (ADT) from the command line:

```
AIR-sdk-path/bin/adt -package -target apk -storetype pkcs12
-keystore yourCertificate.p12 first.apk Main-app.xml first.swf
```

To install it on the device, use the Android ADB tool:

```
android-sdk-path/tools/adb install first.apk
```

If the application is already on your device, use the -r command (for reinstall):

```
android-sdk-path/tools/adb install -r first.apk
```

Conclusion

Congratulations, you have just created and tested your first application. You can expand on it and make it more dynamic by requesting the user to enter a phone number. To do so, provide an input text field, or create a custom-designed numeric UI.

CHAPTER 3

Android

*Anyone can build a fast CPU. The trick
is to build a fast system.*

—Seymour Cray

Android is a mobile operating system initially created by Android Inc., and based on the open source Linux kernel. Linux, created in 1991 by Linus Torvalds, is still one of the most significant examples of open source software ever available.

Google acquired Android Inc., in 2005, and along with other members of the Open Handset Alliance, developed and released Android in 2007. The Android Open Source Project (AOSP) now maintains and expands the Android system. Figure 3-1 shows the Android logo.

Android includes an operating system, middleware, and some key applications. It is designed to be optimal for use in the mobile environment, and is flexible and upgradeable. The most recent versions at the time of this writing are Android 2.3 (called Gingerbread, released in fall 2010), and Android 3.0 (called Honeycomb, released at the beginning of 2011).

Android penetration on mobile devices is rapidly expanding. More information on Android is available at *http://www.tbray.org/ongoing/When/201x/2010/11/14/What-An droid-Is*.

Early feedback on developing applications for Android was not very positive. The system was buggy, there was no bug tracking in place, and very little documentation was available. Nowadays, developing for this system has greatly improved. A public issue tracker is available and an active community has grown (see *http://source.android .com/* and *http://developer.android.com/index.html*). The Android framework enables the reuse and replacement of components. As an AIR developer, you can read these forums to stay informed on system development and native functionality. An additional forum is also maintained on the Adobe site for specific questions regarding AIR for Android: *http://forums.adobe.com/community/air/development/android*.

Figure 3-1. The Android logo

Android Software Development Kit

Android provides great mobile tooling for Java developers to use along with Eclipse or similar editors to write native applications. We will go over some of the tools and how you may want to use them as an AIR developer. But first, let's install the SDK.

Installing the Android SDK

Before we begin, make sure you are running in administrator mode so that you have all the needed permissions and access.

The Android SDK requires Java 1.6 or later, which you can obtain at *http://www.java .com/en/download* or *http://www.oracle.com/technetwork/java/javase/downloads/index .html*. You can download the SDK for Windows, Mac OS (Intel), or Linux at *http:// developer.android.com/sdk/index.html*. The Android SDK only contains the minimum tools to start with. Use the SDK Manager to install or update components.

The SDK directory has different names depending on its version and your platform. It may be named something like *android-sdk_r08-mac.zip* or *android-sdk_r08-win-dows.zip*. For the sake of simplicity, rename it to *androidSDK*. We will use this name to refer to the SDK folder for the rest of the chapter.

Check that you have an Internet connection and an open terminal (or a command prompt on Windows), and enter the following command. If you are not familiar with using the command line, refer to "Using the Command-Line Tool" on page 27, which covers this topic:

```
androidSDK/platform-tools/android update sdk
```

You need Android SDK Tools, revision 6 or later, which might already be installed by default. Click the Settings button and check the "Force https" box; then select the boxes to download SDK Platform Android 2.2, API 8, revision 2. You will need these files in order to use the emulator.

Unfortunately, installation steps change as the SDK evolves. For instance, the *tools* directory in revision 6 was renamed *platform-tools* in revision 8. In addition, version 8 on Windows does not detect the Java Runtime Environment (JRE) and requests that you also install the Java SE JDK (the standard 32-bit version only; the Android SDK does not detect the Java runtime in the 64-bit version). There are other issues with the Windows Android SDK installer on Windows 64-bit machines as well. Please read the documentation to successfully install the SDK for your environment.

On Windows, most Android devices require drivers to communicate with the Android SDK. Instructions for installing these drivers are available on the Android developer website at *http://developer.android.com/sdk/win-usb.html*. If you have difficulty updating Google's USB driver package, try to manually edit the *android_winusb.inf* file in the Android SDK.

Alternatively, with the SDK open, go to Available Packages, select "USB Driver package, revision 3", and click Install Selected. Note that the location of the packages may change with new upgrades. For instance, in newer versions, the packages can be found under Available Packages→Third party add-ons→Google USB driver package, revision 4.

Note that with AIR 2.6, Adobe made the process much easier by bundling the Android USB drivers for most Android devices on Windows.

We will use what is inside the *tools* folder.

If you don't know how to use the command line, read the section "Using the Command-Line Tool" on page 27.

Installing the Android Debug Bridge

ADB is composed of a client that consists of your application, a daemon running on the device or emulator, and a server which runs in the background on your development machine and manages the communication between the client and the daemon. You can read more about it at *http://developer.android.com/guide/developing/tools/adb.html*.

To install an Android application using ADB, type the following at the command prompt:

```
androidSDK/platform-tools/adb install hello.apk
```

To install ADB in debug mode or for the emulator, provide a destination:

```
androidSDK/platform-tools/adb -d install hello.apk
androidSDK/platform-tools /adb -e install hello.apk
```

Let's look at how to test and debug using ADB.

Detecting Your Device

Connect your device to your computer's USB port. Turn on USB storage when prompted, or by exposing the option from the top slide-down menu. Set your device for development by turning on USB debugging under Settings→Application→Development.

In the Terminal window on the Mac, or at the command prompt on Windows, type the following to determine whether the SDK sees your device:

```
androidSDK/platform-tools/adb devices
```

If the SDK detects your device, it will return the ID for it as follows:

```
List of devices attached
HT019P805406    device
```

If it does not detect your device, kill the ADB server and restart it:

```
androidSDK/platform-tools/adb kill-server
androidSDK/platform-tools/adb start-server
```

If all else fails, restart your computer. Once your device is detected, you can start using some of the Android tools.

Using the Dalvik Debug Monitor

You can use the Android Dalvik Debug Monitor (DDM) to test the Android application on your desktop. To launch the GUI, navigate to the *ddms* file under Android→Tools→ddms (ddms.bat on Windows) and double-click it.

You can take device screenshots from live running applications at your device's resolution, which is very handy for documentation. On the console, select Device→Screen Capture. Click Refresh every time you want to see an update of your device screen. The images are recorded at your device screen's resolution.

Selecting Device→File Explorer exposes some of the device's nonprivate file structure, as well as options to pull, push, or delete files on the device.

DDM handles a range of other tasks as well, such as log dumps, thread views, phone call simulation, and memory and performance profiling. You can read more about it at *http://developer.android.com/guide/developing/tools/ddms.html*.

Using the logcat Command

The ADB `logcat` command provides a mechanism for grabbing information from the device and dumping it via USB onto a log screen. Use it to view ActionScript traces and potential errors. More information on this command is available at *http://developer .android.com/guide/developing/tools/adb.html*.

Reading the logs is a great way to learn about the Android OS, which components are involved, and how various requests are managed.

Type the following at the command line:

```
androidSDK/platform-tools/adb logcat
```

If you have the emulator on and the device connected, you can choose the debugging destination:

```
androidSDK/platform-tools/adb -e logcat
androidSDK/platform-tools/adb -d logcat
```

You should now see traces along with native messages. If you use the example from Chapter 2, click the button to send email, send text, or make a phone call to see the trace messages.

Android provides a message filtering system using priority levels from Verbose to Silent. To print messages for the running AIR application alone at all levels of priority, use the following command (replace *applicationID* with your application name as defined in the application descriptor):

```
adb logcat air.applicationID:V *:S
```

To print messages from the currently running AIR application as well as the Activity Manager, use the following:

```
adb logcat air.applicationID:V ActivityManager:| *:S
```

I prefer a simpler approach to only display trace statements and AS error messages. I restrict `logcat` to only print messages with the string `I.air`, as in this command:

```
androidSDK/platform-tools/adb logcat|grep "I.air"
```

or this command:

```
androidSDK/platform-tools/adb logcat|grep "hello" application name
```

During the packaging process, each AIR application has the word *air* added to its `applicationID`. Therefore, using the filter `I.air` guarantees to dump all messages for the currently running AIR application. *I* stands for the *Information* priority level. This level does not display native errors but does display AS error messages.

To clear your Terminal window, on the Mac select Terminal→View→Clear Scrollback. On Windows, type **C:\>cls** at the command prompt.

Before starting a new debug process, clear the logcat buffer:

```
androidSDK/platform-tools/adb logcat -c
```

Accessing the device's filesystem

The Android ADB gives access to some of the device's filesystem. Try this command to display all the applications installed on the device:

```
androidSDK/platform-tools/adb shell pm list packages
```

Using the Virtual Device Manager and Emulator

If you do not have an Android device, use the Runtime emulator to simulate one and test your application. Keep in mind that the Runtime emulator is very slow for both AIR and Android applications, so you should not consider its performance to be an accurate benchmark of how applications will perform on actual devices. The Runtime emulator is located at AIRSDK→Runtimes→AIR→Android→Emulator→Runtime.apk.

First, compile your application for the emulator:

```
androidSDK/bin/adt -package -target apk-debug -storetype pkcs12
-keystore yourCertificate.p12 hello.apk Main-app.xml Main.swf
```

Install the emulator version of the AIR runtime on the emulator:

```
androidSDK/platform-tools/adb -e install AIR-sdk-path/RuntimeEmulator.apk
```

A successful installation displays a message similar to this one:

```
1713 KB/s (6617672 bytes in 3.771s)
pkg: /data/local/tmp/Runtime_Emulator.apk
Success
```

Install the Android Package (APK) file using -e, for *emulator*, as a destination:

```
androidSDK/platform-tools/adb -e install hello.apk
```

Launch the AVD Manager application: on the Mac, select Android SDK→Tools→Android; on Windows, select Android SDK→SDK Setup.exe.

Create an Android Virtual Device (AVD), an emulator, using the AVD Manager application. Select the Virtual Devices option and click New. Give the device a name and select the target API: Android 2.2, API level 8 (if you don't see that option, you need to install the API; go back to Chapter 2 for instructions). The size of the SD card and Skin is optional. Click Create AVD.

Click Start to launch the emulator. The virtual device has a panel on the left representing the face of your device, a group of buttons for all input on the top right, and a keyboard on the bottom right.

Repackage your application with the emulator as a target. In Flash Professional, select File→AIR Android settings→Deployment→Emulator release. When using Flash Builder, enter the following command:

```
androidSDK/bin/adt -package -target apk-emulator -storetype pkcs12
-keystore yourCertificate.p12 hello.apk Main-app.xml Main.swf
```

In Flash Professional, the emulator launches the application automatically. In Flash Builder, install it on the emulator using the Android SDK:

```
androidSDK/platform-tools/adb install hello.apk
```

If you have the device attached and the emulator running, use either -d or -e before the install:

```
androidSDK/platform-tools/adb -e install Main.apk
```

You can read about the emulator in detail on the Android developer website, at *http://developer.android.com/guide/developing/tools/emulator.html* or *http://developer.android.com/guide/developing/tools/othertools.html#android*.

How Does AIR Run on Android?

The packaging of an AIR application includes the compiled *.swf* file, any necessary assets, and bootstrapping code. A bootstrapper is a simple program that activates a more complicated one.

An AIR application starts as any native application. This mechanism is similar to that for AIR desktop applications. The bootstrapper, which is a small piece of Dalvik (*.dex*), checks to see that the AIR runtime is installed. If it is not, it directs the user to get it.

The bootstrapper loads the Runtime library and invokes it, passing it to the application's main *.swf* file. If more than one AIR application is running, the mechanism manages a shared copy of the runtime for all of them.

In some cases, code from the Runtime library also invokes OS functions in Dalvik, the Android virtual machine, and makes Java Native Interface (JNI) calls. It becomes a broadcast subscriber for the specific events related to the application's permissions. It also interfaces with the system for screen display and input events such as gesture and keyboard inputs.

Starting AIR with intent

In the Android environment, applications or the browser can launch other applications and pass arguments to them. I demonstrated this in the example in Chapter 2. An application can receive arguments even if it is already running.

At the time of this writing, AIR applications cannot launch other applications, but they can be launched by others and capture arguments. To test this, install the Android

Advanced Task Killer, a free application for listing running applications and then killing them, or making them active.

If your AIR application is launched by a native application, you can listen to the `Invo keEvent.INVOKE` event:

```
import flash.desktop.NativeApplication;
import flash.events.InvokeEvent;

NativeApplication.nativeApplication.addEventListener
    (InvokeEvent.INVOKE, onInvoke);



function onInvoke(event:InvokeEvent):void {
    trace(event);
    trace(event.arguments);
}
```

Android development using Java is beyond the scope of this book, but this is what launching an application using `intent` would look like:

```
Intent myIntent = new Intent();
myIntent.addCategory(Intent.CATEGORY_LAUNCHER);
myIntent.setAction(Intent.ACTION_MAIN);
myIntent.setFlags(Intent.FLAG_ACTIVITY_NEW_TASK);

myIntent.setClassName("air.NAME_APP", "air.NAME_APP.AppEntry");
startActivity(myIntent);
```

AIR Access to Android APIs

The biggest limitation with AIR for Android at the time of this writing is that it cannot issue Android system notifications (such as notification bar updates), or communicate with other applications. There is also no widget support.

Some experiments have been done to try to overcome this and create a hybrid AIR–Java application for Android. Create two APK files, one with the Android SDK and one with the AIR SDK, then merge them together.

Set up a mechanism such as a network socket for the two processes to communicate at runtime. The `ip` and `port` must be the same. AIR sends messages over sockets to Java to show notifications.

This is not public, nor is it official (at the time of this writing). Expect to read about some developments regarding this, as there is great interest among the developer community for AIR to offer the same (or similar) features to native applications.

Using the Command-Line Tool

The command line is a place where you can run an application, navigate between directories, and perform specific tasks by just typing commands. For a novice, using the command line may seem intimidating at first, but once it's mastered, it's powerful and fast. If you are interested in emerging technology, the command line may be the only way initially to test applications, as UIs are usually the last component built in software development.

A Basic Review

To use the command line on the Mac, open the Terminal window. On Windows, press Shift-Right click and the context menu will display an Open command window. The key is to understand how to point or navigate to the application you want to use, whether you want to use it on its own or to execute commands on other files located in other directories.

Here are some commonly used commands, along with a brief explanation of each:

```
cd dirname          goes to another directory
cd "some name"      if directory's name has space, put it in quotes
cd some\ name       or escape with the backslash
ls                  lists files in a particular directory
.. cd               goes to the parent directory of current directory
cd                  goes to the home directory from wherever you are
```

For the purposes of this chapter, we want to easily run commands from the Android SDK. Let's assume that it is on the desktop. Open the Terminal window; you should be at the top level of your user directory. Type the following:

```
cd Desktop
```

You should now see the path to the desktop. Type the following to see the list of all files on your desktop:

```
ls
```

Or type the following to see their date of creation, size, and permissions for visible and hidden directories:

```
ls -al
```

To run simple commands, you can navigate down to the *tools* directory, or enter the full path using a forward slash between directories followed by the command, as follows:

```
androidSDK/platform-tools/adb devices
```

If you want to access another directory from this location, you need to identify and type long instructions. Let's go over the command to install the AIR runtime emulator to use it with the Android emulator. For the sake of this example, both the Android SDK and the AIR SDK are on the desktop. Type the following command on one line:

```
androidSDK/platform-tools/adb -e install
                AIR_SDK/runtimes/air/android/emulator/Runtime.apk
```

This method works, but as you can see, it is cumbersome.

The PATH environment variable

To avoid typing long paths between directories, you can store them in an environment variable called PATH, which lists directories so that you don't have to provide their full path every time. The shell, a program that reads what you type and responds appropriately, looks for commands in the list of directories stored in PATH.

On the Mac, to check what the variable stores, type:

```
echo $PATH
```

On Windows, type:

```
echo %PATH%
```

Let's add the Android directory to our variable. The value of PATH is the current value plus the new location. Values are separated by a colon and should not have any empty spaces.

This is the instruction for my Mac. I placed the *android* directory on my desktop, renamed to *androidSDK* for convenience:

```
export PATH=$PATH:/Users/Veronique/Desktop/android-sdk/platform-tools
```

 Be careful to follow the instructions exactly as indicated. Do not delete the existing PATH variable. You want to add to it, not replace it. If you are hesitant, practice the command in the preceding paragraph, but without the word export; doing so will only change the PATH variable while the Terminal window is open. For best performance, add the directories less often used at the end.

Now that it is stored, try the same command as before, but without the path to the *android* directory:

```
adb devices
```

For Windows, the principle is the same. Please refer to the instructions on the Adobe website, or go to *http://help.adobe.com/en_US/air/build/WSfffb011ac560372f -71994050128cca87097-8000.html* or *http://polygeek.com/2958_flex_creating-your -first-air-app-for-android-using-flash-builder*.

Conclusion

We have now concluded our introduction on tooling and have built a basic application. Most information from this point on will be tool-agnostic.

CHAPTER 4

Permissions, Certificates, and Installation

It is your work in life that is the ultimate seduction.

—Pablo Picasso

As a mobile application developer, you are a retailer in a global virtual storefront. You can make applications that live in people's pockets. This is exciting.

In Chapter 2, you created an application and installed it on your device. Now it is time to put the application out there for the world to see.

The first and most important consideration is the value of your application as a mobile experience. After that discussion, we will review the various files that compose your Android Package (APK) file, and discuss the process of becoming an official Android developer and putting an application in the Android Market. Finally, we will discuss how to make money from your hard work.

Why Mobile?

The mobile marketplace is a cruel world. Users often download an application on impulse, try it once, and may never open it again if their first impression is negative. You should aim for excellence and simplicity. Define your application in one sentence. Find your niche. Make it unique, if not in concept, then in execution.

Also, you should analyze mobile consumption. An application is often only used for a few minutes at a time. Tasks should be completed quickly or in incremental steps saved on the device. Whatever you do, do not attempt to replicate your existing website. Instead, adapt it for mobile or create a companion application.

The APK File

A variant of the JAR format used for compression and archival, APK is the file format used to distribute and install an Android mobile application. You can open an APK file using an archive tool such as WinZip or StuffIt Expander to see what is inside it. An APK file typically includes *.swf* and *application.xml* files containing assets, as well as a *res* folder which contains icons.

Creating the Application Icon

The default system icon is an Android-green icon. Icons need to be 36×36-, 48×48-, or 72×72-pixel PNG images. They are used for low-, medium-, and high-density screens, respectively.

You should make your icon stand out, while clearly identifying your application. Google provides guidelines on how to make icons, and provides a Photoshop template, at *http://developer.android.com/guide/practices/ui_guidelines/icon_design.html*.

In Flash Professional, go to File→AIR Android Settings→Icon and browse to the icons on your computer.

 If you use an icon of the wrong size in Flash Professional, the IDE will prompt you with a message that reads, "One of the specified icons do not have the correct dimensions."

In Flash Builder, create a directory called *icons* in the *src* folder, and place your icons in it. Right-click on your project and select Properties. Then select ActionScript Build Packaging→Google Android→Package Contents and select the *icons* folder if it is not already selected.

In other tools, add a node to your application descriptor file as follows:

```
<icon>
<image36x36>icons/36.png</image36x36>
<image48x48>icons/48.png</image48x48>
<image72x72>icons/72.png</image72x72>
</icon>
```

Alternatively, if you are using the command line, place all your icons in a folder called *icons* and add it to the end of your statement:

```
AIR-sdk-path/bin/adt -package -target apk -storetype pkcs12
-keystore yourCertificate.p12 hello.apk Main-app.xml Main.swf icons
```

Publish your application one last time. Change your application to release mode if it is in debug mode. In Flash Professional, select File→AIR Android settings. Under the Deployment tab, for "Android deployment type," choose Release.

If you are publishing from the command line, verify that the target is apk:

```
AIR-sdk-path/bin/adt -package -target apk -storetype pkcs12
-keystore yourCertificate.p12 hello.apk Main-app.xml Main.swf
```

Choosing the Application Settings

The application descriptor contains application settings, and should look similar to the following code. Note the required or optional annotation, and default, for each setting.

Here are the required tags:

```
<application xmlns=http://ns.adobe.com/air/application/2.6>
// Last segment specifies the version of AIR required

    <id>com.veronique.MyApplication</id>
    // Universally unique identifier.
    // Android converts ID to a package name by adding
    // "air." to the beginning.
    // Hyphens are converted to underscore
    // and digits are preceded by a capital A.

    <filename>MyApplication</filename>
    // name used for the APK package file

    <versionNumber>1.0.0</versionNumber>
    // contains three integers, up to three digits each

    <initialWindow>
    // properties of initial appearance of the application

        <content>Main.swf</content>
        // root swf

        <fullScreen>false</fullScreen>
        // application takes over the whole screen if true

        <aspectRatio>portrait</aspectRatio>
        // portrait (default) or landscape

        <autoOrients>false</autoOrients>
        // true (default) or false

        <visible>true</visible>

        <renderMode>cpu</renderMode>
        // cpu (default) or gpu

    </initialWindow>

</application>
```

The following tags are optional. They are child nodes of the application tag:

```
<name>Hello World</name>
// or localized
<name>
    <text xml:lang="en">English name</text>
    <text xml:lang="fr">nom français</text>
</name>
// name as it appears on device. Keep it short

<versionLabel>1.0.0</ versionLabel >
// Displayed in installation dialog

<description>
    <text xml:lang="en">English description</text>
    <text xml:lang="fr">Description française</text>
</description>

<copyright></copyright>

<icon>
    <image36x36>icons/36.png</image36x36>
    <image48x48>icons/48.png</image48x48>
    <image72x72>icons/72.png</image72x72>
</icon>

<customUpdateUI>false</customUpdateUI>
    // Update handled by user on double-click or automatic

<allowBrowserInvocation>false</allowBrowserInvocation>
    // can be launched from link in a browser

<android>
        <manifestAdditions>
        <![CDATA[
        <manifest>
        <uses-permission android:name="android.permission.CAMERA"/>
        <uses-permission android:name="android.permission.INTERNET"/>
        // Add all permissions as children of manifest tag

        <supports-screens android:normalScreens="true"/>
            <uses-feature android:required="true"
            android:name="android.hardware.touchscreen.multitouch"/>
            <application android:enabled="true">
                <activity android:excludeFromRecents="false">
                    <intent-filter>
                        <action
                        android:name="android.intent.action.MAIN"/>
                            <category
                            android:name=
                                "android.intent.category.LAUNCHER"/>
                    </intent-filter>
                </activity>
            </application>
        </manifest>
        ]]>
```

```
        </manifestAdditions>
    </android>
```

Setting Permissions

The Android security and privacy model requires permissions to access certain features such as GPS. When clicking the Install button, the user sees the list of permissions and can then make an educated decision to opt out if desired.

Use the permission tag in the application descriptor to list all the permissions needed, as shown in the code below. Permissions cannot be modified at runtime.

Just before installing an application, the Android Market displays the permissions required. Figure 4-1 shows that Queue Manager, an application for managing your Net-flix queue, only requires the Internet permission.

Before submitting your application, verify that you only include the permissions needed. Otherwise, you may filter out a group of users who will not see your application in their version of the Android Market.

```
<uses-permission android:name="android.permission.INTERNET" />
To make network requests. Can be used for remote debugging

<uses-permission android:name="android.permission.WRITE_EXTERNAL_STORAGE" />
To write data to external storage, such as the SDCard

<uses-permission android:name="android.permission.READ_PHONE_STATE" />
Read-only access of phone state. Used to mute AIR in case of incoming call

<uses-permission android:name="android.permission.ACCESS_FINE_LOCATION" />
<uses-permission android:name="android.permission.ACCESS_COARSE_LOCATION" />
Access the location information. Fine for GPS location, Coarse for Cell/Wi-Fi

<uses-permission android:name="android.permission.CAMERA" />
Access the device camera

<uses-permission android:name="android.permission.RECORD_AUDIO" />
Access the device microphone

<uses-permission android:name="android.permission.DISABLE_KEYGUARD" />
<uses-permission android:name="android.permission.WAKE_LOCK" />
Prevents device from dimming, going in sleep mode and activating keyguard

<uses-permission android:name="android.permission.ACCESS_NETWORK_STATE" />
Access information on device network interfaces

<uses-permission android:name="android.permission.ACCESS_WIFI_STATE" />
Access information on device Wi-Fi networks
```

Android offers a lot of other settings, only some of which can be set in AIR but not documented. They should all be added to the Android→Manifest Additions→Manifest node.

Figure 4-1. The Queue Manager application before installation

The Android Launcher activity keeps track of the applications that have been launched. If a long press is applied on the home button, a list of recently run applications appears. If you do not want your application to be on this list, add `excludeFromRecents` to your manifest file as follows:

```
<android>
<manifestAdditions>
    <![CDATA[
    <manifest>
        <application android:enabled="true">
            <activity android:excludeFromRecents="false">
                <intent-filter>
                <action android:name="android.intent.action.MAIN"/>
                <category android:name="android.intent.category.LAUNCHER"/>
                </intent-filter>
```

```
            </activity>
        </application>
    </manifest>
    ]]>
    </manifestAdditions>
</android>
```

Applications are installed on the device memory by default. If you select Set-
tings→Applications→Manage Applications, you will notice that some applications have
the option "Move to SD card" (which then becomes "Move to phone").

However, some Android applications and AIR applications do not have that option. If
you type the following at the command line, all applications will now be moved:

```
adb shell pm setInstallLocation 2
```

To restore the settings, type the following:

```
adb shell pm setInstallLocation 0
```

If you set the installLocation tag to preferExternal, saving internally is not an option.
All of your content, including your application, is stored on the SD card. This could be
helpful for large applications. Keep in mind that the content is accessible to other applications, and therefore is vulnerable. If the SD card is full, the system falls back to an
installation on the device:

```
<android>
    <manifestAdditions>
    <manifest>
        <attribute name="android:installLocation" value="preferExternal"/>
    </manifest>
    </manifestAdditions>
</android>
```

Read the Android recommendation regarding what should not be installed externally,
online at *http://developer.android.com/guide/appendix/install-location.html*.

Users can erase the application data. If you want to prevent them from doing this, you
can add the allowClearUserData attribute to the android node:

```
<manifest>
<application android:allowClearUserData="false" />
</manifest>
```

 At the time of this writing, a bug in Android prevented this setting from
working. It should be fixed in a future release.

You can also fine-tune permissions to add specific requirements. For instance, you may
have an application which only works for devices with a camera auto-focus. You can
add a different type of permission, uses-feature, to inform users of what is needed for
your application:

```
<uses-permission android:name="android.permission.CAMERA" />
<uses-feature android:name="android.hardware.camera" />
<uses-feature android:name="android.hardware.camera.autofocus" />
```

Android throws an error if a required permission is not set, such as for Internet or GPS, but not others, such as reading the phone state or disabling the keyguard. The criterion is what it considered potentially dangerous for the user. In AIR, the application always fails silently.

Native developers have a larger choice of features, and therefore permissions. You can go to *http://developer.android.com/reference/android/Manifest.permission.html* to learn about some of the new possibilities. If you see one that you would like to use, send Adobe a feature request, preferably with a use case so that it can be added to the AIR runtime, by going to *https://www.adobe.com/cfusion/mmform/index.cfm?name=wish form*.

For example, having an API to access contacts would open a lot of possibilities:

```
<uses-permission android:name="android.permission.READ_CONTACTS" />
```

Packaging External Resources

If your application has a lot of art, you may want to keep the art external to the application and load it at runtime. In the AIR for Android settings, if you are using Flash Professional, add the resources to the "Included files" list at the bottom of the General tab.

In Flash Builder, create a directory called *assets* in the *scr* folder, and place your art in it. Right-click on your project and select Properties. Then select ActionScript Build Packaging→Google Android→Package Contents and select the *assets* folder if it is not already selected.

If you are using the command line, list the files or the containing folders at the end of the command line:

```
AIR-sdk-path/bin/adt -package -target apk -storetype pkcs12
-keystore yourCertificate.p12 hello.apk Main-app.xml Main.swf
image.jpg movie.flv data.xml
```

Another way to handle external files is to store them on the SD card and access them via File Access. You cannot remove files included at the time of installation because it would make the application invalid. You can, however, copy them to the SD card. This is the approach you would use if you want to modify them during the life of the application. We will cover this method in Chapter 6.

Signing Your Application with a Certificate

All applications must be signed before being updated to the Android Market. This enables consumers to identify and establish trust with a developer. The developer signs the certificate using a private key. The private key is different from the one you used during development. Typically, a key generally using ADT is only good for five years.

To create a suitable key in Flash Professional, go to File→AIR Android settings→Deployment→Certificate and fill out every field. The publisher name will appear in the Android Market as you enter it. As before, make a note of the password, since you will need it when you compile your application. Choose Type 2048-RSA, Google's recommended type.

The certificate must be valid for 25 years. The system only checks the certificate's expiration date upon installation. If the certificate expires afterward, the application will continue working.

To create a suitable key using AIR ADT and the command line, use the following code, making sure to put your name and country in quotes:

```
AIR-sdk-path/bin/adt -certificate -cn "FirstName LastName" -c "US"
-validityPeriod 25 2048-RSA myCertificate.p12 myPassword
```

More information on this is available on the Android developer website, at *http://devel oper.android.com/guide/publishing/app-signing.html*.

When/if you later upgrade your application, you must use the same certificate, so keep it in a safe place.

Versioning

Versioning gives you the opportunity to submit fixes and updates to your application. A version number consists of three digits separated by dots, as in 1.0.0, referred to as *major.minor.build*. Set the version number in Flash Professional in the Settings window. In Flash Builder, open the application descriptor and change the version number in the XML.

For debugging purposes, you can check the version number at runtime from the `appli cationDescriptor` of the `NativeApplication.nativeApplication` that is an XML object:

```
import flash.desktop.NativeApplication;

var applicationDescription:XML =
NativeApplication.nativeApplication.applicationDescriptor;

var ns:Namespace = applicationDescription.namespace();
// http://ns.adobe.com/air/application/2.6
var currentVersion:String = applicationDescription.ns::versionNumber;
// 1.0.0
```

The update to an application appears on the Android Market quickly.

As mentioned earlier in this chapter, the update can be accomplished in two ways. You can specify your preference in the application descriptor, or the user can specify it manually. The following tag implies that the update is handled by the user upon double-clicking:

```
<customUpdateUI>false</customUpdateUI>
```

If the user installs an update of your application, previously saved data is preserved.

Registering As an Android Developer

To submit your application to the Android Market, you must have or create a Google account and sign up as an Android developer. You also must pay a one-time registration fee of $25 (see *https://market.android.com/publish/signup*).

You should read the Android Market Developer Distribution Agreement (*http://www .android.com/us/developer-distribution-agreement.html*) as well as the content policy which determines what content is allowed (*http://www.android.com/market/terms/de veloper-content-policy.html*).

If you are going to sell applications through the Android Market, you need to set up a merchant account with Google Checkout. For more information on this topic, refer to "Monetizing Your Application" on page 41.

Publishing an Application on the Android Market

An AIR application is packaged as a standard Android application. Therefore, you can distribute it via the Android Market or via another website of your choice.

To publish your application, go to the Developer Console page at *http://market.android .com/publish/Home* and click on the Upload Application button. Figure 4-2 shows the necessary steps to submit an application.

Uploading Assets

Select "Upload assets" to upload the APK file. At the time of this writing, the maximum allowed size for this file is 50 MB. You can also upload at least two screenshots at 320×480, 480×854, or 480×800; one high-resolution, 512×512 icon; one promotional graphic at 180×120; a feature graphic at 1,024×500; and the URL to an optional promotional video (must be YouTube).

Unless you select the Marketing Opt-Out button, Google has the right to promote your application in the Android Market or other Google-owned properties.

Listing Details

Upon selecting "Listing details," you can enter the title, a description, some promotional text, the type, and the category of your application. The default language is

Figure 4-2. Steps to upload an application to the Android Market

English, but you can choose additional languages. As of November 2010, applications need to have a content rating of All, Pre-Teen, Teen, or Mature, as per the Android content policy (see *http://www.android.com/us/developer-content-policy.html*).

Publishing Options

The Android Market Licensing Service is a protection option to prevent users from copying an application from a device. At runtime, it queries the Android Market to obtain the user's licensing status. The License Verification Library (LVL) is a component of the Android SDK. It does increase the file size, so choose it only if you are selling your application.

 LVL is a Java-only API with no integration with ActionScript. At the time of this writing, no solution has been offered to protect applications.

Distributing Applications via Adobe InMarket

Adobe offers a service called InMarket that handles distribution of AIR applications, including credit card processing, hosting, and marketing. You receive 70% of the sales revenue. InMarket has an ActionScript license manager that only works within its system. For more information on InMarket, go to *http://www.adobe.com/products/inmarket/* or *http://www.webkitchen.be/2010/12/02/inmarket-monetizing-your-apps-made-easy/*.

Publishing for the Amazon Market

In March 2011, Amazon opened Appstore for Android, which offers Android games and applications as well as Free Amazon applications.

Note that the Amazon store does not do any filtering, so in your application description, clearly indicate the requirement for at least Android 2.2 and an ARMv7-A processor.

To make your application compatible with this Appstore, you must build an APK specifically for it (build a separate one for the Android market). You must use only AIR 2.6 and up, so that you can overwrite the runtime download URI. Adobe and Amazon are working on a more practical solution. Flash Professional CS5.5 offers a pull-down menu: go to AIR for Android settings→Deployment to target the Google Android Market or the Amazon Appstore.

For more information, read *http://blogs.adobe.com/cantrell/archives/2011/03/air-2-6 -applications-and-the-amazon-appstore-for-android.html*.

Controlling Distribution by Using the MAC Address

You may need to develop an application that is only authorized to run on some devices. You could upload it to a server and give the URL to a selected group, but this method is not very secure.

To monitor installation, use the MAC address of the device. The MAC address is the unique identifier for the hardware, mobile device, or desktop.

First, set the Android permissions to have access to network information:

```
<uses-permission android:name="android.permission.ACCESS_NETWORK_STATE" />
<uses-permission android:name="android.permission.ACCESS_WIFI_STATE" />
```

To obtain the address at runtime, use the NetworkInfo class, which gets a list of interfaces and looks for a hardwareAddress. It is the MAC address for your device:

```
if (NetworkInfo.isSupported) {
    trace("network information is supported");
}

var network:NetworkInfo = NetworkInfo.networkInfo;
for each (var object:NetworkInterface in network.findInterfaces()) {
    if (object.hardwareAddress) {
        trace(object.hardwareAddress);
    }
}
```

The address looks something like this:

```
00:23:76:BB:46:AA.
```

Launching an AIR Application

The first time a user launches an AIR application, the Adobe AIR license agreement will appear. The user only needs to agree to the terms once.

If you are familiar with developing AIR applications on the desktop, you may have noticed a difference here. The installation warning dialog does not appear on the device. The messaging is handled by the operating system when the application is installed, as it is for native Android applications. Also, downloaded applications are stored in the */data/app* directory which is a private directory.

Monetizing Your Application

Before you submit an application, you should become acquainted with other applications already on the Android Market. Visit the AppBrain website (*http://www.appbrain.com/apps/*) or the Android Market website (*https://market.android.com*) to see the current applications.

For reference, the website at *http://www.appbrain.com/apps/popular/adobe-air/* keeps track of the applications developed using AIR.

Paid Applications

Setting up a merchant account with Google Checkout requires that you provide banking and tax information. You only need it for the applications you charge money for. Google's transaction fee is 30% of the price of your application. The arguments for using the Android Market are security, efficiency, and exposure.

It is up to you to decide whether to charge for your application. Your history is public and available to consumers, so charging a fair price is a good long-term business practice.

Unlike Apple and the Apple Store, Google doesn't force you to use the Android Market as a distribution channel. Instead, you can place your application on your web server of choice. Your server MIME type needs to be edited, however. The MIME media type for *.apk* files is `application/vnd.android/package-archive`.

To install an application on a device via a non-Android Market source, select Settings→Applications→Unknown Sources. Unless the application is properly documented, this may reduce your audience.

Mobile Ads

If you want to earn money from your work, you can offer your application for free but receive revenues from embedded advertisements. Read Arron La's story on the revenue he made from his Advanced Task Manager application, at *http://arronla.com/2010/08/android-revenue-advanced-task-manager/*.

The advertisement displayed in your application is one image with a clickable URL. Here is a short list of some mobile advertising companies:

- AdMob (*http://AdMob.com*)
- Smaato (*http://www.smaato.com*)
- Google (*http://www.google.com/mobileads/publisher_home.html*)

You must subscribe to get an application ID. At runtime, your application makes a request to receive advertisement information. Indicate the ad's format (XML is best) and dimensions. Some providers allow you to specify geolocation, age, or gender for targeted ads.

All providers give you an option to test your application with dummy ads before it goes live. Always put the advertisement code in a `try catch` block. You do not want your application to stop functioning because the provider server is down or sends bad data.

At the time of this writing, mobile advertising providers do not offer an AS3 SDK. You need to download the AS2 version and rewrite it for your purposes. Making straight calls in the standalone application does not seem to provide ad impressions. Instead, use the StageWebView API, which allows you to open a web page within your AIR application to simulate the browser experience. We will cover this topic in Chapter 13.

Reporting

Google Market tracks how many users have downloaded your application. But you may want to also know how users interact with your application. You could track, for instance, which part of your product is most popular and which features could be replaced or removed.

Reporting has become a standard component for many applications. This capability tracks user activity and sends the information to a remote service that stores data and provides analysis.

Google Analytics (*http://www.google.com/analytics/*), a popular choice in the nonenterprise market, is free and provides an open source ActionScript API. An ActionScript 3 API for Google Analytics data collection, called gaforflash, is available at *http://code .google.com/p/gaforflash/*. In addition, you can keep up with Google Analytics information by reading the blog at*http://analytics.blogspot.com/2011/01/new-actionscript-3 -library-for-api.html*.

You need to provide a website profile and some geographic information when you register on Google Analytics. A simple example follows.

To set the Internet permission:

```
<uses-permission android:name="android.permission.INTERNET" />
```

To use the `Web ID` property you received from the service:

```
import com.google.analytics.GATracker;
import com.google.analytics.AnalyticsTracker;


var tracker:AnalyticsTracker =
            new GATracker(this, "UA-111-222", "AS3", false);
            // current displayObject
            // Unique Web ID
            // tracking mode
            // debug mode

// button press go to section "game"
function pressButton(event:MouseEvent):void {
    tracker.trackerPageView("game");
    tracker.trackEvent("Button", "click", "parameter1", "parameter2");
    // category
    // action
    // additional parameters as needed
}
```

Conclusion

The distribution model for AIR applications is constantly evolving. Keep informed of new channels. For best practices on mobile distribution, read Jonathan Campos's article, "Learn from my mobile mistakes," at *http://unitedmindset.com/jonbcampos/2010/12/28/learn-from-my-mobile-mistakes/*.

CHAPTER 5

Evaluating Device Capabilities and Handling Multiple Devices

The multitude which does not reduce itself to unity is confusion.

—Blaise Pascal

The premise of mobile AIR is to enable you to create one concept, one code base, and a set of assets to deploy an application on multiple devices effortlessly. AIR for mobile accomplishes this for the most part, but not without challenges. There is a disparity in performance and capabilities among devices, and deploying for a range of screen resolutions requires effort and time even if your art is minimal.

In the near future, mobile devices will approach, and perhaps surpass, the performance of desktop machines. Until then, you must adapt your development style to this limited environment. Every line of code and every asset should be scrutinized for optimization. The AIR runtime has been optimized for devices with limited resources, but this is no guarantee that your code will run smoothly. This part is your responsibility.

In this chapter, we will discuss how to evaluate device capabilities. We will then discuss how to handle multiple screens and orientations.

Hardware

The multitude of Android devices available today makes it difficult to evaluate them all. The subsections that follow discuss the major factors to examine. If you want to know about a specific phone, or if you would like a complete list of Android devices, visit these websites:

http://pdadb.net/
http://en.wikipedia.org/wiki/Category:Android_devices
http://phandroid.com/phones/

The Processor

The CPU, or central processing unit, executes software program instructions. Its speed on mobile devices varies from 500 MHz to 1 GHz. For comparison, the average speed of a desktop computer is around 2.5 GHz.

The instruction set must be ARMv7 or higher to run AIR for Android.

The GPU, or graphics processing unit, is a high-performance processor dedicated to performing geometric calculations on graphics. Its speed is evaluated in millions of triangles processed per second (mt/s), and it ranges on mobile devices from 7 mt/s to 28 mt/s. AIR uses OpenGL ES 2.0-based processors.

The graphics card, display type, and color depth affect display quality.

Memory and Storage

RAM on mobile devices varies from 128 MB to 768 MB, averaging at 512 MB. ROM is an important complementary memory type. On Android, if memory runs out, applications are terminated.

Different types of memory affect the GPU's speed and capacity.

Storage includes the internal memory, expanded by the SD card.

The Camera

Camera quality is often evaluated by the megapixels it can store. The quality of the LED flash and the auto-focus option on the device is also a factor. Some devices include a front camera of lesser quality to use for video telephony.

Sensors

A built-in accelerometer is becoming standard on Android devices, but it is not yet universal. The GPS antenna and driver is used for satellite navigation. Touch technology is a combination of the screen touch overlay, the controller, and the software driver. The number of simultaneous touch points varies, although Android officially only supports two.

The Battery

Battery capability on an Android device is measured in milliamp hours (mAh), and is commercially evaluated by the number of hours of movie play capable on the device. Removable batteries can be replaced by stronger ones if needed.

The Display

Screen size on Android devices is measured as a diagonal, usually in inches.

Resolution is the number of pixels on the screen. The resolution varies between 800×480 and 854×480 on phones, and between 1,024×600 and 1,024×800 on tablets.

The PPI (pixels per inch) or DPI (dots per inch), also called pixel density, is the number of pixels on the screen in relation to the screen's physical size. A device has a defined number of pixels it can display in a limited space. A higher pixel density is preferable on devices viewed at close range.

Table 5-1 lists the screen size, resolution, and PPI on some popular Android and Apple devices.

Table 5-1. Feature comparison of popular Android devices

Device	Screen size (inches)	Resolution	PPI
Samsung Galaxy Tab	7	1,024×600	170
iPad	9.7	1,024×768	132
iPad 2	9.7	1,024×768	136
Motorola Xoom	10.1	1,280×800	160
Nexus One	3.7	800×480	254
Droid 2	3.7	854×480	265
iPhone 4	3.5	960×640	326

Software

At the time of this writing, Android's latest operating system is 3.0 and is called Honeycomb.

The process for upgrading the Android operating system is very different from the Apple model, which requires the device to be synced with iTunes. Android uses an "over the air approach" to push upgrades. Manufacturers slowly push upgrades to phones, sometimes over several months. Not all devices receive upgrades, so developing for established versions instead of recently released versions may guarantee you a broader audience.

If you are not sure what version is installed on your device, select Settings→About phone→Android version (on some devices, this information is available under "Software information"). Your phone system must have at least Android 2.2, called Froyo, to run AIR for Android. The Adobe AIR runtime is not accessible on the Android Market for earlier versions.

Performance

The device's performance is measured by its speed of execution and how much it can hold in memory. Methods and tools can be used to perform a benchmark. We will cover this topic in Chapter 19. For a quick analysis, try the AIRBench application developed by Christian Cantrell, from Adobe, and read his blog at *http://blogs.adobe.com/ cantrell/archives/2010/10/using-airbench-to-test-air-across-android-phones.html*.

AIRBench tests devices' capabilities, but also runs performance analyses. I used it on three different devices. Table 5-2 shows the performance results I achieved in milliseconds (lowest numbers show best performance).

Table 5-2. AIRBench performance results for the Samsung Galaxy Tab, Droid 2, and Nexus One devices

Test	Samsung Galaxy Tab	Droid 2	Nexus One
Parse a 145 KB XML file	103	128	142
Allocate 8,192 KB of memory	85	23	57
Write, read, and delete a 1,024 KB file	147	97	3,646
Insert, select, and delete 500 rows of data in an SQLite database	636	751	875
Perform several string operations	336	488	470
Perform an SHA256 hash on a 45 KB image	117	145	151
Calculate sunrise and sunset times for 10 cities 100 times	156	183	128
Calculate frame rate	60	60	60

Capabilities

You can request information on the device at runtime to automate some of the presentation of your application. The Android Market, unlike the Apple Store, does not separate applications between phones and tablets. Be prepared for all devices.

Rather than trying to make your application look identical on all devices, adapt the layout for the resolution used.

The `flash.system.Capabilities` class provides information on the environment. To determine that your application is running on a mobile device, use `cpuArchitecture`:

```
import flash.system.Capabilities;

if (Capabilities.cpuArchitecture == "ARM") {
    trace("this is probably a mobile phone");
}
```

Alternatively, you can compare `screenDPI` and `screenResolutionX`. Here is the code to calculate the diagonal dimension of the screen:

```
var dpi:int = Capabilities.screenDPI;
var screenX:int = Capabilities.screenResolutionX;
var screenY:int = Capabilities.screenResolutionY;
var diagonal:Number = Math.sqrt((screenX*screenX)+(screenY*screenY))/dpi;
if (diagonal < 5) {
    trace("this must be a mobile phone");
}
```

You can also store the screenDPI that will be used to scale and position your assets, as demonstrated further in the section "Creating Content for Multiple Screens" on page 50:

```
var dpi:int = Capabilities.screenDPI;
```

Orientation

To control the look of your application, you can define the application's scaling and alignment. The scaleMode as set in the following code prevents automatic scaling and the align setting always keeps your application at the upper-left corner. When you choose auto-orient, it is added automatically in Flash Builder Mobile:

```
import flash.display.StageScaleMode;
import flash.display.StageAlign;

stage.scaleMode = StageScaleMode.NO_SCALE;
stage.align = StageAlign.TOP_LEFT;
```

Android devices equipped with an accelerometer can determine device orientation. As the user moves the hardware, your content rotates. Define a custom background color to prevent distracting white borders from appearing while in transition:

```
[SWF(backgroundColor="#999999")]
```

If you always want your application in its original aspect ratio, in Flash Professional select File→AIR Android settings, and under the General tab, deselect "Auto orientation". In Flash Builder, under Mobile Settings, deselect "Automatically reorient".

To get the initial orientation, use the following:

```
var isPortrait:Boolean = getOrientation();

function getOrientation():Boolean {
    return stage.stageHeight > stage.stageWidth;
}
```

To listen for a device's orientation and set a stage resize on the desktop, set autoOr ients to true:

```
<initialWindow>
    ...
    <autoOrients>true</autoOrients>
</initialWindow>
```

and register for the Event.RESIZE event:

```
import flash.events.Event;

stage.addEventListener(Event.RESIZE, onResize);
stage.dispatchEvent(new Event(Event.RESIZE);

function onResize(event:Event):void {
    trace(stage.stageWidth, stage.stageHeight);
}
```

The event is fired when your application first initializes, and then again when the device changes orientation. If you create an application to be deployed on the desktop, the event fires when the browser window is resized.

Another API is available for orientation changes. It uses `StageOrientationEvent` and detects changes in many directions. It is not as universal as `RESIZE`, but it does provide information on the orientation before and after the event.

The default orientation is up and right:

```
import flash.events.StageOrientationEvent;

if (stage.supportsOrientationChange) {
    stage.addEventListener(StageOrientationEvent.ORIENTATION_CHANGE,
                                                        onChange);
}

function onChange(event:StageOrientationEvent):void {
    trace(event.beforeOrientation);
    trace(event.afterOrientation);
    // default
    // rotatedLeft
    // rotatedRight
}
```

The goal is to use this information to position and perhaps resize your assets as needed. We will discuss this next.

Creating Content for Multiple Screens

To make your application universal, create the core code once and write the environment detection and presentation-specific code on top.

Android 1.6 and later provide support for multiple screens and resolutions. Even though AIR does not have access to Android compatibility features, it is insightful to understand this approach.

The platform divides screen sizes and resolutions into three general sizes: large, normal, and small. Applications provide images or layouts and the sizes they support as part of the manifest file. Android stores the files in folders named *drawable* and uses the appropriate size based on the device dimension and dpi. If a size is missing, it uses what is available and scales it up or down as needed. If the manifest file declares that multiple screen support is not available, the platform may display the application at medium size on a black background.

For more information, review the Android documentation provided at *http://developer .android.com/guide/practices/screens_support.html* and *http://developer.android.com/ guide/topics/resources/index.html*.

Flash Builder provides dynamic layout capabilities to manage pixel-level differences in screen resolution and orientation. It offers a scaling mechanism to handle different pixel densities across devices. Existing components have new skins and functionality designed for mobile form factors. New components are added to support mobile-specific UI patterns. The entire application is scaled automatically, and its font size adjusted, if the application property `authorDensity` is set to `true`. More information on this is available at *http://labs.adobe.com/technologies/flexsdk_hero/samples/*.

Asset Scaling and Positioning

You can scale and position your assets dynamically once you have collected the device's capabilities and current state. As a general rule, do not use absolute or hardcoded values.

Use the `screenDPI` property to convert inches to pixels, the unit needed for assets:

```
function toPixels(inches:Number):int {
    return Math.round(Capabilities.screenDPI*inches);
}
```

Here is the same function using the metric system to convert millimeters to pixels, which is easier for those educated outside the United States:

```
function toPixels(mm:Number):int {
    return Math.round(Capabilities.screenDPI*(mm/25.4));
}
```

Shift your thinking to inches to determine the dimension you want. Then use it to convert your asset to pixels. The following creates a sprite of 10×10 inches, or 100×100 pixels:

```
var box:Sprite = new Sprite();
box.graphics.beginFill(0x999999);
var pos:int = toPixels(10);
box.graphics.drawRect(0, 0, pos, pos);
box.graphics.endFill();
addChild(box);
```

Dynamic positioning

Once the art is created at the right size, position it dynamically.

In this example, the sprite is positioned in the center of the screen. Adjust the position to offset it in relation to the registration point (see Figure 5-1):

```
// registration point is at upper-left corner as defined earlier
box.x = stage.stageWidth * 0.5 - box.width*0.5;
box.y = stage.stageHeight * 0.5 - box.height*0.5;
```

For an object whose registration point is in the middle, the x and y positions do not need an offset (see Figure 5-2):

```
box.x = stage.stageWidth;
box.y = stage.stageHeight;
```

In this example, a sprite with a registration point at the upper left is positioned at the bottom of the screen (see Figure 5-3):

```
box.y = stage.stageHeight - box.height;
```

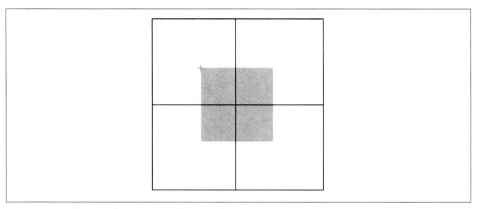

Figure 5-1. Offsetting the sprite in relation to the registration point

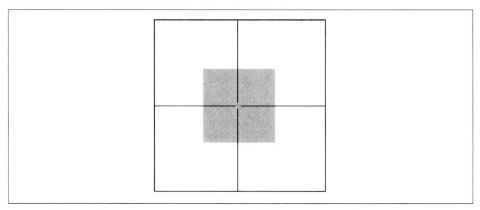

Figure 5-2. Sprite whose registration point is in the middle, requiring no offset

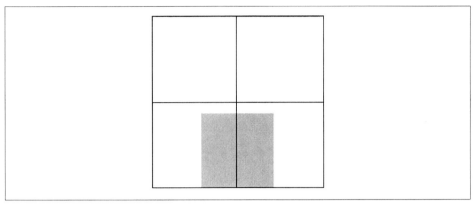

Figure 5-3. Sprite whose registration point is at the upper left, positioned at the bottom of the screen

In this example, the sprite is positioned one-quarter of the way down from the upper-left corner (see Figure 5-4):

```
box.x = stage.stageWidth*0.25;
box.y = stage.stageHeight*0.25;
```

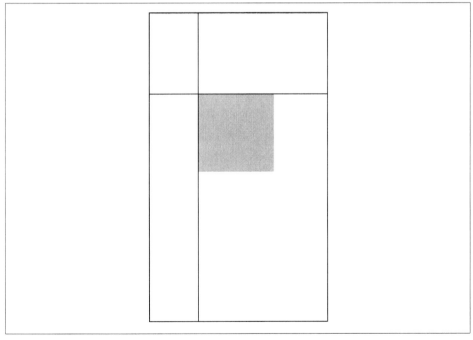

Figure 5-4. Sprite positioned one-quarter of the way down the upper-left corner

If your application is displayed full screen, use `stage.FullScreenWidth` and `stage.Full ScreenHeight` instead.

Sometimes the simplest solution is to group your art and center it, and then fill the borders with a colored background as for a picture frame.

Using a grid layout as a starting point is a good approach for multiple screen deployment. The website at *http://960.gs/* provides some ideas.

Vector Graphics or Bitmaps?

Vector graphics scale well, are reusable, and reduce production time, but they can render slowly. Bitmaps render quickly but do not scale well. Enhancement can be done in both areas.

Using vector graphics

Create your vector art at medium size and resize it on the fly based on the device's resolution and PPI. Then use `cacheAsBitmap` or `cacheAsBitmapMatrix` based on the transformation applied to improve its rendering performance. If you want to apply a filter, draw it into a bitmap.

Using bitmaps

You can choose from several techniques when using bitmaps. For instance, you can create art at different resolutions and choose the right one for the device's resolution. This guarantees fidelity, but at the cost of packaging extra assets. Alternatively, you can create the bitmap at the highest possible resolution and then scale it down if needed. Keep your art light so that you don't waste too much bandwidth.

Other techniques, commonly used in game production, are sprite sheet production and blitting. We will cover all these topics in depth in Chapter 16.

Developing a Deployment Strategy

If you create an application to deploy on Android, iOS, and the desktop, use different compilation processes. In Flash Professional, create different Flash files and document classes.

In Flash Builder, create separate projects. Define the project dimension in the `initial Window` tag of the descriptor file. If you are only developing for the Android platform, your `Main` class should handle the device's capabilities and instructions on layout, as described earlier.

Considering Connectivity

Unlike with the desktop experience, you cannot assume your user is always connected when using a mobile device. She might be moving in and out of networks. Be prepared to display a message if your application is not able to function because of this.

At startup and during the life of your application, you can check the state of connectivity. AIR on the desktop has this functionality, but it is not part of the package for AIR for Android. Rest assured: the classes you need are available. Go to the AIR SDK and navigate to Frameworks→Projects→AIR→Core→src→AIR→Net. Copy all four `air.net` classes into the *src* directory on Flash Builder and next to your document class in Flash Professional. Change the package name from *package air.net* to just *package*.

You can check the status on `URLMonitor` for an HTTP request or on `SocketMonitor` for a socket connection request. Both classes extend from the `ServiceMonitor` class.

Here is an example of an HTTP request:

```
import URLMonitor;
import SocketMonitor;
import flash.net.URLRequest;
import flash.events.StatusEvent;

var monitor:URLMonitor =
    new URLMonitor(new URLRequest("http://www.google.com"));

monitor.pollInterval = 1000;
monitor.addEventListener(StatusEvent.STATUS, onStatus);
monitor.start();

function onStatus(event:StatusEvent):void {
    monitor.stop();
    trace(event.code); // Service.available or Service.unavailable
    trace(event.target.available); // true or false
```

Conclusion

In this chapter, we discussed what you need to do to develop for multiple devices. Schedule a reasonable amount of time up front to plan for differences and specifics. The investment will pay off when you test your application on phones and tablets and see it working as expected. This is when you will notice and enjoy the benefits of universal deployment.

This concludes the book's introductory chapters. We will now dive into the various APIs specific to Android development.

CHAPTER 6

Opening and Closing an Application and Saving Data

The difference between a bad programmer and a good one is whether he considers his code or his data structures more important. Bad programmers worry about the code. Good programmers worry about data structures and their relationships.

—Linus Benedict Torvalds

In Android, every application, also called an activity, is given a unique user ID and runs in its own process. The system—more specifically, the Activity Manager—manages the life cycle of applications and provides a common activity stack.

The application life cycle has three states: active, paused, and stopped. The Activity Manager keeps track of the list of application processes currently running, in order, from newest to oldest. If memory is needed, the oldest application is terminated first. It may receive an event first or be terminated at once.

The decision is therefore very much a result of the user's interaction and history, with the current activity being the most important. AIR applications on Android are treated as any other application, as we will see in this chapter.

While an application has a limited life cycle, it has the ability to save persistent data. Android provides an SQLite database, document-like data, as well as an internal state, which is a simple set of name/value pairs associated with an activity.

AIR uses its own APIs to save data. The AIR runtime comes with an SQLite engine and access to the filesystem. It also provides local shared objects, a cookie-like solution. We will go over all of these options.

The AIR Application

`NativeApplication` represents your AIR application. It belongs to the *flash.desktop* package and inherits from `EventDispatcher`. It is a singleton automatically created when the application launches. You can get a reference to it via the static property `NativeApplication.nativeApplication`.

`NativeApplication` dispatches application-specific events such as `invoking` and `exiting` and has application-specific properties such as `icon` and `systemIdleMode`. Some of its properties, created for AIR on the desktop, are not relevant to the mobile environment, such as `activeWindow` and `openedWindows`, because there are no multiple windows in this environment.

Opening the Application

When you first start your application by clicking on its icon or via another process, the previously active application moves to the background. Your application launches and comes to the foreground to occupy the home screen. Navigating between native applications or between a native application and an AIR-developed application is identical.

Android does not currently provide the option of a startup screen. You may experience a black screen while the application is setting up. Test your application and rework your initialization process if setup takes too long. As a workaround, make your root application a simple movie with a loading indicator graphic. Once it is loaded and rendered (listen for the `ADDED_TO_STAGE` event), load your main application in it using the `Loader` class. The main application *.swf* file must be in the list of Included Files so that it lives in the application directory.

By default, your application occupies the screen underneath the 38-pixel-tall status bar that displays information such as network signal, battery life, time, and notifications. If you wish to hide this bar and go full screen, in Flash Professional select Full Screen under File→AIR Android settings→General. In Flash Builder, add the following node as a child of the `<initialWindow>` node in the application descriptor:

```
<fullScreen>true</fullScreen>
```

Closing the Application

If another application is selected, yours is moved to the background but continues to play and does not close. Typically, `NativeApplication` dispatches an exiting event when it starts the closing process. You can register for that event and be prepared to act quickly according to your application needs:

```
import flash.desktop.NativeApplication;
import flash.events.Event;
```

```
NativeApplication.nativeApplication.addEventListener(Event.EXITING, onExit);

function onExit(event:Event):void {
    // save application's current state
}
```

However, the Android OS may choose to terminate background processes immediately if RAM is needed. In some cases, such as receiving a phone call, there is no guarantee that NativeApplication will have a chance to dispatch the exiting event before being shut down. It is therefore a good practice to save critical data often while the application is active. We will discuss how to save data locally later in this chapter.

The Android OS closes applications that were inactive the longest first. If you want to immediately shut down a particular application, select Settings→Applications→Manage applications→Running, click the desired icon, and press "Force stop." You can also use third-party task killer applications, which conveniently display all the applications currently running in one selection.

The Android UX guidelines recommend using the back or home button as an exit button. But you may choose to shut down your AIR application via code when it moves to the background, or make it a user option while it is running to run the following method:

```
NativeApplication.nativeApplication.exit();
```

Moving Between the Background and Foreground

NativeApplication dispatches an event when it moves to the background. It also dispatches an event when it becomes the active application again. Set listeners if you wish to react to these events:

```
NativeApplication.nativeApplication.addEventListener
    (Event.ACTIVATE, onActivate);

NativeApplication.nativeApplication.addEventListener
    (Event.DEACTIVATE, onDeactivate);
```

Improvements were made in Flash Player 10.1 and AIR 2.0 to conserve memory and battery life. When an application is no longer active, it goes into sleep mode, it stops rendering, and its frame rate drops to 4 fps. This number was chosen because socket connections and the like tend to break at lower frame rates. If AIR doesn't have any persistent connections, you can go as low as 0 fps. The command to change the frame rate is:

```
stage.frameRate = 0;
```

Some items are kept active. For instance, audio keeps playing, video with or without an audio track continues running, sensor listeners such as those for the accelerometer and geolocation are not removed, and timers keep running. Listen to Event.

DEACTIVATE and change the default behavior as needed when receiving the event. This is not done automatically, so you are responsible for managing this.

The following code shows how a video plays and pauses whenever the application is in the foreground or background:

```
import flash.desktop.NativeApplication;
import flash.events.Event;
import flash.media.Video;
import flash.net.NetConnection;
import flash.net.NetStream;

var stream:NetStream;

NativeApplication.nativeApplication.addEventListener
                         (Event.ACTIVATE, onActivate);
NativeApplication.nativeApplication.addEventListener
                         (Event.DEACTIVATE, onDeActivate);

var video:Video = new Video(640, 270);
var nc:NetConnection = new NetConnection();
nc.connect(null);
stream = new NetStream(nc);
stream.client = {};
video.attachNetStream(ns);
addChild(video);
stream.play("yourMovie.mp4");

function onDeActivate(event:Event):void {
    stream.pause();
}
function onActivate(event:Event):void {
    stream.resume();
}
```

When a user receives a phone call, allowing your audio to play over the conversation would equate to a poor user experience. Add the READ_PHONE_STATE permission to your application descriptor file. It allows AIR to mute audio while the call is in progress:

```
<uses-permission android:name="android.permission.READ_PHONE_STATE" />
```

When the application goes to the background, take the opportunity to trigger the garbage collector. It is not recommended that you use this too often because it takes time and can affect performance, but a deactivate state may be a natural break point:

```
system.gc();
```

 Information on battery life and free memory is not currently exposed in AIR for Android. Let's hope it is in a future release. It is available for the RIM Playbook to monitor the state of the device.

Setting Back, Menu, and Search Buttons

The system uses the buttons at the base of your device for navigation and search functions. Except for the home button, you can override their default behavior to use them in your AIR application.

Note that AIR currently cannot communicate with the native user interface and does not have access to the Options menu triggered by pressing the Menu key. The Options menu can hold up to six items; if additional items are stored, it displays a More menu item which reveals an expanded menu. If you want to create a native-like look and feel, you can design a similar-looking menu in your application.

Register for a keyboardEvent.KEY_DOWN event and track which soft key was pressed by identifying its keyCode. Call event.preventDefault() to catch the event before it triggers the default navigation and replace it with your desired behavior:

```
import flash.ui.Keyboard;
import flash.events.KeyboardEvent;

stage.addEventListener(KeyboardEvent.KEY_DOWN, onKey);

function onKey(event:KeyboardEvent):void {
    switch (event.keyCode) {
        case Keyboard.BACK:
            event.preventDefault();
            trace("go back within the AIR application");
            break;
        case Keyboard.MENU:
            event.preventDefault();
            trace("display a custom menu");
            break;
        case Keyboard.SEARCH:
            event.preventDefault();
            trace("perhaps use as a help button");
            break;
    }
}
```

No keyboard event is dispatched for the home soft key.

Keep in mind that overriding the back button default behavior is against Android UX guidelines. Some users may give your application a bad review because of it.

A trick I often use is to override these buttons during development to test various cases at runtime. I may, for instance, use the search button to increment a variable, add a listener, or display a benchmarking tool.

Overriding a Dimmed Screen

After your application is idle for a while, the OS makes the device screen go into dimming mode and sets your device to auto-lock if your settings request it. Note that this is different from AIR on the desktop. On the desktop, playing a video at full screen automatically blocks screensavers and power-saving modes. It does not happen automatically on Android.

If you wish to override this behavior during a certain activity, you need to set the following permissions:

```
<uses-permission android:name="android.permission.WAKE_LOCK" />
<uses-permission android:name="android.permission.DISABLE_KEYGUARD" />
```

For convenience, place this code in your document class or where you first set up your application settings. Import the needed classes:

```
import flash.desktop.NativeApplication;
import flash.desktop.SystemIdleMode;
```

Tell the native application to stay awake:

```
NativeApplication.nativeApplication.systemIdleMode
                = SystemIdleMode.KEEP_AWAKE;
```

To set the native application to normal behavior again, use this code:

```
NativeApplication.nativeApplication.systemIdleMode
                = SystemIdleMode.NORMAL;
```

Keep in mind that blocking the idle behavior has a negative impact on battery life. Test it and use it with caution.

Why and How to Save Data

As I mentioned previously, you don't have full control over when your application becomes inactive or is terminated. Think of your application flow and building blocks and determine which states are important to save and under what circumstances.

Saving data is essential for a good user experience and for continuity. Saving should be considered when the application is about to exit, when it goes to the background, and at small intervals while your application is active.

To keep your audience engaged, avoid having them go over the same introductory steps every time they launch your application. Instead, bring them directly to the application's core. Your application may be the scheduler of an event occurring over several days. Keep track of the date it was last used and display it first the next time the application is opened.

Persistent data may be an important component of your application, as in a game where the usernames and scores are saved and can be improved upon. If your game was interrupted in the middle of game play, keep track of its progress and display it in the same state the next time it is visible.

Data may be an essential part of your application if the user has the opportunity to build a library of information to manipulate and save over time. If your application is a utility for collecting a selection of images, a storage mechanism is the core of its functionality.

Internal or External Storage?

Let's consider where to save data first. Data can be saved internally or externally.

Internally, *File.ApplicationDirectory* is the directory where your application and its assets are installed. AIR made this directory read-only because it is not writable on all systems. Instead, you can write to *File.ApplicationStorageDirectory*, the storage directory allocated to your application. Use this location to save fairly small amounts of data and information such as preferences and user settings. For example, your application data should not occupy more than a portion of the application's full size.

If your application is removed, the data saved in storage is deleted along with it.

Users can erase the data by selecting Settings→Applications→Manage Applications→Application→Clear Data. They will be alerted to the consequences with a warning that reads, "All of this application's data will be deleted permanently. This includes all files, settings, accounts, databases and so on." Android provides the option to set `allowClearUserData` to `false` to prevent users from clearing data. At the time of this writing, this feature is not available in the Flash Professional and Flash Builder permissions panel.

Data can also be saved internally in the memory cache allocated to your application. To use this approach, create a temporary file or folder and save data in it. This is a good place to save noncritical information such as downloaded data files that may not have a lasting value, or temporary saved files. If your application is removed, the data saved in the cache is also deleted.

Users can erase the cache under Settings→Applications→Manage Applications→Application→Clear Cache. Android does not provide the option to prevent clearing the cache.

Externally, data can be saved on the device's SD card under the *File.documentsDirectory* directory, also referred to as *File.userDirectory* or *File.desktopDirectory*. Use this approach for any relatively large amounts of data, such as images or video or temporary files. Create a directory with your application name to keep it distinct from other applications' data.

Writing to the card requires a permission, which needs to be added to the descriptor file. If you don't have this permission, AIR will throw a runtime error:

```
<uses-permission android:name=
                 "android.permission.WRITE_EXTERNAL_STORAGE" />
```

Before installing any data, make sure the user's phone has an SD card:

```
if (File.userDirectory)
    // proceeds with saving data
```

You can use this approach as a way for one application to write data and another application to access that data.

If your application is deleted, the data is not deleted automatically. However, the data is visible, and can therefore be removed by the user even if your application is not. If the user removes the SD card, the data becomes unavailable.

A word of warning: during development, if you are using Flash Professional to install your application on the device, every uninstall/reinstall deletes previously saved data, including updates. In Flash Builder, you can prevent this behavior from occurring by unchecking the "Clear application data" box on each Launch option when you first create your project. If the user installs an update of your application, however, previously saved data is preserved.

 The user may delete data, cache, and SD card content. Make sure to check for the existence of a file before reading or writing to it to avoid runtime errors. The exception to this rule is the local `SharedObject`, which handles this automatically.

It is better to use filenames than paths to guarantee consistency across devices and platforms, and the `resolvePath` method to refine the path. We will cover this further in "The Filesystem" on page 66.

Here is the list of directories and their equivalent paths:

/data/data/app.appId/app/assets

```
app:/
File.applicationDirectory
```

/data/data/app.appID/appID/Local Store

```
app-storage:/
```

/data/data/app.appID/appID/Local Store

```
File.applicationStorageDirectory
```

/sdcard

```
File.documentsDirectory
File.userDirectory
File.desktopDirectory
```

/data/data/app.appId/cache

```
File.createTempDirectory()
File.createTempFile()
```

There are several ways to save persistent application data on your device. The amount of space your data requires, and the complexity of the data, will determine which approach to take. We will discuss these options next.

Local SharedObject

This is a simple and convenient approach to saving small amounts of data on your device (100 KB maximum). You don't need to manage where the data is saved and if it already exists—this is handled automatically for you.

The SharedObject static class belongs to the *flash.net* package and inherits from Even tDispatcher.

A Flash shared object is similar to a browser cookie, but it does not expire and it has a default size limit of 100 KB. The object is written in the proprietary ActionScript Message Format (AMF). You can store data types such as String, Array, XML, Number, Data, Object, and ByteArray. An application can only access its own SharedObject data. A single application can have multiple shared objects.

To use this approach, first get a reference to your application's shared object. The getLocal() method creates it if it does not already exist:

```
import flash.net.SharedObject;
var so:SharedObject = SharedObject.getLocal("myApplication");
```

The preceding code creates a new directory in the application storage area and a shared object inside it called myApplication.sol.

To add data to a shared object, add attributes to its data (the data object itself is read-only). Here we are storing a string, an array, a boolean, and an object:

```
so.data.animal = "Hamster";
so.data.food = ["Grains", "Avocado", "Carrot"];
so.data.isVegetarian = true;
so.data.stuff = {toy:"Wheel", house:"Cage"};
```

To save these new attributes to the persistent local file, call the flush method. For devices, it is recommended that you save data right away to avoid losing the data if the application is terminated. Saving data can be performance-intensive, so carefully plan when your application initiates a save:

```
so.flush();
```

If you wish to monitor the save process, create a String variable to store what the flush method returns. If the result is pending, set a listener to trace the reason the data was not stored:

```
import flash.net.SharedObjectFlushStatus;
import flash.events.NetStatusEvent;

var flushStatus:String = so.flush();
if (flushStatus != null) {
    switch(flushStatus) {
        case SharedObjectFlushStatus.PENDING:
            so.addEventListener(NetStatusEvent.NET_STATUS,
                                        onFlushStatus);
            break;
        case SharedObjectFlushStatus.FLUSHED:
```

```
            trace("success");
            break;
        }
    }

    function onFlushStatus(event:NetStatusEvent):void {
        trace(event.info.code);
    }
```

To check that an attribute exists, do the following:

```
if (so.data.animal == undefined) {
    trace("What are you?");
} else {
    trace("Hello again, ", so.data.animal);
}
```

To display all the attributes, use:

```
for (var i:String in so.data) {
    trace("prop", i, ": ", so.data[i]);
}
// prop food : Grains,Avocado,Carrot
// prop isVegetarian : true
// prop stuff : [object, Object]
// prop animal : Hamster
```

To check the size of the shared object, use:

```
so.size;
// 140
```

If you wish to remove an attribute, use the `delete` command. Setting the variable to `undefined` or `null` changes its value but doesn't remove it:

```
delete so.data.animal;
```

If you wish to remove all of the attributes, use the `clear()` method. This method will also delete the shared object itself:

```
so.clear();
```

The Filesystem

The filesystem should be familiar to anyone who owns a computer. It is responsible for the hierarchical organization of files and projects, with the option to read, write, move, and delete files. In AIR for Android, files can only be created and manipulated in the application storage directory or on the SD card.

The `File` class belongs to the *flash.filesystem* package and inherits from the `FileRefer` ence class. It represents the path to a directory or a file, regardless of whether the directory or file exists or has not yet been created.

You can create a `File` object to the path of the file you want to access, here the application storage area. The `resolvePath` function creates the path from the current location which is the *.swf* file that is currently running:

```
import flash.filesystem.File;
var file:File
    = File.applicationStorageDirectory.resolvePath("hello.txt");
```

Data is read or written using `FileStream`. Create it, open it, and close it after the operation is complete.

The `FileStream` method you should use depends on the type of data you are encoding. For text files, use `readUTFBytes` and `writeUTFBytes`. For a `ByteArray`, use `readBytes` and `writeBytes`, and so on. To get a complete list of methods, refer to *http://help.adobe.com/en_US/FlashPlatform/reference/actionscript/3/flash/filesystem/FileStream.html*.

Writing data to the file

Use the `FileMode.WRITE` method to write data to the file. In the following example, we are creating a folder if one does not already exist, and then we are creating a file in the folder:

```
import flash.filesystem.File;
import flash.filesystem.FileStream;
import flash.filesystem.FileMode;

var folder:File
        = File.applicationStorageDirectory.resolvePath("greetings");
    if (!folder.exists) {
        folder.createDirectory();
}
var file:File = folder.resolvePath("hello.txt");
```

Note that although a reference to the new file has been created, the file will not exist until data is saved in it. Let's write a simple string:

```
var fileStream:FileStream = new FileStream();
fileStream.open(file, FileMode.WRITE);
fileStream.writeUTFBytes("Can you hear me?");
fileStream.close();
```

To make your file unique, save the data as part of the name as follows:

```
var now:Date = new Date();
var name:String = "file" +
now.getDay() + "_" + now.getHours() + "_" +
now.getMinutes() + "_" + now.getSeconds();
```

Reading a file

Use the `FileMode.READ` method to read a file. In the following example, if the file doesn't exist, we don't need to read its data:

```
var file:File
    = File.applicationStorageDirectory.resolvePath("greetings/hello.txt");
if (!file.exists) {
        return;
}
var fileStream:FileStream = new FileStream();
fileStream.open(file, FileMode.READ);
var string:String = fileStream.readUTFBytes(fileStream.bytesAvailable);
fileStream.close();
trace(string); // Can you hear me?
```

Deleting a file

Let's delete the file first:

```
var file:File
    = File.applicationStorageDirectory.resolvePath("greetings/hello.txt");
if (file.exists) {
        file.deleteFile();
}
```

Now let's delete the directory. Note the boolean passed in the `deleteDirectory` function. This is to prevent errors. If the boolean is set to **true**, the folder is deleted only if the directory exists:

```
var folder:File
    = File.applicationStorageDirectory.resolvePath("greetings");
folder.deleteDirectory(true);
```

Choosing between synchronous and asynchronous mode

You have a choice of synchronous or asynchronous mode (`fileStream open` or `openAsync`). The former uses the application's main thread, so the application does not execute any other process until a command is completed. Use `trace catch` to capture any errors. The latter uses a different thread and runs in the background. You need to set listeners to be notified when the command is in progress or completed. Only one mode can be used at a time.

Asynchronous mode is often preferred for mobile development. Choosing one method over the other is also a function of how large the data set is, as well as if the saved data is needed in the current state of your application and the desired user experience.

The write and read examples shown earlier use a synchronized method. To trace errors, use a `try catch` statement:

```
try {
    var string:String = fileStream.readUTFBytes(fileStream.bytesAvailable);
    fileStream.close();
} catch(error:Error) {
```

```
        trace(error.message);
    }
```

In this asynchronous example, we read a text file and store it when it is received in its entirety:

```
import flash.events.Event;
import flash.events.ProgressEvent;

var fileStream:FileStream;
var file:File
        = File.applicationStorageDirectory.resolvePath("hello.txt");
if (!file.exists) {
        return;
}

fileStream = new FileStream();
fileStream.addEventListener(ProgressEvent.PROGRESS, onProgress);
fileStream.addEventListener(Event.COMPLETE, onComplete);
fileStream.openAsync(file, FileMode.READ);

function onProgress(event:ProgressEvent):void {
    trace(fileStream.bytesAvailable);
}

function onComplete(event:Event):void {
    fileStream.removeEventListener(ProgressEvent.PROGRESS, onProgress);
    fileStream.removeEventListener(Event.COMPLETE, onComplete);
    var bytes:uint = fileStream.bytesAvailable;
    fileStream.close();
}
```

Writing data and saving it to temporary files

You can write and save data to a temporary directory or file. The data is saved to the application cache. This method is particularly useful if you have data you want to temporarily save during the life of the application while keeping memory free. You can create a directory or a file:

```
var tempDirectory:File = File.createTempDirectory();
var tempFile:File = File.createTempFile();
trace(tempDirectory.nativePath, tempDirectory.isDirectory);
trace(tempFile.nativePath, tempFile.isDirectory);
```

Keep a variable reference to the data while the application is running, and delete the file when the application quits. If you want to make the cache data persistent, save its path using its nativePath property, and save its name using its name property, in a SharedObject or another file in the application storage directory. Finally, another good place to save temporary files is the SD card:

```
tempFile.deleteFile();
tempDirectory.deleteFile();
```

Unlike AIR on the desktop, when files are deleted they are removed immediately because the device doesn't have a trash folder. The following command gives the same result as the ones shown earlier:

```
tempFile.moveToTrash();
tempDirectory.moveToTrash();
```

In addition to these features, you can also add data to the end of a file; when updating the file, you can read it and write to it at the same time. Also useful is the ability to copy files and folders and move them to another location. You can use this technique to move some the application assets to the SD card. Note, however, that you should never delete any files that came installed with your application, because that will invalidate it.

Using the SQLite Database

Using the SQLite database system is another solution for saving local persistent data, and it is the preferred solution if your information is somewhat complex, if you want the option to organize it in different ways, or if you want to keep it private.

The AIR runtime contains an SQL database engine to create, organize, retrieve, and manipulate the data, using the open source Structured Query Language Lite (SQLite) database system. It does not use the Android OS SQLite framework.

The SQL classes compose the bulk of the *flash.data* package. Once again, you have a choice between synchronous and asynchronous mode. For the sake of simplicity, we will use synchronous mode in our examples.

Creating the database file

If the database doesn't exist yet, create it and save it as a single file in the filesystem:

```
import flash.filesystem.File;

function createDatabase():void {
    var file:File =
        File.applicationStorageDirectory.resolvePath("myData.db");
    if (file.exists) {
        trace("I already exist, ready to be used");
    } else {
        trace("I did not exist, now I am created");
    }
}
```

It is usually a good idea to keep the database in the *ApplicationStorageDirectory* directory so that it is not accessible by other applications and it is preserved when the application is updated. If you want to save it to the SD card instead, the path should be:

```
var file:File = File.documentsDirectory.resolvePath("myData.db");
```

Opening the database file

The SQLConnection class is used to create queries or execute them. It is essential that it is a class variable, not a local variable, so that it doesn't go out of scope.

```
import flash.data.SQLConnection;
var connection:SQLConnection;

connection = new SQLConnection();
```

To open the connection pointing to your database file, call the open method and pass the File reference:

```
import flash.events.SQLEvent;
import flash.events.SQLErrorEvent;

try {
    connection.open(file);
    trace("connection opened");
} catch(error:Error) {
    trace(error.message);
}
```

Creating the table

An SQL database is organized into tables. Each table consists of columns representing individual attributes and their values. Create the table according to your needs by giving each column a name and a data type. The table will have as many rows as items, or records, created.

> SQLite stores the expected data types such as Integer, Text, Real, and Null. It also supports the BLOB type, a raw binary data type which stores information exactly as it was input. This is particularly useful for storing a ByteArray. You can read about SQLite at *http://www.sqlite.org/data type3.html*.

You communicate to the database by creating an SQLStatement object and then sending its sqlConnection property to the connection that is open. Next, write the command to its text attribute as a string, and finally, call its execute method.

In this example, we are creating a new table called geography using the statement CREATE TABLE IF NOT EXISTS to guarantee that it is only created once. It has three columns: an id column which self-increments and functions as the primary key, a country column of type Text, and a city column of type Text. The primary key is a unique identifier to distinguish each row. Figure 6-1 shows the geography table:

id	country	city

Figure 6-1. The geography table's fields

```
import flash.data.SQLStatement;
import flash.data.SQLMode;

var statement:SQLStatement = new SQLStatement();
statement.sqlConnection = connection;
var request:String =
    "CREATE TABLE IF NOT EXISTS geography ("
    + "id INTEGER PRIMARY KEY AUTOINCREMENT, country TEXT, city TEXT )";
statement.text = request;

try {
    statement.execute();
} catch(error:Error) {
    trace(error.message);
}
```

Adding data

Once the table is created, data is added using an INSERT INTO statement and some values:

```
var statement:SQLStatement = new SQLStatement();
statement.sqlConnection = connection;
var insert:String =
    "INSERT INTO geography (country, city) VALUES ('France', 'Paris')";
statement.text = insert;

try {
    statement.execute();
} catch(error:Error) {
    trace(error.message);
}
```

If the data is dynamic, you can use the following syntax. Note that unnamed parameters are used, therefore relying on the automatically assigned index value. Figure 6-2 shows the result:

```
addItem({country:"France", city:"Paris"});

function addItem(object:Object):void {
    var statement:SQLStatement = new SQLStatement();
    statement.sqlConnection = connection;
var insert:String = "INSERT INTO geography (country, city) VALUES (?, ?)";
statement.text = insert;
statement.parameters[0] = object.country;
statement.parameters[1] = object.city;

try {
        statement.execute();
        trace("item created");
```

id	country	city
0	France	Paris

Figure 6-2. The geography table with some dynamic data added

```
    } catch(error:SQLError) {
        trace(error.message);
    }
}
```

As an alternative, you can use the following syntax. Here we assume named parameters that work much like an associate array. Figure 6-3 shows the result:

```
addItem({country:"United States", city:"New York"});

function addItem(object:Object):void {
    var statement:SQLStatement = new SQLStatement();
    statement.sqlConnection = connection;
var insert:String =
    "INSERT INTO geography (country, city) VALUES (:co, :ci)";
statement.text = insert;
statement.parameters[":co"] = object.country;
    statement.parameters[":ci"] = object.city;

try {
        statement.execute();
        trace("item created");
    } catch(error:SQLError) {
        trace(error.message);
    }
}
```

id	country	city
0	France	Paris
1	United States	New York

Figure 6-3. The geography table with dynamic data and named parameters added

Using either of these two dynamic approaches facilitates re-use of the same SQL statement to add many items, but is also more secure because the parameters are not written in the SQL text. This prevents a possible SQL injection attack.

Requesting data

Data is requested by using the SELECT statement. The result is an SQLResult that you can get as a property of the SQLStatement: statement.getResult(). Each row item is received as an object with property names corresponding to the table column names. Note the use of the * in place of the columns' name to get the entire table:

```
import flash.data.SQLResult;

var statement:SQLStatement = new SQLStatement();
statement.sqlConnection = connection;
statement.text = "SELECT * FROM geography";

statement.addEventListener(SQLEvent.RESULT, selectionReceived);
statement.execute();

function selectionReceived(event:SQLEvent):void {
    statement.removeEventListener(SQLEvent.RESULT, selectionReceived);

var result:SQLResult = statement.getResult();
if (result != null) {
        var rows:int = result.data.length;
        for (var i:int = 0; i < rows; i++) {
            var row:Object = result.data[i];
            trace(row.id + "" + row.country + "" + row.city);
        }
    }
}
```

Instead of requesting the entire table, you may want to receive only one item in the table. Let's request the country that has New York as a city. Execute(1) only returns the item stored under table ID 1:

```
var statement:SQLStatement = new SQLStatement();
statement.sqlConnection = connection;
statement.text = "SELECT country FROM geography WHERE city = 'New York'";
try {
    statement.execute(1);
    var result:SQLResult = statement.getResult();
    if (result.data != null) {
        trace(result.data[0].country);
    }
} catch(error:Error) {
    trace("item", error.message);
}
```

Let's make the same request again, passing the city as dynamic data:

```
getCountry("New York");

function getCountry(myCity:String):void {
    var statement:SQLStatement = new SQLStatement();
    statement.sqlConnection = connection;
    statement.text = "SELECT country FROM geography WHERE city = :ci";
    statement.parameters[":ci"] = myCity;
    try {
        statement.execute(1);
        var result:SQLResult = statement.getResult();
        if (result.data != null) {
            trace(result.data[0].country);
```

```
        }
    } catch(error:Error) {
        trace("item", error.message);
    }
}
```

Editing existing data

Existing data can be modified. In this example, we're searching for the country United States and changing the city to Washington, DC. Figure 6-4 shows the result:

```
modifyItem("United States", "Washington DC");

function modifyItem(myCountry:String, myCity:String):void {
    var statement:SQLStatement = new SQLStatement();
    statement.sqlConnection = connection;
    var updateMessage:String =
        "UPDATE geography SET city = :ci where country = :co";
    statement.text = updateMessage;
    statement.parameters[":co"] = myCountry;
    statement.parameters[":ci"] = myCity;
    try {
        statement.execute();
        trace("all removed");
    } catch(error:Error) {
        trace("item", error.message);
    }
}
```

id	country	city
0	France	Paris
1	United States	Washington DC

Figure 6-4. The geography table with existing data modified

Now let's look for the country France and delete the row that contains it (see Figure 6-5). We are using the DELETE FROM statement. Note that deleting a row does not modify the IDs of the other items. The ID of the deleted row is no longer usable:

```
function deleteItem(myCountry:String):void {
    var statement:SQLStatement = new SQLStatement();
    statement.sqlConnection = connection;
    var deleteMessage:String = "DELETE FROM geography where country = :co";
    statement.text = deleteMessage;
    statement.parameters[":co"] = myCountry;
    try {
        statement.execute();
        trace("all removed");
    } catch(error:Error) {
        trace("item", error.message);
```

```
        }
    }
```

id	country	city
1	United States	Washington DC

Figure 6-5. The geography table with row 0 deleted

As you have seen, you can do a lot while working within a structure you create.

Embedding a Database

Sometimes you may want to install your application with a database that is already prepopulated. In such a case, you should include the *db* file when you package your application. In Flash Professional, select File→AIR Android Settings→General→Included files, click the plus sign (+), and browse to the *db* file. In Flash Builder, place the *db* file in the *src* directory.

To make changes to the database, first you need to move it from *applicationDirectory* to *applicationStorageDirectory*. As discussed previously, *applicationDirectory* is a read-only directory.

Now check that the database is embedded:

```
var embedded:File = File.applicationDirectory.resolvePath("embeddedDB.db");
if (embedded.exists) {
    trace("database was embedded");
    // move on to the next step
} else {
    trace("database was not embedded");
}
```

Next, check that it has not yet been copied. If it does not exist yet, copy the database over:

```
var local:File =
    File.applicationStorageDirectory.resolvePath("myDatabase.db");
if (!local.exists) {
    embedded.copyTo(local);
}
```

Try to keep the embedded database small. If it is substantial in size, consider copying it asynchronously using the copyToAsync method.

Once the database is copied to the editable directory, you can use it as you would any other database. Note that the original database cannot be deleted. Any attempt to change the application package would make it invalid.

Using Encrypted Local Storage

AIR has an encryption functionality which you can use to store sensitive data. The data is encrypted using AES-CBC 128-bit. Although this capability is not available for Android at the time of this writing, it is worth discussing in case it is added in the future.

The EncryptedLocalStorage static class belongs to the *flash.data* package and inherits from Object. The data is application-specific and can only be retrieved from within its security sandbox. It is saved as a ByteArray and requires a key.

To encrypt the data, use:

```
import flash.utils.ByteArray;
import flash.data.EncryptedLocalStore;

function write():void {
    var myData:ByteArray = new ByteArray();
    myData.writeUTFBytes("my very sensitive data");
    EncryptedLocalStore.setItem("myKey", myData);
}
```

To decrypt the data, use:

```
function read():void {
    var myData:ByteArray = EncryptedLocalStore.getItem("myKey");
    if (myData != null) {
        trace(myData.readUTFBytes(myData.bytesAvailable));
    }
}
```

To remove the data, use:

```
function delete():void {
    EncryptedLocalStore.removeItem("myKey");
}
```

Conclusion

We covered a lot of material in this chapter. Being able to save data expands your application's functionality and allows you to customize it to your users' needs. It is also an important feature on mobile devices where local data access is so much quicker—and cheaper, especially if your audience uses 3G—than remote data.

CHAPTER 7

Multitouch Technology

Touch has a memory.

—John Keats

Put a young child in front of a computer and see her reach for the screen to grab moving pixels. Touching an element to impact it is the most natural form of input.

Over the past few years, there has been an explosion of innovation utilizing the latest research in haptic technology, including everything from touch-based computers such as the iPhone and Microsoft Surface to tangible user interfaces such as the Reactable to gesture-based motion tracking as in Microsoft's Kinect.

The keyboard and the mouse that we have grown accustomed to using to communicate with our digital tools are perhaps now becoming outdated. The human hand, and even the entire human body, may be the interaction method of the future.

This is what we will cover in this chapter.

A Brief History

The first multitouch system designed for human input was developed in 1982 by Nimish Mehta of the University of Toronto. Bell Labs, followed by other research labs, soon picked up on Mehta's idea. Apple's 2007 launch of the iPhone, which is still the point of reference today for multitouch experiences and gestures, popularized a new form of user interaction.

More recently, Microsoft launched Windows 7, Adobe added multitouch and gesture capability to Flash Player and AIR, and a range of smartphones, tablets, and laptops that include multitouch sensing capability have become available or are just entering the market. Common devices such as ATMs, DVD rental kiosks, and even maps at the local mall are increasingly equipped with touch screens.

For an in-depth chronology, please read Bill Buxton's article at *http://www.billbuxton .com/multitouchOverview.html*.

Exploring the use of alternate input devices in computing is often referred to as *physical computing*. For the past 20 years, this research has advanced considerably, but only recently has it been reserved for exhibitions or isolated equipment installations. These advances are now starting to crop up in many consumer electronics devices, such as the Nintendo Wii, Microsoft Xbox, and Sony PlayStation Move.

A playful example of a human–computer interface is the Mud Tub. Created by Tom Gerhardt in an effort to close the gap between our bodies and the digital world, the Mud Tub uses mud to control a computer. For more information, go to *http://tomger hardt.com/mudtub/*.

For our purposes, we will only use clean fingers and fairly predictable touch sensors.

What Is Multitouch and Gesture?

Multitouch is a technology that is capable of detecting one or more touches (typically via a finger) and movements on a surface simultaneously. A *gesture* is a series of touches recognized as a pattern and registered as a single event. The reading and interpretation of touches is a task an ambitious developer can tackle, but luckily, platforms are increasingly doing the job for us.

How Does It Work?

The number of touch screen manufacturers is growing rapidly and their engineers are constantly researching new and improved ways to detect touches. The technology is a combination of ingenious hardware and clever software.

Resistive technology requires two flexible sheets, electrically conductive, with vertical and horizontal lines for precision location. The sheets are separated by an air gap or microdots. When pressed firmly, they make contact and a change in the electrical current is registered and sent to a controller. This technology is very accurate and fairly inexpensive, but it does not support multitouch and does not work well with gestures.

Capacitive technology uses a surface made of insulator-like glass, also called a ground plane, and coated with a transparent conductor. Voltage is applied to the surface. The finger works as the capacitor that modifies the surface's electrostatic field—more specifically, the coupling between row and column electrodes. The controller can determine the location of the touch from the change in capacitance as measured from the four corners of the surface. This technology is durable and accurate, except when the screen is small or the user is wearing gloves, and it is used in many modern PDAs, such as the iPhone and Android-based devices.

Other technologies, used in nonmobile devices or equipment in a controlled environment, include *infrared*, *acoustic digitizer*, and *in-cell*.

The Multitouch Class

The Flash platform synthesizes gestures across platforms. It also provides the tools needed to access the raw touch data. While support for individual APIs can vary, some level of touch capability is currently compatible with Windows 7, iOS, Mac OS X, Android, and RIM.

The `flash.ui.Multitouch` class is a recent addition to the ActionScript language to support user input. The Android platform supports multitouch, but it is always a good practice to test the device's capabilities:

```
import flash.ui.Multitouch;

if (Multitouch.supportsGestureEvents == true) {
    trace(Multitouch.supportedGestures);
}
```

The `supportedGestures` property returns an array of gestures that your specific device understands. This is particularly important to test if you use unusual gestures. For instance, the list of gestures for the Nexus One is:

```
gestureZoom, gestureRotate, gesturePan, gestureSwipe, gestureTwoFingerTap
```

For a summary of gesture definitions across platforms, see the handy reference at *http://www.lukew.com/ff/entry.asp?1071*.

Testing support for multitouch is done separately:

```
if (Multitouch.supportsTouchEvents == true) {
    trace(Multitouch.maxTouchPoints);
}
```

The `maxTouchPoints` property returns the number of touches supported simultaneously. Most Android devices currently support two points. We will come back to this in the section titled "The TouchEvent Class" on page 88.

The `flash.ui.MultitouchInputMode` class provides the mechanism to select the mode of input the application uses. Only one mode can be active at a time.

When using the mode `NONE`, all events are interpreted as `mouseEvent`. This is the default mode:

```
import flash.ui.MultitouchInputMode;
Multitouch.inputMode = MultitouchInputMode.NONE
```

With the `GESTURE` mode, all events are interpreted as `GestureEvent`:

```
Multitouch.inputMode = MultitouchInputMode.GESTURE;
```

With the `TOUCH_POINT` mode, all events are interpreted as `touchEvent`:

```
Multitouch.inputMode = MultitouchInputMode.TOUCH_POINT
```

The mode can be changed at runtime, but you should use it only if you have a case that requires it and if it is not confusing to the user. Only one mode, the last one chosen, is possible at a time.

The GestureEvent Class

A GestureEvent is the interpretation of multiple points as a recognizable pattern. The Flash platform offers three gesture classes: GestureEvent, TransformGestureEvent, and PressAndTapGestureEvent. Gestures cannot be detected in sequence. The user must finish the first gesture, lift her fingers, and then start the next gesture.

Here is how to set a listener for the event type you want to receive:

```
Multitouch.inputMode = MultitouchInputMode.GESTURE;
stage.addEventListener(TransformGestureEvent.GESTURE_ZOOM, onZoom);
```

Gesture events have a phase property that is used to indicate the progress of the gesture. Its value is BEGIN when the finger is first pressed down; UPDATE while the finger is moving; and END when the finger leaves the screen. Another phase, ALL, is for events such as swipes or two-finger taps, which only return one phase.

A typical use for the phase property is to play one sound when the gesture begins and another sound when it ends:

```
import flash.ui.MultitouchInputMode;
import flash.events.GesturePhase;
import flash.events.TransformGestureEvent

function onZoom(event:TransformGestureEvent):void {
    if (event.phase == GesturePhase.BEGIN) {
        // play hello sound
    } else if (event.phase == GesturePhase.END) {
        // play good bye sound
    }
}
```

Gesture events have other properties related to position, as well as some that are relevant to their particular type. One gesture event, TransformGestureEvent, has many types, which we will discuss in the following subsections.

 All of the illustrations in the following subsections courtesy of Gesture-Works (*http://www.gestureworks.com*).

The Zoom Gesture

The zoom gesture is also referred to as pinching. With this gesture, the user places two fingers on the object, increasing and decreasing the distance between the fingers to scale the object up and down in size (see Figure 7-1).

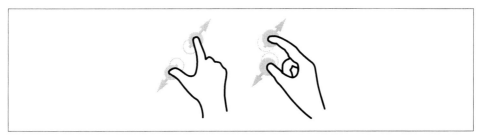

Figure 7-1. The zoom gesture

The following code creates a sprite and scales it according to the movement being performed:

```
import flash.ui.Multitouch;
import flash.ui.MultitouchInputMode;
import flash.display.Sprite;
import flash.events.TransformGestureEvent;

var sprite:Sprite;

Multitouch.inputMode = MultitouchInputMode.GESTURE;

sprite = new Sprite();
sprite.x = stage.stageWidth * 0.5;
sprite.y = stage.stageHeight * 0.5;
var g:Graphics = sprite.graphics;
g.beginFill(0xFF6600);
g.drawCircle(0, 0, 150);
g.endFill();
sprite.addEventListener(TransformGestureEvent.GESTURE_ZOOM, onZoom);

sprite.x = stage.stageWidth * 0.5;
sprite.y = stage.stageHeight * 0.5;

function onZoom(event:TransformGestureEvent):void {
    sprite.scaleX *=  event.scaleX;
    sprite.scaleY *=  event.scaleY;
}
```

The event.scaleX and event.scaleY values are used to calculate the relative distance between the two fingers.

The Rotate Gesture

You can rotate an object using two different gestures. With the first gesture, you place one finger on the object and move the second finger around it. With the second gesture, you spread the two fingers apart and rotate one clockwise and the other counterclockwise (see Figure 7-2). The latter seems to work better on small devices.

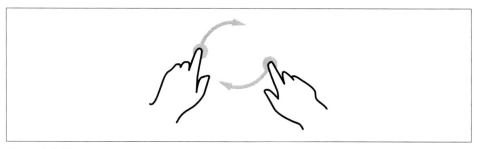

Figure 7-2. The rotate gesture

Here we use the drawing API to create a sprite with a rectangle shape:

```
import flash.display.Sprite;
import flash.events.TransformGestureEvent;
import flash.ui.Multitouch;
import flash.ui.MultitouchInputMode;

var sprite:Sprite;

Multitouch.inputMode = MultitouchInputMode.GESTURE;

sprite = new Sprite();
sprite.x = stage.stageWidth * 0.5;
sprite.y = stage.stageHeight * 0.5;
var g:Graphics = sprite.graphics;
g.beginFill(0xFF6600);
g.drawRect(-150, -150, 300, 300);
g.endFill();
sprite.addEventListener(TransformGestureEvent.GESTURE_ROTATE, onRotate);


sprite.x = stage.stageWidth * 0.5;
sprite.y = stage.stageHeight * 0.5;


function onRotate(event:TransformGestureEvent):void {
    event.currentTarget.rotation += event.rotation;
}
```

The event.rotation value is the cumulated rotation change relative to the position of the stage. Notice how I drew the rectangle so that it is centered in the middle of the sprite. The default position is top left, so offset your art to have its registration point in the center of the pixels.

The following code moves the child sprite to be offset by half its dimension:

```
someParent.x = 0;
someParent.y = 0;
someChild.x = - someChild.width * 0.5;
someChild.y = - someChild.height * 0.5;
```

Bitmaps are also offset according to the dimension of their bitmapData:

```
var bitmapData:BitmapData = new BitmapData();
var bitmap:Bitmap = new Bitmap(bitmapData);
bitmap.x = - bitmapData.width * 0.5;
bitmap.y = - bitmapData.height * 0.5;
```

The Pan Gesture

You use a pan gesture to reveal an object that is off-screen if it is larger than the screen. The use of two fingers is not immediately intuitive. This gesture seems to work best when using a light touch. Figure 7-3 shows an example.

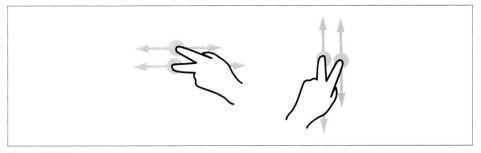

Figure 7-3. The pan gesture

In this example, we are drawing a 1,000-pixel-long rectangle with a sine wave on it. The wave is so that you can see the sprite move when you pan:

```
Multitouch.inputMode = MultitouchInputMode.GESTURE;
var sprite:Sprite;

function createArt():void {
    sprite = new Sprite();
    addChild(sprite);

    var g:Graphics = sprite.graphics;
    g.beginFill(0xFFCCFF);
    g.drawRect(0, 550, 1000, 200);
    g.endFill();
    g.lineStyle(3, 0xFF0000);
    // 650 is an arbitrary pixel position
    g.moveTo(2, 650);

    // draw a sin wave
    var xpos:Number = 0;
    var ypos:Number = 0;
    var angle:Number = 0;
    for (var i:int = 0; i < 200; i++) {
        xpos += 5;
        ypos = Math.sin(angle)*100 + 650;
        angle += 0.20;
        sprite.graphics.lineTo (xpos, ypos);
    }
```

```
        stage.addEventListener(TransformGestureEvent.GESTURE_PAN, onPan);
    }

    function onPan(event:TransformGestureEvent):void {
        // move the sprite along with the motion
        sprite.x += event.offsetX;
    }
```

offsetX is the horizontal magnitude of change since your finger made contact with the screen as it is moving across the screen.

The Swipe Gesture

A swipe gesture is often used as a way to dismiss an element as though you are pushing it off-screen. The direction of the swipe is defined by a single integer. Left to right and bottom to top returns -1. Right to left and bottom to top returns 1. Figure 7-4 shows an example of the swipe gesture.

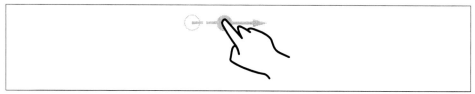

Figure 7-4. The swipe gesture

The following code simulates the act of reading a book. Swiping from left to right brings you further in the book. Swiping in the other direction returns you to the beginning of the book:

```
    import flash.events.TransformGestureEvent;
    import flash.text.TextField;
    import flash.text.TextFormat;

    var pageText:TextField;
    var counter:int = 1;

    function createArt():void {
        var textFormat:TextFormat = new TextFormat();
        textFormat.size = 90;
        textFormat.color = 0xFF6600;

        // create a text field to display the page number
        pageText = new TextField();
        pageText.x = 100;
        pageText.y = 200;
        pageText.autoSize = TextFieldAutoSize.LEFT;
        pageText.defaultTextFormat = textFormat;
        pageText.text = "Page " + counter;
        addChild(pageText);
```

```
    // create a listener for a swipe gesture
    stage.addEventListener(TransformGestureEvent.GESTURE_SWIPE, onSwipe);
}

function onSwipe(event:TransformGestureEvent):void {
    counter -= event.offsetX;
    if (counter < 1) counter = 1;
    pageText.text = "Page " + counter;
}
```

The offsetX value is used to decrement or increment the page number of the book.

The Press and Tap Gesture

The press and tap gesture, PressAndTapGestureEvent, only has one type: GESTURE_PRESS_AND_TAP. This gesture is more complicated than the others, and users may not figure it out without instructions. Unlike the previous gestures, this gesture happens in two steps: first one finger is pressed and then another finger taps (see Figure 7-5). It is really two events synthesized as one.

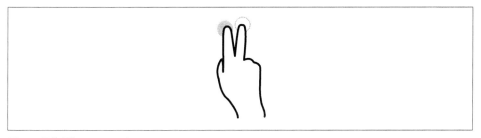

Figure 7-5. The press and tap gesture

The following code creates an elegant UI for selecting a menu and then tapping to access its submenu, as a context menu:

```
import flash.events.PressAndTapGestureEvent;

stage.addEventListener(PressAndTapGestureEvent.GESTURE_PRESS_AND_TAP,
                                    onPressAndTap);

function onPressAndTap(event:PressAndTapGestureEvent):void {
    trace(event.tapLocalX);
    trace(event.tapLocalY);
    trace(event.tapStageX);
    trace(event.tapStageY);
}
```

 The press and tap gesture is not supported by most devices at the time of this writing. I have provided this information in case the repertoire of gestures broadens in the future.

The Two-Finger Tap Gesture

GestureEvent only has one type, GESTURE_TWO_FINGER_TAP, and it is not supported by Android at the time of this writing. A tap is similar to a mouse click, but it requires making contact on a limited spatial area, with the two fingers close together, in a short time period. Figure 7-6 shows an example of a two-finger tap.

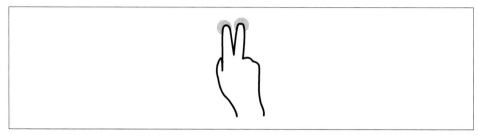

Figure 7-6. The two-finger tap gesture

The two-finger tap is a good gesture for a strong statement, as when you want the user to make a decision. You could use it, for instance, to pause and play a video:

```
import flash.events.PressAndTapGestureEvent;

sprite.addEventListener(GestureEvent.GESTURE_TWO_FINGER_TAP, onTwoFinger);

function onTwoFinger(event:GestureEvent):void {
    // play or pause video
}
```

The TouchEvent Class

A touch event is similar to a mouse event, except that you can have multiple inputs at once. Because this event uses more power, you should only use it if you need to capture more than one point. If you only need to track one point, the mouse event will work well even though your mouse is now a finger.

Touches are also called raw touch data because you receive them as is. If you want to interpret them as gestures, you need to write the logic yourself or use a third-party library.

First, set the input mode to TOUCH_POINT:

```
import flash.ui.Multitouch;
import flash.ui.MultitouchInputMode;
import flash.events.TouchEvent;

Multitouch.inputMode = MultitouchInputMode.TOUCH_POINT;
```

TOUCH_TAP is similar to a mouse up event. The following code creates a simple application where every touch creates a new circle:

```
import flash.events.TouchEvent;

Multitouch.inputMode = MultitouchInputMode.TOUCH_POINT;

stage.addEventListener(TouchEvent.TOUCH_TAP, onTouchTap);

function onTouchTap(event:TouchEvent):void {
    var sprite:Sprite = new Sprite();
    sprite.graphics.lineStyle(25, Math.random()*0xFFFFFF);
    sprite.graphics.drawCircle(0, 0, 80);
    sprite.x = event.stageX;
    sprite.y = event.stageY;
    addChild(sprite);
}
```

The touchPointID is a new and important event property. Each new touch has a unique ID associated with it, from TOUCH_BEGIN to TOUCH_END. touchPointID gives you a way to identify and store every point and associate data with it if needed.

In this example, we use an Object to store the ID as a property and associate it with a sprite. To drag and drop the sprites, we use the startTouchDrag and stopTouchDrag methods:

```
var touches:Object = {};

stage.addEventListener(TouchEvent.TOUCH_BEGIN, onTouchBegin);
stage.addEventListener(TouchEvent.TOUCH_END, onTouchEnd);

function onTouchBegin(event:TouchEvent):void {
    var sprite:Sprite = createCircle(event.stageX, event.stageY);
    addChild(sprite);

    // store the touchPointID and the sprite
    touches[event.touchPointID] = sprite;
    // drag the sprite
    sprite.startTouchDrag(event.touchPointID, true);
}

function onTouchEnd(event:TouchEvent):void {
    // retrieve the sprite using the touchPointID
    var sprite:Sprite = touches[event.touchPointID];
    // stop drag and destroy
    stopTouchDrag(event.touchPointID);
    sprite.graphics.clear();
    removeChild(sprite);
    touches[event.touchPointID] = null;
}

function createCircle(x:int, y:int):Sprite {
    var sprite:Sprite = new Sprite();
    sprite.graphics.lineStyle(25, Math.random()*0xFFFFFF);
    sprite.graphics.drawCircle(0, 0, 100);
    sprite.x = x;
    sprite.y = y;
```

```
        return sprite;
}
```

As we discussed earlier, `Multitouch.maxTouchPoints` determines how many touches a device can support. Many Android devices only support the detection of two simultaneous touch points.

 A current bug in Android will always report to AIR that two touch points are available, but this will not limit the number of simultaneous touch point events that may be dispatched. For example, if a device supports five touch points, it may still report that it only supports two, but will dispatch events for all five. This bug should be resolved in an upcoming release.

There is no built-in mechanism to prevent a new touch if the maximum has been reached. In fact, expect unpredictable behavior such as the oldest touch no longer functioning. To prevent this, keep a count of how many points are present and stop the code from executing if you have reached the limit:

```
var pointCount:int = 0;

function onTouchBegin(event:TouchEvent):void {
    if (pointCount == Multitouch.maxTouchPoints) {
    return;
    }
    pointCount++;
    // create new sprite
}

function onTouchEnd(event:TouchEvent):void {
    pointCount--;
    // remove old sprite
}
```

Let's create an application using touch events and the drawing API. On `TouchBegin`, a new sprite is created and associated with a touch ID. It draws on `TouchMove` and is removed on `TouchEnd`. Draw using two fingers or two separate users:

```
Multitouch.inputMode = MultitouchInputMode.TOUCH_POINT;

var touches:Object = {};

stage.addEventListener(TouchEvent.TOUCH_BEGIN, onTouchBegin);
stage.addEventListener(TouchEvent.TOUCH_MOVE, onTouchMove);
stage.addEventListener(TouchEvent.TOUCH_END, onTouchEnd);

function onTouchBegin(event:TouchEvent):void {
    var sprite:Sprite = new Sprite();
    addChild(sprite);
    sprite.graphics.lineStyle(3, Math.random()*0xFFFFFF);
    sprite.graphics.moveTo(event.stageX, event.stageY);
    touches[event.touchPointID] = sprite;
}
```

```
function onTouchMove(event:TouchEvent):void {
    var sprite:Sprite = touches[event.touchPointID];
    sprite.graphics.lineTo(event.stageX, event.stageY);
}

function onTouchEnd(event:TouchEvent):void {
    var sprite:Sprite = touches[event.touchPointID];
    sprite.graphics.clear();
    removeChild(sprite);
    touches[event.touchPointID] = null;
}
```

Other available events are TOUCH_OUT, TOUCH_OVER, TOUCH_ROLL_OUT, and TOUCH_ROLL_OVER.

 There is a known bug on the Nexus One in which two points that are too close together get swapped or returned reverse values. The issue does not seem to exist on other devices.

The GestureWorks Library

Ideum, a design company specializing in museum work, developed and sells a library for detecting multitouch and gestures for Flash Professional CS5 and Flash Builder 4.0. Called GestureWorks (see *http://gestureworks.com*), the library supports all the gestures we have discussed thus far.

GestureWorks provides unique gestures such as flip/flick which calculates acceleration, 3D tilt, and a multitouch gesture scroll. It also supports continuous transitional and concurrent gesturing, which means you can use multiple gestures, such as move, rotate, and scale, simultaneously.

GestureWorks also includes a simulator for testing touch-based interactions within your application if you do not have ready access to touch-based screens. This should facilitate a quicker and smoother development process.

Lastly, GestureWorks comes with many examples, including a Google Maps example which demonstrates the expected gestures when manipulating a map. This will give you a head start if you are interested in applications using geocoding.

Designing for Touch

Designing for touch can be tricky. Here are some tips on creating the best user experience.

First, multitouch and gesture interaction requires testing of various devices. You should never use the emulator for final testing, however. Even though AIR enables you to develop for multiple platforms, it is dependent on the device and the operating system, and the result is not always a uniform experience. GestureWorks, discussed in the preceding section, may address some of this issue; the library's detection of gestures is superior to the AIR library.

In addition, you should review your code carefully. Make it lean to achieve optimal performance, as gesture responsiveness should not lag. Keep your display list small and use `event.stopPropagation` to prevent bubbling.

Careful design is also essential. Your hit area should be larger than what you design for the desktop. Make your buttons and hot areas large and obvious. The various software companies make different recommendations on the size of clickable assets. While pixel sizes are important, when using touch as an interaction model the actual physical size and resolution of the LCD in relation to your finger will dictate the design and can change from device to device. You should also create a safe area between interactive elements so that you limit incidental touches on different UI elements.

Also, you should know your repertoire of gestures well and use it appropriately, especially for small devices. Use only the simplest gestures and do not assume your choice of gesture is obvious. Test with actual users before deploying your application. If you plan to distribute your application globally, pay special attention to your choice of gestures, as cultural differences sometimes dictate what is expected.

Finally, the reinforcement of UI and visual hints should always be considered. If you provide instructions, use a step-by-step instruction application in which the user executes the expected gesture. Stay away from a written list of instructions.

Conclusion

Although the mouse has evolved to touch technology, the keyboard has hardly changed since the creation of the typewriter. Many small devices and tablets offer digital keyboards, but none of them are an ideal solution on their own. They rely on spellchecking and a customized dictionary to compensate for fingers that type the wrong key and ease the cumbersome user experience.

Perhaps a better approach is to move away from the traditional keyboard and to think of using gestures. Palm OS proposed Graffiti in 1996 as a shorthand handwriting recognition system (*http://en.wikipedia.org/wiki/Graffiti_(Palm_OS)*). Samsung offers the Swype key that allows you to enter a word in a continuous gesture by tracing a path between letters (*http://www.swypeinc.com/product.html*). 8pen proposes a hierarchical keyboard (*http://www.the8pen.com/index.html*).

Let's see what the future will bring.

CHAPTER 8

Accelerometer

You may hate gravity, but gravity does not care.

—Clayton Christensen

The ability to detect motion opens a world of possibilities for interaction and game design. Motion sensor technology can be used to create an intuitive, life-like user interface, a control mechanism in gaming, or a new kind of brush for animation.

In this chapter we will discuss how to detect motion, and we will go over some examples that make use of this information.

What Is a Motion Sensor?

Your Android device contains an onboard sensor that measures acceleration along the perpendicular axes—on the x-axis from left to right, on the y-axis from bottom to top, and on the z-axis from back to front. It calculates the forces affecting the device, both gravity and user movement. Figure 8-1 depicts acceleration measurement along the perpendicular axes on an Android device.

The Accelerometer Class

The `flash.sensors.Accelerometer` class is an addition to ActionScript to support receiving messages from the device's motion sensor. It is a subclass of the `EventDis patcher` class. The `flash.events.AccelerometerEvent` class is a new `Event` class that returns the sensor's updated information.

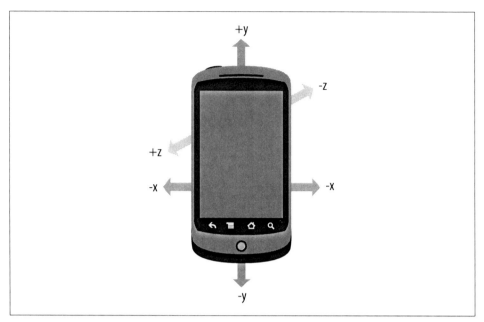

Figure 8-1. Measuring acceleration along the perpendicular axes on an Android device

When using these classes, you should first check at runtime that the user's device has a motion sensor and that it is available for reading. Look at the value of the `isSupported` boolean property:

```
import flash.sensors.Accelerometer;
if (Accelerometer.isSupported == false) {
    return;
}
```

The accelerometer `muted` property is `false` if the user blocks access to the accelerometer sensor. Android devices do not provide an option to disable access at the time of this writing, so you can ignore it.

Now create an instance of the `Accelerometer` class. This is essential to make the accelerometer variable a class variable, not a local variable, to guarantee that it is not removed from memory:

```
var accelerometer:Accelerometer;
accelerometer = new Accelerometer();
```

Next, set an `AccelerometerEvent` to receive updates for the device sensor:

```
import flash.events.AccelerometerEvent;

accelerometer.addEventListener(AccelerometerEvent.UPDATE, onUpdate);
```

A timer starts ticking the moment the application is initialized and returns a `time stamp` value in milliseconds. This is useful if you want to average activity over time:

```
function onUpdate(event:AccelerometerEvent):void {
    trace(event.accelerationX);
    trace(event.accelerationY);
    trace(event.accelerationZ);
    trace(event.timestamp);
}
```

The event returns a floating point for each axis that ranges between –1.0 and 1.0. The values indicate the force pulling your device from both gravity and the user's motion. If your device is not moving, the only acceleration measured is gravity that is, of course, active.

Earth's gravity is best known as the phenomenon that gives weight to objects with mass and causes them to free-fall to the ground when dropped. It is also an acceleration because a falling object keeps going faster and faster.

Acceleration is measured in meters/second^2. At the surface of the Earth, acceleration is 1G (for g-force), about 9.8 m/s^2 or 32 ft/s^2. After one second, an object is falling at 1 G (9.8 m/s), after two seconds at 2 G (19.6 m/s), and so on, hence s^2.

Motion values are not locked into the default portrait aspect ratio. If the screen orientation changes, the `Accelerometer` class takes care of adjusting the values so that they are set according to the stage axis, not the device axis.

Visualizing the Values

It is not very intuitive to make sense of the accelerometer values. Let's build an application to draw the values in a way that may clarify them.

In Figure 8-2, each axis is represented, from top to bottom, by a colored bar: green for the x-axis, red for the y-axis, and blue for the z-axis. The gray vertical line in the middle of the screen represents the zero point or rest state.

Notice that if you tilt the device in a more abrupt way, values change more rapidly. Let's now animate objects around the screen responding in real time to the user's motion.

A Simple Animation

Let's create a simple animation along the x- and y-axes. A multiplier is used to boost the values so that our ball object moves around the screen at a reasonable rate:

```
import flash.display.Shape;

const MULTIPLIER:Number = 8.0;
var accelerometer:Accelerometer;
var ball:Shape;
```

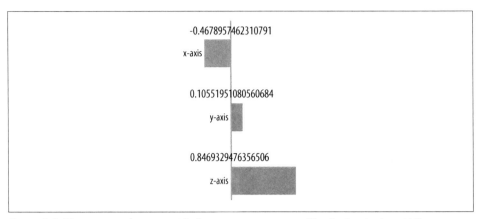

Figure 8-2. The x-, y-, and z-axes, with the rest state represented by the line in the middle

```
ball = new Shape();
ball.graphics.beginFill(0xFF9900);
ball.graphics.drawCircle(0,0, 50);
ball.graphics.endFill();
ball.x = stage.stageWidth/2;
ball.y = stage.stageHeight/2;
ball.cacheAsBitmap = true;
addChild(ball);

accelerometer = new Accelerometer();
accelerometer.addEventListener(AccelerometerEvent.UPDATE, onUpdate);

function onUpdate(event:AccelerometerEvent):void {
    ball.x -= event.accelerationX * MULTIPLIER;
    ball.y += event.accelerationY * MULTIPLIER;
}
```

Move your device and see how the ball follows your movement. As before, if you move in a more abrupt fashion, the ball will also move faster.

This is a good first try, but there is a lot we can do to improve responsiveness and animation.

Updates and Screen Rendering

The device defines the frequency of sensor updates. You cannot obtain this information through the Android or AIR API. You can, however, overwrite it to conserve battery life. The value is in milliseconds:

```
accelerometer.setRequestedUpdateInterval(30);
```

Do not use every `AccelerometerEvent` update to redraw the screen. This drains the battery and moves too fast for the frame rate at which the screen is redrawn. Instead, store the value on update and redraw the screen on the `ENTER_FRAME` event. You will notice a much smoother animation and better overall performance:

```
import flash.events.Event;
import flash.events.AccelerometerEvent;
import flash.sensors.Accelerometer;

const MULTIPLIER:Number = 20.0;
var vx:Number = 0.0;
var vy:Number = 0.0;
var accelerometer:Accelerometer;

accelerometer = new Accelerometer();
accelerometer.addEventListener(AccelerometerEvent.UPDATE, onUpdate);
stage.addEventListener(Event.ENTER_FRAME, onEnterFrame);

function onUpdate(event:AccelerometerEvent):void {
    vx = event.accelerationX * MULTIPLIER;
    vy = event.accelerationY * MULTIPLIER;
}

function onEnterFrame(event:Event):void {
  event.stopPropagation();
  ball.x -= vx;
  ball.y += vy;
}
```

Notice the `event.stopPropagation` method called in the `onUpdate` function. It is important to eliminate unnecessary steps, especially if you have a deep `displayList`.

 The event flow sends an event throughout the display list, from the top, looking for event listeners that may have been defined along the way and then bubbled back up. `StopPropagation()` stops the process as soon as the event finds the target.

Setting Boundaries

Keep your animation within the boundaries of your screen. Set the values of the boundaries, and only move the ball if the position change is within them:

```
var radius:int;
var xBounds:int;
var yBounds:int;
var newX:Number = 0.0;
var newY:Number = 0.0;

radius = ball.width;
xBounds = stage.stageWidth - radius;
yBounds = stage.stageHeight - radius;

function onEnterFrame(event:Event):void {
  event.stopPropagation();
```

```
        newX = ball.x - vx;
        newY = ball.y + vy;

        if (newX > radius && newX < xBounds) {
            ball.x = newX;
        }
        if (newY > radius && newY < yBounds) {
            ball.y = newY;
        }
    }
}
```

In this example, the boundaries are defined by xBounds and yBounds. They represent the dimension of the stage minus the radius of the ball being animated.

Rotating Toward the Center

In this example, the ball turns toward the center of the screen while it is moving. Making an element react to its environment brings it to life.

With the following code, the larger ball now contains a small ball that is off-centered so that the rotation is visible:

```
import flash.events.Event;

var ball:Shape;
var centerX:int = stage.stageWidth/2;
var centerY:int = stage.stageHeight/2;
var newX:Number = 0.0;
var newY:Number = 0.0;

ball = new Shape();
ball.graphics.beginFill(0xFF3300);
ball.graphics.drawCircle(0,0, 30);
ball.graphics.beginFill(0x3300FF);
ball.graphics.drawCircle(10,10, 10);
ball.graphics.endFill();
ball.x = stage.stageWidth/2;
ball.y = stage.stageHeight/2;
ball.cacheAsBitmap = true;
addChild(ball);

function onEnterFrame(event:Event):void {
    event.stopPropagation();

    newX = ball.x - vx;
    newY = ball.y + vy;

    if (newX > radius && newX < xBounds) {
        ball.x = newX;
    }
    if (newY > radius && newY < yBounds) {
        ball.y = newY;
    }
```

```
            var dx:int = centerX - ball.x;
            var dy:int = centerY - ball.y;
            var radians:Number = Math.atan2(dy, dx);
            ball.rotation = radians*180/Math.PI;
        }
```

Shake Me

Shaking the device is a novel and yet intuitive interaction. You can use it to detect the user's strength, to simulate a real object as in the game Ask the Magic Eight Ball, or simply as a reset button.

Shaking can be defined as a drastic motion, and therefore as a relatively large change of value over time. To detect the force of shaking, you can compare acceleration values against a threshold regardless of the orientation. In this example, if a value on any of the axes goes above the threshold of 1.5, the motion is considered a shake:

```
    const THRESHOLD:Number = 1.5;

    function onUpdate(event:AccelerometerEvent):void {
        if (event.accelerationX > THRESHOLD || event.accelerationY > THRESHOLD
                                    || event.accelerationZ > THRESHOLD ) {
            trace("strong enough");
            var max:Number =
            Math.max(event.accelerationX, event.accelerationY,
                                    event.accelerationZ);
            trace("you are ", max.toString(), "strong");
        }
    }
```

To detect an actual shaking motion, vary the condition for each coordinate and check the value in both directions. Generally, shaking happens more along the x-axis, happens somewhat less along the y-axis, and is relatively insignificant along the z-axis. This is because a natural human motion is to move one's arm from left to right. To reflect this, the threshold for x is 2.5. The threshold for y is twice that value, and the threshold for z is three times that value.

The boolean `isMeasuring` allows for clean reading of all the axes together. It is set to `true` when it starts to capture values and `false` only after all the accelerometer axes have been captured:

```
    const THRESHOLD:Number = 2.5;
    var isMeasuring:Boolean = false;
    var isShaking:Boolean = false;
    var accelerometer:Accelerometer;

    accelerometer = new Accelerometer();
    accelerometer.addEventListener(AccelerometerEvent.UPDATE, onUpdate);

    function onUpdate(event:AccelerometerEvent):void {
        if (isMeasuring) {
            return;
```

```
    }
    isMeasuring = true;
    if (Math.abs(event.accelerationX) > THRESHOLD) {
        isShaking = true;
    }
    if (Math.abs(event.accelerationY) > THRESHOLD*2) {
        isShaking = true;
    }
    if (Math.abs(event.accelerationZ) > THRESHOLD*3) {
        isShaking = true;
    }
    if (isShaking) {
        // we have a shake
    }
    isMeasuring = false;
}
```

Using the same kind of analysis, you could imagine capturing other device gestures, such as a circle or a zigzag motion. For such motion, though, timing would need to be incorporated.

Smoothing Out Values

Accelerometer sensors are prone to spurious results. Accelerometer values are not always coming across at a regular pace, and users can make erratic movements. If you want to avoid a jittery effect, smooth out the values. You can do this by combining previous readings with the current reading and leaving out a range of values according to a defined filter.

There are two approaches to accomplishing this. A *high-pass filter* is used for an application that is looking for rapid changes by weighting the current reading more than the previous reading. A good use case for a high-pass filter is detecting a shake motion, as in our previous example. A *low-pass filter* is used for an application that is looking for fine-tuned, stable values. This type of filter would be used in a game of precision, such as carefully pushing an object toward a target.

When testing these filters, the values start adjusting as expected after a few seconds.

Using a high-pass filter

The high-pass filter works with a fixed filter. Try different filter values until you achieve the effect you are looking for:

```
const FILTER:Number = 0.10;
var high:Number = 0.0;
var oldHigh:Number = 0.0;

function onUpdate(event:AccelerometerEvent):void {
    var ax:Number = event.accelerationX;
    high = ax - (ax*FILTER) + oldHigh * (1.0 - FILTER);
    oldHigh = high;
}
```

Let's go over the formula. `ax` is the new accelerometer value on the x-axis. `high` is the adjusted value after applying the filter formula, and `oldHigh` is the cumulated value over time.

`ax` is reduced by one-tenth of its value. For instance, if `ax` is equal to 3:

```
high = ax - (ax*FILTER)
3 - (3*0.10)
3 - 0.30
2.70
```

Let's say that initially `oldHigh` is equal to zero, but over time, it is equal to 2. The following code reduces `oldHigh` by one-tenth:

```
oldHigh = oldHigh * (1.0 - FILTER));
2 * (1.0 - 0.10);
2 * 0.90
1.80
```

The new `high` value is 4.5:

```
2.70 + 1.80
4.5
```

Let's examine these values over time. Returning to our shake example, to test the code with the high-pass filter, the threshold value is increased:

```
const THRESHOLD:Number = 5.0;
var isMeasuring:Boolean = false;
var isShaking:Boolean = false;
const FILTER:Number = 0.10;
var high:Number = 0.0;
var oldHigh:Number = 0.0;

function onUpdate(e:AccelerometerEvent):void {
if (isMeasuring) {
        return;
}
isMeasuring = true;

var ax:Number = event.accelerationX;
high = ax - (ax*FILTER) + oldHigh * (1.0 - FILTER);
oldHigh = high;

if (Math.abs(high) > THRESHOLD) {
        isShaking = true;
}
if (isShaking) {
    // we have a shake
}
isMeasuring = false;
}
```

Using a low-pass filter

The low-pass filter has the effect of changing slowly and stabilizing the input. It is handy for rotating art for a flight simulation or a rowing boat.

The low-pass filter looks as follows:

```
const FILTER:Number = 0.10;
var low:Number = 0.0;
var oldLow:Number = 0.0;

function onUpdate(event:AccelerometerEvent):void {
    var ax:Number = accelerationX;
    low = ax * FILTER + oldLow * (1.0 - FILTER);
    oldLow = low;
}
```

Keep in mind that the more you filter the value, the more lag you will get in response because the average converses more slowly to the current value of the sensor.

Conclusion

When developing applications using an accelerometer, draw the user in and keep her interested. It is the seduction of a digital device that feels tactile.

CHAPTER 9

Camera

*The camera is an instrument that teaches people
how to see without a camera.*

—Dorothea Lange

Now that mobile devices and cameras are one and the same device, everyone is a photographer. With mobile devices running email and SMS applications, everyone is also a publisher.

If you want to create an application that uses or creates pictures, you can do so by accessing some of the Android APIs. For instance, you can access the Gallery application, also called the Media Library, to select and display an image. You can add an image to the Gallery from AIR. You also can open the native camera to take a picture or shoot a video. And as we will discuss in this chapter, you can do all of this from within your AIR application.

The Gallery Application and the CameraRoll Class

The Gallery application is the display for the repository of images located on the SD card and accessible by various applications. Launch it, choose an image, and then select Menu→Share. A list of applications (such as Picasa, Messaging, and Email) appears, a convenient way to upload media from the device to another destination (see Figure 9-1).

The `flash.media.CameraRoll` class is a subclass of the `EventDispatcher` class. It gives you access to the Gallery. It is not supported for AIR desktop applications.

 When the native camera application launches, it looks for the SD card. If your device is connected to your development computer with USB storage turned on, the card is already mounted on this filesystem and is not accessible. Make sure you turn off USB storage to test your application during development.

Figure 9-1. The Gallery application

Selecting an Image

You can test that your device supports browsing the Gallery by checking the `supports BrowseForImage` property:

```
import flash.media.CameraRoll;

if (CameraRoll.supportsBrowseForImage == false) {
    trace("this device does not support access to the Gallery");
    return;
}
```

If your device does support the Gallery, you can create an instance of the `CameraRoll` class. Make it a class variable, not a local variable, so that it does not lose scope:

```
var cameraRoll:CameraRoll = new CameraRoll();
```

You can add listeners for three events:

- A `MediaEvent.SELECT` when the user selects an image:

```
import flash.events.MediaEvent;

cameraRoll.addEventListener(MediaEvent.SELECT, onSelect);
```

- An `Event.CANCEL` event if the user opts out of the Gallery:

```
import flash.events.Event;
cameraRoll.addEventListener(Event.CANCEL, onCancel);

function onCancel(event:Event):void {
    trace("user left the Gallery", event.type);
}
```

- An `ErrorEvent.ERROR` event if there is an issue in the process:

```
import flash.events.ErrorEvent;
cameraRoll.addEventListener(ErrorEvent.ERROR, onError);

function onError(event:Event):void {
```

```
        trace("Gallery error", event.type);
    }
```

Call the `browseForImage` function to bring the Gallery application to the foreground:

```
cameraRoll.browseForImage();
```

Your application moves to the background and the Gallery interface is displayed, as shown in Figure 9-2.

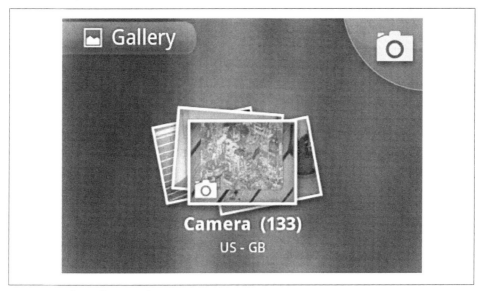

Figure 9-2. The Gallery interface

 When you are using the native camera, it comes to the foreground, your AIR application moves to the background, and the `NativeApplication Event.DEACTIVATE` event is called. Make sure that if you registered for that event, you don't have any logic that could interfere with the running of your application, such as exiting. Likewise, when the native camera application quits and your AIR application comes back to the foreground, `Event.ACTIVATE` is called.

When you select an image, a `MediaEvent` object is returned. Use its `data` property to reference the image and cast it as `MediaPromise`. Use a `Loader` object to load the image:

```
import flash.display.Loader;
import flash.events.IOErrorEvent;
import flash.events.MediaEvent;
import flash.media.MediaPromise;

function onSelect(event:MediaEvent):void {
    var promise:MediaPromise = event.data as MediaPromise;
    var loader:Loader = new Loader()
```

```
loader.contentLoaderInfo.addEventListener(Event.COMPLETE, onImageLoaded);
loader.contentLoaderInfo.addEventListener(IOErrorEvent.IO_ERROR,onError);
loader.loadFilePromise(promise);
}
```

The concept of `MediaPromise` was first introduced on the desktop in a drag-and-drop scenario where an object doesn't yet exist in AIR but needs to be referenced. Access its `file` property if you want to retrieve the image `name`, its `nativePath`, or its `url`.

The `url` is the qualified domain name to use to load an image. The `nativePath` refers to the hierarchical directory structure:

```
promise.file.name;
promise.file.url;
promise.file.nativePath;
```

Let's now display the image:

```
function onImageLoaded(event:Event):void {
    addChild(event.currentTarget.content);
}
```

Only the upper-left portion of the image is visible. This is because the resolution of the camera device is much larger than your AIR application stage.

Let's modify our code so that we can drag the image around and see all of its content. We will make the image a child of a sprite, which can be dragged around:

```
import flash.events.MouseEvent;
import flash.display.DisplayObject;
import flash.geom.Rectangle;

var rectangle:Rectangle;

function onImageLoaded(event:Event):void {
    var container:Sprite = new Sprite();
    var image:DisplayObject = event.currentTarget.content as DisplayObject;
    container.addChild(image);
    addChild(container);

    // set a constraint rectangle to define the draggable area
    rectangle = new Rectangle(0, 0,
                        -(image.width - stage.stageWidth),
                        -(image.height - stage.stageHeight)
                        );
    container.addEventListener(MouseEvent.MOUSE_DOWN, onDown);
    container.addEventListener(MouseEvent.MOUSE_UP, onUp);
}

function onDown(event:MouseEvent):void {
    event.currentTarget.startDrag(false, rectangle);
}

function onUp(event:MouseEvent):void {
    event.currentTarget.stopDrag();
}
```

It may be interesting to see the details of an image at its full resolution, but this might not result in the best user experience. Also, because camera resolution is so high on most devices, there is a risk of exhausting RAM and running out of memory.

Let's now store the content in a BitmapData, display it in a Bitmap, and scale the bitmap to fit our stage in AIR. We will use the Nexus One as our benchmark first. Its camera has a resolution of 2,592×1,944. The default template size on AIR for Android is 800×480. To complicate things, the aspect ratio is different. In order to preserve the image fidelity and fill up the screen, you need to resize the aspect ratio to 800×600, but some of the image will be out of bounds.

Instead, let's resize the image to 640×480. The image will not cover the whole stage, but it will be fully visible. Take this into account when designing your screen.

First, detect the orientation of your image. Resize it accordingly using constant values, and rotate the image if it is in landscape mode:

```
import flash.display.Bitmap;
import flash.display.BitmapData;


const MAX_HEIGHT:int = 640;
const MAX_WIDTH:int = 480;

function onImageLoaded(event:Event):void {
    var bitmapData:BitmapData = Bitmap(event.target.content).bitmapData;
    var bitmap:Bitmap = new Bitmap(bitmapData);

    // determine the image orientation
    var isPortrait:Boolean = (bitmapData.height/bitmapData.width) > 1.0;

    if (isPortrait) {
        bitmap.width = MAX_WIDTH;
        bitmap.height = MAX_HEIGHT;
    } else {
        bitmap.width = MAX_HEIGHT;
        bitmap.height = MAX_WIDTH;
        // rotate a landscape image
        bitmap.y = MAX_HEIGHT;
        bitmap.rotation = -90;
    }
    addChild(bitmap);
}
```

The preceding code is customized to the Nexus One, and it will not display well for devices with a different camera resolution or screen size. We need a more universal solution.

The next example shows how to resize the image according to the dynamic dimension of both the image and the stage. This is the preferred approach for developing on multiple screens:

```
function onImageLoaded(event:Event):void {
    var bitmapData:BitmapData = Bitmap(event.target.content).bitmapData;
    var bitmap:Bitmap = new Bitmap(bitmapData);

    // determine the image orientation
    var isPortrait:Boolean = (bitmapData.height/bitmapData.width) > 1.0;

    // choose the smallest value between stage width and height
    var forRatio:int = Math.min(stage.stageHeight, stage.stageWidth);

    // calculate the scaling ratio to apply to the image
    var ratio:Number;
    if (isPortrait) {
        ratio = forRatio/bitmapData.width;
    } else {
        ratio = forRatio/bitmapData.height;
    }
    bitmap.width = bitmapData.width * ratio;
    bitmap.height = bitmapData.height * ratio;

    // rotate a landscape image and move down to fit to the top corner
    if (!isPortrait) {

        bitmap.y = bitmap.width;
        bitmap.rotation = -90;
    }
    addChild(bitmap);
}
```

Beware that the browseForImage method is only meant to load images from the Gallery.
It is not for loading images from the filesystem even if you navigate to the Gallery. Some
devices bring up a dialog to choose between Gallery and Files. If you try to load an
image via Files, the application throws an error. Until this bug is fixed, set a listener to
catch the error and inform the user:

```
cameraRoll.browseForImage();
cameraRoll.addEventListener(ErrorEvent.ERROR, onError);

function onError(event:Event):void {
    if (event.errorID == 2124) {
        trace("you can only load images from the Gallery");
    }
}
```

If you want to get a list of all the images in your Gallery, you can use the filesystem as
follows:

```
var gallery:File = File.userDirectory.resolvePath("DCIM/Camera");
var myPhotos:Array = gallery.getDirectoryListing();
var bounds:int = myPhotos.length;

for (var i:uint = 0; i < bounds; i++) {
    trace(myPhotos[i].name, myPhotos[i].nativePath);
}
```

Adding an Image

You can add an image to the Gallery from within AIR. To write data to the SD card, you must set permission for it:

```
<uses-permission android:name="android.permission.WRITE_EXTERNAL_STORAGE" />
```

Check the `supportsAddBitmapData` property to verify that your device supports this feature:

```
import flash.media.CameraRoll;
if (CameraRoll.supportsAddBitmapData == false) {
    trace("You cannot add images to the Gallery.");
    return;
}
```

If this feature is supported, create an instance of `CameraRoll` and set an `Event.COM PLETE` listener. Call the `addBitmapData` function to save the image to the Gallery. In this example, a stage grab is saved.

This feature could be used for a drawing application in which the user can draw over time. The following code allows the user to save his drawing, reload it, and draw over it again:

```
var cameraRoll:CameraRoll;

cameraRoll = new CameraRoll();
cameraRoll.addEventListener(ErrorEvent.ERROR, onError);
cameraRoll.addEventListener(Event.COMPLETE, onComplete);
var bitmapData:BitmapData =
    new BitmapData(stage.stageWidth, stage.stageHeight);
bitmapData.draw(stage);
cameraRoll.addBitmapData(bitmapData);

function onComplete(event:Event):void {
    // image saved in gallery
}
```

Remember that the image that is saved is the same dimension as the stage, and therefore it has a much smaller resolution than the native camera. At the time of this writing, there is no option to specify a compression, to name the image, or to save it in a custom directory. AIR follows Android naming conventions, using the date and time of capture.

The Camera Application and the CameraUI Class

You can access the native camera within AIR. Your application needs to have the permission for it. In Flash Professional, select File→AIR Android settings→Permissions→Camera. In Flash Builder, select CAMERA under Mobile Settings→Permissions.

The `flash.media.CameraUI` class is an addition to the ActionScript language to support the device's native camera application. It is a subclass of the `EventDispatcher` class. It is only supported on AIR for mobile applications.

This object allows you to launch the native camera application to take an image or shoot a video while your AIR application moves to the background. The image is stored in the Gallery along with the other images.

 Android's support for the front camera became available with the Gingerbread version. At the time of this writing, AIR does not support the front camera, but it will in a future release.

To use this class, first you must verify that your device supports access to the camera by checking the `CameraUI.isSupported` property:

```
import flash.media.CameraUI;
if (CameraUI.isSupported == false) {
    trace("You cannot use the native camera.");
    return;
}
```

If camera access is supported, create an instance of the `CameraUI` class and call its `launch` function. This function expects one parameter of type `MediaType` to specify picture or video mode. Choosing a level of compression is not an option at the time of this writing:

```
import flash.media.MediaType;

var cameraUI:CameraUI = new CameraUI();
cameraUI.launch(MediaType.IMAGE);
```

The camera application is now active and in the foreground. The AIR application moves to the background.

To receive camera events, set listeners before launching the camera. A `Media Event.COMPLETE` is dispatched after a picture is taken, an `Event.CANCEL` if no media is selected, and an `ErrorEvent` if there is an error in the process:

```
cameraUI.addEventListener(MediaEvent.COMPLETE, onComplete);
cameraUI.addEventListener(Event.CANCEL, onCancel);
cameraUI.addEventListener(ErrorEvent.ERROR, onError);
```

Once the event is received, the camera application automatically closes and the AIR application moves back to the foreground.

On select, a `MediaEvent` object is returned. From this point on, the process is identical to receiving an image from the Gallery. Please refer to "Selecting an Image" on page 104 for details:

```
function onComplete(event:MediaEvent):void {
    var promise:MediaPromise = event.data as MediaPromise;
    var loader:Loader = new Loader();
```

```
        loader.contentLoaderInfo.addEventListener(Event.COMPLETE, onImageLoaded);
        loader.contentLoaderInfo.addEventListener(IOErrorEvent.IO_ERROR,onError);
        loader.loadFilePromise(promise);
    }

    function onImageLoaded(event:Event):void {
        var bitmapData:BitmapData = Bitmap(event.target.content).bitmapData;
        var bitmap:Bitmap = new Bitmap(bitmapData);

        var isPortrait:Boolean = (bitmapData.height/bitmapData.width) > 1.0;
        var forRatio:int = Math.min(stage.stageHeight, stage.stageWidth);

        var ratio:Number;
        if (isPortrait) {
            ratio = forRatio/bitmapData.width;
        } else {
            ratio = forRatio/bitmapData.height;
        }
        bitmap.width = bitmapData.width * ratio;
        bitmap.height = bitmapData.height * ratio;

        if (!isPortrait) {
            bitmap.y = stage.stageHeight;
            bitmap.rotation = -90;
        }
        addChild(bitmap);
    }
```

We will discuss the use of `CameraUI` with `MediaType.VIDEO` in Chapter 12.

Uploading to a Remote Server

Images can be uploaded to a remote server if you have access to one. You need the Internet permission to add this functionality:

```
<uses-permission android:name="android.permission.INTERNET" />
```

This process is identical to what you would do in a desktop application:

```
import flash.net.URLRequestMethod;
import flash.filesystem.File;

var request:URLRequest = new URLRequest("server url");
request.method = URLRequestMethod.POST;
var uploadFile:File = new File(promise.file.url);
uploadFile.upload(request);
```

EXIF Data

EXIF stands for Exchangeable Image File. EXIF data is low-level information stored in JPEG images. EXIF was created by the Japan Electronic Industries Development Association (JEIDA) and became a convention adopted across camera manufacturers,

including on mobile devices. You can read about the EXIF format at *http://en.wikipedia*
.org/wiki/Exchangeable_image_file_format and *http://www.exif.org/Exif2-2.PDF*.

EXIF data can include the date and time the image was created, the camera manufac-
turer and camera settings, location information, and even a thumbnail image. Visit
Jeffrey Friedl's website at *http://regex.info/exif.cgi* and load a JPEG image to see the
information it contains.

In AIR for Android, you could use the geolocation API to get location information and
associate it with the photo you just shot, but it is more efficient to get this information
directly from the image if it is available. To store image location on an Android device
when taking a picture, the user must have Location & Security→Use GPS Satellites
selected and then turn on the camera's Store Location option.

Several open source AS3 libraries are available for reading EXIF data. I chose the one
by Kenichi Ishibashi. You can download his library using Subversion at *http://code*
.shichiseki.jp/as3/ExifInfo/. Ishibashi's `Loader` class uses the `loadBytes` function and
passes its data as a `ByteArray` to access the raw data information. Import his package
to your class.

Our first example loads an image from the Gallery, reads its thumbnail data, and displays it. Note that thumbnail creation varies among devices and is not always available.
Check that it exists before trying to display it:

```
import flash.display.Loader;
import flash.display.MovieClip;
import flash.media.CameraRoll;
import flash.media.MediaPromise;
import flash.events.MediaEvent;
import flash.events.Event;
import flash.net.URLRequest
import jp.shichiseki.exif.*;

var loader:ExifLoader;
var cameraRoll:CameraRoll;

function Exif1() {
    if (CameraRoll.supportsBrowseForImage) {
        init();
    }
}

function init():void {
    cameraRoll = new CameraRoll();
    cameraRoll.addEventListener(MediaEvent.SELECT, onSelect);
    cameraRoll.browseForImage();
}

function onSelect(event:MediaEvent):void {
    var promise:MediaPromise = event.data as MediaPromise;
    loader = new ExifLoader();
    loader.addEventListener(Event.COMPLETE, imageLoaded);
    loader.load(new URLRequest(promise.file.url));
```

```
    }

    function imageLoaded(event:Event):void {
        var exif:ExifInfo = loader.exif as ExifInfo;

        if (exif.thumbnailData) {
            var thumbLoader:Loader = new Loader();
            thumbLoader.loadBytes(exif.thumbnailData);
            addChild(thumbLoader);
        }
    }
}
```

The next example also lets you choose an image from the device's Gallery and display its geographic information. The user must have GPS enabled and must have authorized the camera to save the location when the picture was taken:

```
import flash.display.Loader;
import flash.display.MovieClip;
import flash.media.CameraRoll;
import flash.media.MediaPromise;
import flash.events.MediaEvent;
import flash.events.Event;
import flash.net.URLRequest;
import flash.text.TextField;
import flash.text.TextFormat;
import flash.text.TextFieldAutoSize;
import jp.shichiseki.exif.*;

var cameraRoll:CameraRoll;
var loader:ExifLoader;

if (CameraRoll.supportsBrowseForImage) {
    cameraRoll = new CameraRoll();
    cameraRoll.addEventListener(MediaEvent.SELECT, onSelect);
    cameraRoll.browseForImage();
}

function onSelect(event:MediaEvent):void {
    var promise:MediaPromise = event.data as MediaPromise;
    loader = new ExifLoader();
    loader.addEventListener(Event.COMPLETE, onImageLoaded);
    loader.load(new URLRequest(promise.file.url));
}

function onImageLoaded(event:Event):void {
    var exif:ExifInfo = loader.exif as ExifInfo;

    var textFormat:TextFormat = new TextFormat();
    textFormat.size = 40;
    textFormat.color = 0x66CC99;

    var where:TextField = new TextField();
    where.x = 50;
    where.y = 200;
    where.defaultTextFormat = textFormat;
```

```
    where.autoSize = TextFieldAutoSize.LEFT;
    addChild(where);

    if (exif.ifds.gps) {
        var gpsIfd:IFD = exif.ifds.gps;

        var exifLat:Array = gpsIfd["GPSLatitude"] as Array;
        var latitude:Number = shorten(exifLat, gpsIfd["GPSLatitudeRef"]);
        var exifLon:Array = gpsIfd["GPSLongitude"] as Array;
        var longitude:Number = shorten(exifLon, gpsIfd["GPSLongitudeRef"]);

        where.text = latitude + "\n" + longitude;
    } else {
        where.text = "No geographic \information";
    }
}

function shorten(info:Array, reference:String):Number {
    var degree:Number = info[0] + (info[1]/60) + (info[2]/3600);
    // position from Greenwich and equator
    if (reference == "S" || reference == "E") {
        degree * -1;
    }
    return degree;
}
```

Base 60 is commonly used to store geographic coordinates in degrees. Degrees, minutes, and seconds are stored separately. Put them back together and sign them depending on whether they are south of the equator and east of Greenwich Mean Time.

Displaying latitude and longitude is not very helpful, nor is it interesting for most users. But you can render a static map using latitude and longitude or retrieve an address.

We will come back to these topics in Chapter 10.

Conclusion

Images are among the most popular types of content for mobile applications, whether users are cataloguing the images or manipulating them. You now have all the tools to create one of your own.

Geolocation

Without geography, you're nowhere.

—Jimmy Buffett

The ability to locate exactly where you are on Earth via consumer products has become commonplace, yet the technology is empowering. If you own a GPS-capable cellular phone, you have this technology at your fingertips.

In this chapter, we will discuss the geolocation API for accessing location information from an Android device.

Geolocation Classes

The `flash.events.GeolocationEvent` class is a new `Event` object that contains updated geolocation information. The new `flash.sensors.Geolocation` class is a subclass of the `EventDispatcher` class. It listens for and receives information from the device's location sensor in the form of a `GeolocationEvent`.

To use the geolocation classes, first you must add the necessary permissions. In Flash Professional, enable `ACCESS_FINE_LOCATION` and `ACCESS_COARSE_LOCATION` device permissions under File→AIR Android Settings→Permissions. In Flash Builder, select `ACCESS_NETWORK_STATE` and `ACCESS_WIFI_STATE` under Mobile Settings→Permissions. To make changes, append your application manifest file as follows:

```
<uses-permission android:name="android.permission.ACCESS_FINE_LOCATION" />
<uses-permission android:name="android.permission.ACCESS_COARSE_LOCATION" />
```

Fine location refers to GPS communication, while coarse location refers to network communication. I will explain the difference between the two later in this chapter.

If your location permissions are not set up, your application will fail silently.

During development and testing, you must select the checkboxes on your device in Android Settings→Location and Security→Use GPS satellites and Android Settings→Location and Security→Use wireless networks to enable both sensors, as shown in Figure 10-1.

Figure 10-1. Enabling sensors for wireless networks and GPS satellites

Next, verify that the device running your application supports geolocation:

```
import flash.sensors.Geolocation;
import flash.events.GeolocationEvent;

if (Geolocation.isSupported) {
    // geolocation supported
}
```

Now let's write a simple application to listen to geolocation event updates. Make geolocation a class variable, not a local variable, to guarantee that it does not get out of scope:

```
import flash.sensors.Geolocation;
import flash.events.GeolocationEvent;

var geolocation:Geolocation;

if (Geolocation.isSupported) {
    geolocation = new Geolocation();
    geolocation.addEventListener(GeolocationEvent.UPDATE, onTravel);
}

function onTravel(event:GeolocationEvent):void {
    trace(event.latitude);
```

```
        trace(event.longitude);
    }
```

You should see your current latitude and longitude in degrees as floating-point values. My home location, for instance, is latitude 40.74382781982420 and longitude 74.00146007537840.

The user has the ability to enable or disable access to the location sensor on the device. Check the geolocation muted boolean property when you first run your application to see its value. You should also create a listener to receive status updates in case the property changes while the application is running:

```
import flash.events.StatusEvent;

if (!geolocation.muted) {
    geolocation.addEventListener(StatusEvent.STATUS, onStatusChange);
} else {
    // inform the user to turn on the location sensor
}

function onStatusChange(event:StatusEvent):void {
    trace("status:" + event.code);
    if (event.code == "Geolocation.Muted") {
        // inform the user to turn on the location sensor
    }
}
```

If muted is true, or if event.code is equal to Geolocation.Muted, display a message to the user requesting the need for location data.

The GeolocationEvent Class

A GeolocationEvent.UPDATE event is delivered when the listener is first created. Then, it is delivered when a new location update is received from the device/platform. An event is also delivered if the application wakes up after being in the background.

Using the geolocation API drains the battery very quickly. In an effort to save battery life, control the frequency of updates by setting an update interval on the geolocation object. Unless you are moving very quickly and want to check your speed, you don't need to check your location more than once every few seconds or minutes:

```
geolocation.setRequestedUpdateInterval(10000);
```

If not specified by you, the updates are based on the device/platform default interval. Look up the hardware documentation if you want to know the device default interval; this is not something you can get in the Android or AIR API.

The Earth is divided using a grid system with latitude from the equator toward the North and South Poles and longitude from Greenwich, England, to the international date line in the Pacific Ocean. Values are positive from the equator going north and from Greenwich going east. Values are negative from the equator going south and from Greenwich going west.

The `GeolocationEvent` properties are as follows:

- `event.latitude` ranges from –90 to 90 degrees and `event.longitude` ranges from –180 to 180 degrees. They are both of data type `Number` for greater precision.

- `event.horizontalAccuracy` and `event.verticalAccuracy` are in meters. This value comes back from the location service and represents how accurate the data is. A small number represents a better reading. Less than 60 meters is usually considered GPS accurate. This measurement may change as the technology improves.

- `event.timeStamp` is in milliseconds and starts counting from the moment the application initializes. If you need to get a regular update, use a timer instead of `GeolocationEvent` because it may not fire up at regular intervals.

- `event.altitude` is in meters and `event.speed` is in meters/second.

- `event.heading`, moving toward true north, is an integer. It is not supported on Android devices at the time of this writing, and it returns a value of `NaN` (Not a Number). However, you can calculate it by comparing longitude and latitude over time to determine a direction, assuming your device moves fast enough.

When your application moves to the background, the geolocation sensor remains active. If you want to overwrite the default behavior, listen to `Native Application Event.DEACTIVATE` to remove the event listener and `Event.ACTIVATE` to set it again.

When you first register for geolocation updates, AIR sets location listeners. It also queries for the `LastKnownLocation` and sends it as the first update. Because it is cached, the initial data may be incorrect until a first real location update is received.

Locating a Device Using Global Positioning System and Network/WiFi Technology

The Android platform uses both GPS and network/WiFi to locate a device. There is no direct way to specify a unique location source, but a workaround is to only add the relevant permission, fine or coarse as defined earlier, in the manifest file.

Using GPS

GPS is a manmade navigation system. Satellites in space constantly broadcast messages with their ephemeris, or position in the sky, and the time. Your mobile device, as a GPS receiver, uses the messages received to determine the distance to each satellite by measuring the transit time of the message. Using triangulation, the device is able to determine its own position as latitude and longitude or on a map. Other information derived from this is direction and speed, calculated from changes in position. Visit the TomTom site for a simple explanation and good graphics on how GPS works (*http://www.tomtom .com/howdoesitwork/page.php?ID=8&CID=2&Language=1*).

GPS is the most accurate positioning technology, and it provides the most frequent updates. However, it is not always available, particularly indoors. It also consumes the most battery power.

Position acquisition is often not very accurate initially, but it improves over time. The GPS sensor can take several minutes to get a proper position from satellites. Do not make your application full screen so that the status bar is hidden from the user so that they cannot see network activity and signal strength. If a GPS connection is established, a GPS icon is visible on the top right. If it is trying to establish or fix a lost GPS connection, the icon will blink.

Signal-to-noise ratio

SNR is an algorithm that compensates for inaccurate or ambiguous results due to interference and multipath errors. Interference could be due to weather conditions or signals bouncing off mountains or large buildings. A multipath error is a problem with signals from multiple satellites arriving out of sync if one of them experiences interference.

Assisted GPS

Assisted GPS, also called A-GPS, is used to improve the startup performance or Time To First Fix (TTFF). In this mode, your device uses cell tower positions and triangulates from there to get an initial location quickly. It then switches to GPS when it is available and accurate enough. Figure 10-2 shows GPS Test, an application developed by Chartcross Ltd. It displays the position and signal strength of satellites within view as obtained by the device's GPS receiver.

Using the Cellular Network and WiFi

If GPS is not available, your application will switch over to cell/WiFi. The network system is a combination of cell towers, WiFi hotspots, and IP-based geolocation. Cell tower signals, although not affected by architecture or bad weather, are less accurate and are dependent on the infrastructure. WiFi hotspots are very precise with enough data points but are only available in urban areas.

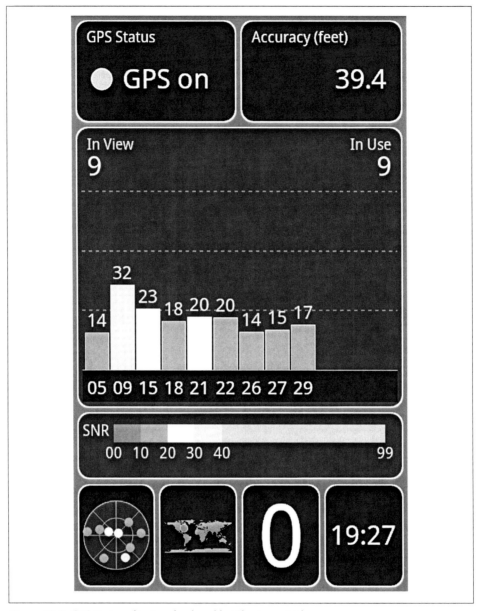

Figure 10-2. GPS Test application developed by Chartcross Ltd.

How to Know if GPS or WiFi Is Active

The static `flash.net.NetworkInfo` class provides information about the network interfaces on computers and on some mobile devices. Your application needs permission to access network information. Add it to your application manifest as follows:

```
<uses-permission android:name="android.permission.ACCESS_NETWORK_STATE" />
<uses-permission android:name="android.permission.ACCESS_WIFI_STATE" />
```

Check that it is supported on your device:

```
if (NetworkInfo.isSupported) {
    // network information supported
}
```

NetworkInfo stores a list of possible network interfaces that you can get by calling:

```
import flash.net.NetworkInfo;

var network:NetworkInfo = NetworkInfo.networkInfo;
for each (var object:NetworkInterface in network.findInterfaces()) {
    trace(object.name);
}
```

For example, the list of interfaces for the Nexus One, Droid 2, and Samsung Galaxy Tab is:

```
mobile, WIFI, mobile_mms, mobile_supl, mobile_dun, mobile_hipri
```

You can find out which method is active, and its name, using the following code:

```
import flash.net.NetworkInterface;

var network:NetworkInfo = NetworkInfo.networkInfo;
for each (var object:NetworkInterface in network.findInterfaces()) {
    trace(object.name);
    if (object.active) {
        if (object.name == "WIFI") {
            // you are using wifi

        } else {
            // you are using GPS
        }
    }
}
```

AIR and Android

The AIR API, under the hood, uses the Android LocationManager class to receive location and accuracy information. It also receives additional information about satellites and fixes, but it doesn't expose this information at the time of this writing.

If you are interested in seeing the Android process, use the Android command logcat, as explained in Chapter 3, and read the logs for SensorManager, Sensors, GpsLocationProvider, and LocationManager:

```
androidSDK/tools/adb logcat
```

On Android, if you want to simulate geolocation coordinates, select Settings→Applications→Development→Mock locations. This is a setting you could choose if you are using the emulator to simulate an itinerary without actually being there. As the time of this writing, it is not supported in AIR for Android:

```
<uses-permission android:name="android.permission.ACCESS_MOCK_LOCATION" />
```

Reverse Geocoding

Unless you are displaying a map, providing an address or nearby points of interest is more tangible than latitude and longitude.

Reverse geocoding is the process of reverse-coding a point location to fetch a readable address and place name. It is widely used in combination with location-based services (LBS) to retrieve local weather data or business information, as well as by public safety services such as Enhanced 911. Such information is not immediately available, but there are free services that provide it.

The Yahoo! Geocoding API is well documented and reliable. You need to apply for an application ID that is required as an argument in your requests. It is not exclusive to mobile use and can be used in the browser, assuming it has a way to detect location. Go to *http://developer.yahoo.com/geo/placefinder/* and read the "How Do I Get Started" section to request an ID. You need to log in with a Yahoo! account and fill out the form. Provide the URL of a website, even though it will not be used on the device.

First, add the permission to go out to the Internet:

```
<uses-permission android:name="android.permission.INTERNET" />
```

In this example, I am receiving the latitude and longitude data from `Geolocation Event` and passing it along with my required `applicationID` and `gFlags = R` for reverse geocoding:

```
import flash.events.GeolocationEvent;
import flash.events.Event;
import flash.events.IOErrorEvent;
import flash.net.URLLoader;
import flash.net.URLRequest;
import flash.net.URLRequestMethod;
import flash.net.URLVariables;
import flash.sensors.Geolocation;

var geolocation:Geolocation;
const YAHOO_URL:String = "http://where.yahooapis.com/geocode";
const applicationID:String = "GET_YOUR_ID_ON_YAHOO_SITE";
var loader:URLLoader;
```

Set the geolocation listener:

```
if (Geolocation.isSupported) {
    geolocation = new Geolocation();
    geolocation.addEventListener(GeolocationEvent.UPDATE, onTravel);
}
```

Request reverse geolocation data from the Yahoo! service passing the coordinates:

```
function onTravel(event:GeolocationEvent):void {
    var request:URLRequest = new URLRequest(YAHOO_URL);
    var variables:URLVariables = new URLVariables();
    variables.q = event.latitude.toString() + "\n"
                + event.longitude.toString();
    variables.gflags = "R";
    variables.appid = applicationID;
    request.data = variables;
    request.method = URLRequestMethod.GET;

    loader = new URLLoader();
    loader.addEventListener(Event.COMPLETE, onLocationLoaded);
    loader.addEventListener(IOErrorEvent.IO_ERROR, onLocationLoaded);
    loader.load(request);
}

function onError(event:IOErrorEvent):void {
    trace("error", event);
}
```

Parse the XML received from the service to get city and country information:

```
function onLocationLoaded(event:Event):void {
    loader.removeEventListener(Event.COMPLETE, onLocationLoaded);
    geolocation.removeEventListener(GeolocationEvent.UPDATE, onTravel);
    var xml:XML = new XML(event.target.data);
    var city:String = xml.Result.city.text();
    var country:String = xml.Result.country.text();
    trace(xml);
}
```

The XML comes back with a `ResultSet.Result` node, which includes a street address, city, and country. For example, this is the result for my office building located in New York City's Times Square:

```
<Result>
    <quality>99</quality>
    <latitude>40.757630</latitude>
    <longitude>-73.987167</longitude>
    <offsetlat>40.757630</offsetlat>
    <offsetlon>-73.987167</offsetlon>
    <radius>500</radius>
    <name>40.7576303 -73.98716655000001</name>
    <line1>230 Rodgers &amp; Hammerstein Row</line1>
    <line2>New York, NY  10036-3906</line2>
    <line3/>
    <line4>United States</line4>
    <house>230</house>
    <street>Rodgers &amp; Hammerstein Row</street>
    <xstreet/>
    <unittype/>
    <unit/>
    <postal>10036-3906</postal>
    <neighborhood/>
    <city>New York</city>
    <county>New York County</county>
```

```
        <state>New York</state>
        <country>United States</country>
        <countrycode>US</countrycode>
        <statecode>NY</statecode>
        <countycode>NY</countycode>
        <hash/>
        <woeid>12761367</woeid>
        <woetype>11</woetype>
        <uzip>10036</uzip>
    </Result>
```

This address is actually correct for this particular location. It is not my postal address, but it is where I am currently sitting on the west side of the building.

Other interesting data in the XML is `woeid` and `woetype` ("woe" is short for Where On Earth). GeoPlanet (*http://developer.yahoo.com/geo/geoplanet/guide/*) was developed by Yahoo! as a way to identify some features on Earth in a unique, language-neutral manner. This is particularly important because many places in the world have the same name, such as Paris, France, and Paris, Texas.

`woeid` is a 32-bit unique and nonrepetitive identifier. Numbers follow a hierarchy such as country, state, and city. `woetype` is the type used to identify a place—in this case, 11 refers to the postal code.

Twitter and Flickr are currently using the GeoPlanet system.

Maps

Several geocoding systems and companies offer web services for the consumer market. They all provide similar features. A map is received. It is drawn or a composite of satellite pictures or street tiles is drawn, the latter being more common for mobile devices. It can pan and zoom. Geographical locations or points of interest are represented in the form of markers. Additional features include custom itineraries, the display of specific areas in color, driving and biking directions, and business searches.

Some of the better-known geocoding systems are Google Maps, Yahoo! Maps, Bing Maps, GeoNames, and USC Geocoder. As the technology is rapidly growing, this list may soon expand or change. A lot of map services get their information from NAVTEQ and Tele Atlas, companies that sell databases of geodata, or from MaxMind which sells IP geolocation data. Google now has its own full set of geodata, gathered by its street-view cars.

Launching Google Maps

As we previously discussed, you can collect a point location (latitude, longitude) using the `Geolocation` class, and pass it to the device using a URI handler. It then presents the user with the option of using the native Maps application or launching Google Maps in the browser:

```
<uses-permission android:name="android.permission.INTERNET" />

import flash.events.GeolocationEvent;
import flash.net.navigateToURL;
import flash.net.URLRequest;
import flash.sensors.Geolocation;

function onTravel(event:GeolocationEvent):void {
    geolocation.removeEventListener(GeolocationEvent.UPDATE, onTravel);
    var long:String = event.longitude.toString();
    var lat:String = event.latitude.toString();
    navigateToURL(
        new URLRequest("http://maps.google.com/?q=" + lat + "," + long));
}
```

Note that if you navigate to *http://maps.yahoo.com* instead, launching the native Google Maps is not an option.

The major hurdle with this approach is that your application is now in the background and there is no direct way to go back to it unless you press the device's native back button.

The Android SDK has a library for embedding maps into native applications with interactivity. AIR doesn't support this feature at the time of this writing, but there are many other ways to offer a map experience to your audience. To demonstrate some of the map features within AIR, we will use the Yahoo! Maps Web Services (*http://devel oper.yahoo.com/maps*) and Google Maps API family (*http://code.google.com/apis/ maps/*).

Static Maps

A static map may be sufficient for your needs. It provides a snapshot of a location; although it doesn't offer pan or zoom, it does load relatively quickly, even over GPS.

The Yahoo! Map Image API

The Yahoo! Map Image API from Yahoo! Maps (*http://developer.yahoo.com/maps/rest/ V1/*) provides a reference to a static map image based on user-specified parameters. This API requires an `applicationID`. It doesn't set a restriction on how to use the service, it serves images up to 1,024×1,024, and it has few customizable options.

To use the API, send a `URLRequest` with your parameters. In return, you receive the path to the image which you then load using a `Loader` object. The next example uses the point location from geolocation, the stage dimensions for the image size, and 1 for street level (zoom goes up to 12 for country level):

```
import flash.display.Loader;
import flash.events.GeolocationEvent;
import flash.events.Event;
import flash.net.URLLoader;
import flash.net.URLRequest;
```

```
import flash.sensors.Geolocation;

var geolocation:Geolocation;
const YAHOO_URL:String =
    "http://local.yahooapis.com/MapsService/V1/mapImage";
const applicationID:String = "YOUR_YAHOO_APP_ID";
var urlLoader:URLLoader;
var loader:Loader;

function findLocation():void {
    if (Geolocation.isSupported) {
        geolocation = new Geolocation();
        geolocation.addEventListener(GeolocationEvent.UPDATE, onTravel);
    }
}

function onTravel(event:GeolocationEvent):void {
    var request:String = "?appid=YOUR_APPI"
                    + "&latitude=" + event.latitude
                    + "&longitude=" + event.longitude
                    + "&zoom=1"
                    + "&image_height=" + stage.stageHeight
                    + "&image_width=" + stage.stageWidth;

    urlLoader = new URLLoader();
    urlLoader.addEventListener(Event.COMPLETE, onXMLReceived);
    urlLoader.load(new URLRequest(YAHOO_URL + request));
}

function onXMLReceived(event:Event):void {
    urlLoader.removeEventListener(Event.COMPLETE, onXMLReceived);
    geolocation.removeEventListener(GeolocationEvent.UPDATE, onTravel);

    var xml:XML = XML(event.currentTarget.data);
    loader = new Loader();
    loader.contentLoaderInfo.addEventListener(Event.COMPLETE, onLoaded);
        loader.load(new URLRequest(xml));
}

function onLoaded(event:Event):void {
    event.currentTarget.removeEventListener(Event.COMPLETE, onLoaded);
    this.addChild(event.currentTarget.content);
}
```

You should see a map of where you are currently located.

The Google Static Maps API

The Google Static Maps API (*http://code.google.com/apis/maps/documentation/stati cmaps/*) offers more features than the Yahoo! product, but at the time of this writing, it enforces a rule whereby static maps can only be displayed as browser content unless you purchase a Google Maps API Premier license. An AIR application is not considered browser content. Read the terms carefully before developing a commercial product using this API.

With this service, a standard HTTP request returns an image with the settings of your choice.

The required parameters are as follows:

- center for location as an address or latitude/longitude (not required with marker)
- zoom from 0 for the Earth to 21 for a building (not required with marker)
- size (up to 640×640 pixels)
- sensor (with or without use of GPS locator)

The maximum image size is 640×640. Unless you scale the image up in size, it will not fill the screen on most Android devices. Optional parameters are mobile, format, map type, language, markers, visible, and path.

The following example requests a 480×640 image of Paris centered on the Eiffel Tower:

```
<uses-permission android:name="android.permission.INTERNET" />

import flash.display.Loader;
import flash.net.URLRequest;
import flash.events.Event;

const GOOGLE_URL:String = "http://maps.google.com/maps/api/staticmap?"

function loadStaticImage():void {
    var request:String = "center=Eiffel+Tower,Paris,France
                          &zoom=16&size=480x640&sensor=false";
    var loader:Loader = new Loader();
    loader.contentLoaderInfo.addEventListener(Event.COMPLETE, imageLoaded);
    loader.load(new URLRequest(GOOGLE_URL + request));
}

function imageLoaded(event:Event):void {
    event.currentTarget.removeEventListener(Event.COMPLETE, imageLoaded);
    addChild(event.currentTarget.content);
}
```

You should see on your screen the map of Paris, as shown in Figure 10-3.

Let's make another request using a dynamic location. The sensor parameter is now set to true and we are adding the mobile parameter. The image size is also dynamic, choosing whichever value is the smallest between Google restricted values and our stage size. And we are now using the hybrid version of the maptype:

```
import flash.display.Loader;
import flash.net.URLRequest;
import flash.sensors.Geolocation;

const GOOGLE_URL:String = "http://maps.google.com/maps/api/staticmap?"

var geolocation:Geolocation = new Geolocation();
geolocation.addEventListener(GeolocationEvent.UPDATE, onTravel);
```

```
function onTravel(event:GeolocationEvent):void {
    geolocation.removeEventListener(GeolocationEvent.UPDATE, onTravel);
    loadStaticImage(event.latitude, event.longitude);
}

function loadStaticImage(lat:Number, long:Number):void {
    var width:int = Math.min(640, stage.stageWidth);
    var height:int = Math.min(640, stage.stageHeight);

    var request:String = "center=" + lat + "," + long +
                         "&zoom=15
                         &size=" + width + "x" + height +
                         "&maptype=hybrid&mobile=true&sensor=true";

    var loader:Loader = new Loader();
    loader.contentLoaderInfo.addEventListener(Event.COMPLETE, imageLoaded);
    loader.load(new URLRequest(GOOGLE_URL + request));
}

function imageLoaded(event:Event):void {
    event.currentTarget.removeEventListener(Event.COMPLETE, imageLoaded);
    addChild(event.currentTarget.content);
}
```

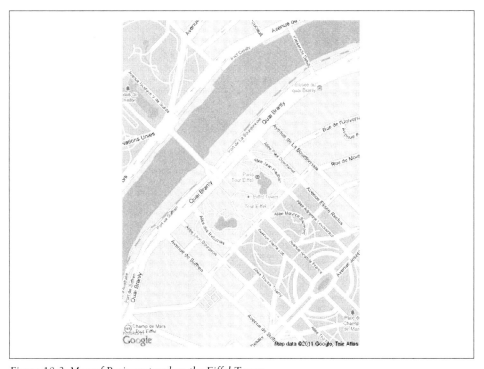

Figure 10-3. Map of Paris centered on the Eiffel Tower

The center parameter can be substituted for one or multiple markers. A marker can be given a color and a label, or it can be customized. And we are now using the road map version of the maptype:

```
function loadStaticImage(lat:Number, long:Number):void {
    var width:int = Math.min(640, stage.StageWidth);
    var height:int = Math.min(640, stage.StageHeight);

    var request:String = "markers=size:large|color:blue|label:L|"
                    + lat + "," + long
                    + "&zoom=16"
                    + &size=" + width + "x" + height +
                    "&maptype=roadmap&mobile=true&sensor=true";

    var loader:Loader = new Loader();
    addChild(loader);
    loader.load(new URLRequest(googleURL + request));
}
```

This is again a low-impact but limited solution. The user only sees an image that cannot be scaled and is only given basic information. Let's now look at using actual maps.

Dynamic Maps

Yahoo! and Google both provide well-documented AS3 libraries for use with their map APIs. The only restriction for both is a maximum of 50,000 uses per day.

 Maps are slow to initialize. Create placeholder art to display instead of the default gray rectangle, and display an attractive loading animation. Do not forget to remove the art after the map appears. Any art under the map would slow down its performance.

The Google Maps API for Flash

With the Google Maps API for Flash (*http://code.google.com/apis/maps/documentation/flash/*), Flex developers can embed Google maps in Flash applications. Sign up for a Google Maps API key and download the Flash SDK. Use version 20 or up (*map_1_20.swc* or *map_flex_1_20.swc*), as version 19 has a known issue with ResizeE vent. Add the path to the *.swc* file in the library path and set Default Linkage to "Merged into code". As you will see, this API offers a wealth of options that are easy to implement.

To set the library path in Flash Professional, go to File→Publish Settings. Click the tool icon next to Script. Select the Library Path tab and click the Flash icon to navigate to the *.swc* file. Once you've imported the file, change Default Linkage to "Merged into code".

In Flash Builder, right-click your project, go to Properties→ ActionScript Build Path, and click Add SWC to navigate to the *.swc* file. "Merged into code" is the default setting.

Create a `Map` object as well as `key` and `url` properties. Entering both your API key and the site URL you submitted when you applied for the key is required even though you are not displaying the map in your website but rather as a standalone Android application.

The `sensor` parameter, also required, states whether you use a GPS sensor. It needs to be a string, not a boolean. The map size, defined by `setSize`, is set dynamically to the dimensions of the stage.

When the map is ready, the geolocation listener is set up. After the first update is received, the `setCenter` function is called with location, zoom level, and the type of map to use. Finally, the zoom control is added. Figure 10-4 shows the result:

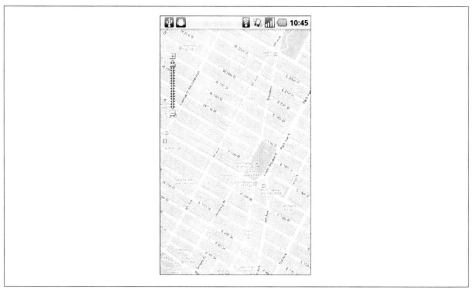

Figure 10-4. My current location

```
<uses-permission android:name="android.permission.INTERNET" />

import com.google.maps.Map;
import com.google.maps.MapEvent;
import com.google.maps.MapType;
import com.google.maps.LatLng;
import flash.geom.Point;
import flash.sensors.Geolocation;
import flash.events.GeolocationEvent;
import com.google.maps.controls.ZoomControl;

const KEY:String = YOUR_API_KEY;
const SITE:String = YOUR_SITE;
var map:Map;
var geolocation:Geolocation;

map = new Map();
map.key = KEY;
map.url = SITE;
map.sensor = "true";
map.setSize(new Point(stage.stageWidth, stage.stageHeight));
map.addEventListener(MapEvent.MAP_READY, onMapReady);

function onMapReady(event:MapEvent):void {
    geolocation = new Geolocation();
    geolocation.addEventListener(GeolocationEvent.UPDATE, onTravel);
    addChild(map);
}

function onTravel(event:GeolocationEvent):void {
    geolocation.removeEventListener(GeolocationEvent.UPDATE, onTravel);
    map.setCenter(new LatLng(event.latitude, event.longitude),
                  18, MapType.NORMAL_MAP_TYPE);
    map.addControl(new ZoomControl());
}
```

Add a marker as landmarks and navigation control. Here the marker is customized to have a shadow, a blue color, and a defined radius. When you click on it, an information window opens with text content:

```
import com.google.maps.MapMouseEvent;
import com.google.maps.overlays.Marker;
import com.google.maps.overlays.MarkerOptions;
import com.google.maps.InfoWindowOptions;

var options:Object = {hasShadow:true,
                       fillStyle: new FillStyle({color:0x0099FF, alpha:0.75}),
                       radius:12
                };
var marker:Marker =
        new Marker(new LatLng(45.7924, 15.9696), new MarkerOptions(options));
marker.addEventListener(MapMouseEvent.CLICK, markerClicked);
map.addOverlay(marker);

function markerClicked(event:MapMouseEvent):void {
```

```
        event.currentTarget.openInfoWindow
            (new InfoWindowOptions({content:"hello"}));
    }
```

Styled Maps support

In October 2010, Google announced support for Styled Maps on Flash, included in
Flash SDK version 20 and up (see *http://code.google.com/apis/maps/documentation/*
flash/maptypes.html#StyledMaps). This addition gives you control over color scheme
and customization of markers and controls. It makes your map look more unique or
match your brand and design. You can also write or draw over the map. The Google
Geo Developers Blog (*http://googlegeodevelopers.blogspot.com/2010/10/five-great*
-styled-maps-examples.html) shows some examples of how Styled Maps has been used.

Google Maps 5

Google Maps 5 was released in December 2010. It provides 3D building rendering,
dynamic vector-based map drawing, and offline reliability. If you would like to see it
supported in AIR, file a software request on the Adobe site, *http://www.mobilecrunch*
.com/2010/12/16/google-maps-5-with-3d-buildings-now-available-for-android/.

EXIF Data and the Map Object

In Chapter 9, we saw how a JPEG image stores location information if the user allows
that feature. Let's look at an example in which the user can choose an image from the
camera roll, read its location information, and display the corresponding map:

> For an explanation on the use of the CameraRoll API and Kenichi
> Ishibashi's EXIF library, please review Chapter 9.

```
import com.google.maps.Map;
import com.google.maps.MapEvent;
import com.google.maps.LatLng;
import com.google.maps.MapType;
import com.google.maps.overlays.Marker;
import com.google.maps.overlays.MarkerOptions;
import flash.events.Event;
import flash.events.MediaEvent;
import flash.media.CameraRoll;


import flash.net.URLRequest;
import jp.shichiseki.exif.*;

public static KEY:String = YOUR_API_KEY;
public static SITE:String = YOUR_SITE;
```

```
var cameraRoll:CameraRoll;
var exifLoader:ExifLoader;
var map:Map;
```

Create your Map object as before:

```
map = new Map();
map.url = SITE;
map.key = KEY;
map.sensor = "false";
map.setSize(new Point(stage.stageWidth, stage.stageHeight));
map.addEventListener(MapEvent.MAP_READY, onMapReady);
addChild(map);
```

Get an image from the device Gallery using the CameraRoll API:

```
function onMapReady(event:MapEvent):void {
    map.setCenter
        (new LatLng(40.736072, -73.992062), 14, MapType.NORMAL_MAP_TYPE);
    if (CameraRoll.supportsBrowseForImage) {
        var camera:CameraRoll = new CameraRoll();
        camera.addEventListener(MediaEvent.SELECT, onImageSelected);
        camera.browseForImage();
    }
}
```

After the user selects an image, create an instance of the ExifLoader class and pass it the photo url. It will load the image and read its EXIF data:

```
function onImageSelected(event:MediaEvent):void {
    exifLoader = new ExifLoader();
    exifLoader.addEventListener(Event.COMPLETE, onExifRead);
    exifLoader.load(new URLRequest(event.data.file.url));
}
```

If the image contains geolocation information, it is used to draw the map and a marker at the exact location:

```
function onImageLoaded(event:Event):void {
    var exif:ExifInfo = reader.exif;

    if (exif.ifds.gps) {
        var gpsIfd:IFD = exif.ifds.gps;
        var exifLat:Array = gpsIfd["GPSLatitude"] as Array;
        var latitude:Number = shorten(exifLat, gpsIfd["GPSLatitudeRef"]);
        var exifLon:Array = gpsIfd["GPSLongitude"] as Array;
        var longitude:Number = shorten(exifLon, gpsIfd["GPSLongitudeRef"]);


        var marker:Marker;
        var parts:Array;
        marker = new Marker(new LatLng(latitude, longitude));
        map.addOverlay(marker);
        map.setCenter(new LatLng(latitude, longitude));
    }
}
```

```
function shorten(info:Array, reference:String):Number {
    var degree:Number = info[0] + (info[1]/60) + (info[2]/3600);
    // position from Greenwich and equator
    if (reference == "S" || reference == "E") {
        degree * -1;
    }
    return degree;
}
```

The speed Property

We are all familiar with a car speedometer, which tells you how fast you are driving. Although not nearly as precise, geolocationEvent has a speed property which you can use in some applications. You can imagine an application for parasailing, parachuting, or skiing, or if you prefer to remain on the ground, a measuring tool for a remote-controlled toy.

The speed is returned in meters/second. It is a good unit for small-distance measurement. To convert to kilometers/hour, use:

```
event.speed * 3.6;
```

If you are not familiar with the metric system, convert the speed to feet/second as follows:

```
event.speed * 3.2808399;
```

To convert to miles/hour, use:

```
event.speed * 2.23693629; // or (event.speed*3600)/1609.344
```

Conclusion

Geolocation has inspired the development of many kinds of applications. Here are just a few:

- Foursquare is a geo-based mobile phone application designed to enable users to share their location with friends and add comments on places visited. You earn points when you discover a new place and badges for interesting locations, and you become the mayor of a location if you are its most frequent visitor.

- Geocaching is a worldwide high-tech treasure hunt. A geocacher places an object, also called a geocache, pinpoints its location using GPS, and shares the geocache location online. To play, you enter your postal code, choose a geocode from a list, store the coordinates on your device, and start hunting. Once you find the physical object, you add your name to a logbook and put the object back or replace it with another object of similar value. You can share stories and photos of your experience.

- The Complex Network of Global Cargo Ship Movements pieced together the routes of cargo ships over the course of a year using a GPS-based vessel tracking system (*http://www.wired.com/wiredscience/2010/01/global-shipping-map/*). The marine traffic website displays vessels around the world in real time. The system is based on the Automatic Identification System (AIS) automated tracking system. The International Maritime Organization requires vessels to carry an AIS transponder on board, which transmits their position, speed, and course, among some other static information such as the vessel's name, dimensions, and voyage details (for more information, go to *http://www.marinetraffic.com/ais/*).

- SiliconSky GPS developed a prototype of an asthma inhaler with built-in GPS tracking capability (*http://news.cnet.com/8301-17938_105-10228982-1.html*). It tracks asthma inhaler use trends, including the exact time and the geographic location of inhaler users, to better monitor the health issue.

- Nike has partnered with Apple to create NikePlus (*http://judgeseyesonly.com/nike plus_video.html*), a running shoe that comes equipped with a GPS sensor and transmits your location data to your iPod.

- To expose the technology which makes all this possible, GoSatWatch tracks and predicts visible satellites, and displays their path and their location (*http://www .gosoftworks.com/GoSatWatch/GoSatWatch.html*).

CHAPTER 11

Microphone and Audio

Sound is the vocabulary of nature.

—Pierre Schaeffer

Audio has a place in mobile applications. Perhaps music is the core element of your project, or sound bites are the final touch to make your application look polished.

This chapter will review what ActionScript has to offer with audio on Android devices. First we will use the microphone, an enhanced modern digital Dictaphone of sorts. Then we will explore the various ways to use audio in your application.

The Microphone

You can use the microphone in many applications on a mobile device. For example, you can take quick audio notes. You can add an audio caption to your photograph. You can even create a DJ multitrack tool with a convenient multitouch interface.

`flash.media.Microphone` is a static class for monitoring and capturing audio from the device's native microphone. It is a subclass of the `EventDispatcher` class.

Your application needs the audio permission to use it:

```
<uses-permission android:name="android.permission.RECORD_AUDIO"/>
```

First make sure your device has a microphone and gives you access to it:

```
import flash.media.Microphone;

if (Microphone.isSupported) {
    // continue on
}
```

If it does, create a reference to it through its `getMicrophone` method. On Android devices, you only have access to one microphone:

```
var microphone:Microphone = Microphone.getMicrophone();
```

The microphone has several properties that you can set to improve your recording.

gain works as a volume multiplier and has a value between 0 and 100. The default value is 50 or a multiplier of 1. Any value above 50 boosts the microphone and below reduces it.

```
microphone.gain = 100;
```

You want to boost the microphone to the maximum, not only because the mobile hardware is of a lesser quality than your desktop, but also because your users may be outdoors, or in a noisy place, while using your application:

rate defines the sample rate and impacts the quality of the input audio. A higher sample rate gives a better sound quality but requires more memory on playback and takes more storage room. The sample rate is measured in kilohertz (kHz) with values of 5, 8, 11, 22, and 44. Considering that the microphone is only mono, a value of 22 should be sufficient. Try a smaller rate depending on your application's needs:

```
microphone.rate = 22;
```

activityLevel is a read-only property that returns the amount of sound detected, from 0 to 100. It can be used as a visual aid for users to monitor how loud they should be speaking:

```
var level:Sprite = new Sprite();
level.x = stage.stageWidth*0.5;
level.y = stage.stageHeight*0.5;
level.graphics.beginFill(0xFF6600);
level.graphics.drawCircle(0, 0, 100);
level.graphics.endFill();

// while recording
level.width = microphone.activityLevel * 3;
level.height = microphone.activityLevel * 3;
```

silenceLevel represents the amount of noise needed to activate the microphone. The default is 10, but you can modify this using setSilenceLevel. A second optional parameter is the amount of time before a silent state starts:

```
microphone.setSilenceLevel(0, 3000);
```

Recording Audio

When recording, the device buffers the microphone input. Create a ByteArray object to store the audio data. Create a reference to the microphone and add a listener to the SampleDataEvent.SAMPLE_DATA event:

```
import flash.media.Microphone;
import flash.utils.ByteArray;
import flash.events.SampleDataEvent;

var bytes:ByteArray = new ByteArray();
```

```
var microphone:Microphone=Microphone.getMicrophone();
if (microphone!= null) {
    microphone.gain = 100;
    microphone.rate = 22;
    microphone.setSilenceLevel(0, 4000);
    microphone.addEventListener(SampleDataEvent.SAMPLE_DATA, recording);
}

function recording(event:SampleDataEvent):void {
    while(event.data.bytesAvailable) {
    var sample:Number = event.data.readFloat();
        bytes.writeFloat(sample);
    }
}
```

To stop the recording, remove the event listener. You can do this in code using a timer:

```
import flash.utils.Timer;
import flash.events.TimerEvent;

var timer:Timer = new Timer(5000);
timer.addEventListener(TimerEvent.TIMER, stopRecording);
timer.start();

function stopRecording(event:TimerEvent):void {
    microphone.removeEventListener(SampleDataEvent.SAMPLE_DATA, recording);
    timer.reset();
}
```

You can also let the user click a button to stop the recording. In this case, be aware of the memory and storage being used. You may want to prompt the user if the recording has been going on for more than a few seconds.

Playing Back Audio

Create a sound object and a listener to read the samples stored in ByteArray. You must set the position on the first bytes to rewind to the beginning of the recording.

Audio data is made of samples; 8,192 samples is the maximum amount of data that can be written to a sound at one time. If you try to play more samples, you will get a runtime error. If you provide fewer than 2,048 samples, the application will assume the sound reached its end and will stop:

```
import flash.media.Sound;

if (bytes.length > 0) {
    bytes.position = 0;
    var sound:Sound = new Sound();
    sound.addEventListener(SampleDataEvent.SAMPLE_DATA, playback);
    sound.play();
}

function playback(event:SampleDataEvent):void {
    var sample:Number;
```

```
        for (var i:int = 0; i < 8192; i++) {
            if (bytes.bytesAvailable > 0) {
                sample = bytes.readFloat();
                event.data.writeFloat(sample); // channel left
                event.data.writeFloat(sample); // channel right
            }
        }
    }
}
```

Note that even though the microphone is monophonic in Flash, sound data needs to be written to both left and right output channels. If you don't do this, the recording playback will be twice the speed at which it was recorded because two samples will run in one stereo sample of the sound object.

Saving a Recording

Let's now save your recording on the device. In the following examples, we are saving the audio files on the SD card. Your application needs permission to write to external storage. If you do not have this permission, AIR will throw a runtime error:

```
<uses-permission android:name=
"android.permission.WRITE_EXTERNAL_STORAGE"/>
```

 When the native camera application launches, it looks for the SD card. If your device is connected to your development computer with USB storage turned on, the card is not accessible. Make sure you turn off USB storage to test your application during development.

The BLOB type

At the time of this writing, there is no native library in which to save an MP3 file that can be played back into the application at runtime. As an alternative, you can save the bytes in an SQLite database as BLOB data. The BLOB type is raw binary data that stores information exactly as it was input. To review the use of SQLite, please read Chapter 6.

In this section, we will compress the file to reduce its size. First, let's create a database and a table to store the audio files:

```
import flash.data.SQLConnection;
import flash.events.SQLEvent;
import flash.data.SQLStatement;
import flash.errors.SQLError;
import flash.filesystem.File;

var connection:SQLConnection;

// open connection to database
connection = new SQLConnection();
connection.addEventListener(SQLEvent.OPEN, openDatabase);
var file:File = File.documentsDirectory.resolvePath("Dictaphone.db");
connection.open(file);
```

```
function openDatabase(event:SQLEvent) {
    connection.removeEventListener(SQLEvent.OPEN, openDatabase);
    createTable();
}

// create or open table
function createTable():void {
    var statement:SQLStatement = new SQLStatement();
    statement.sqlConnection = connection;
    var request:String =
        "CREATE TABLE IF NOT EXISTS mySounds (" +
        "id INTEGER PRIMARY KEY AUTOINCREMENT, " +
        "audio BLOB )";
    statement.text = request;
    try {
        statement.execute();
    } catch(error:SQLError) {
        trace(error.message, error.details);
    }
}
```

Now we'll compress the audio and save it in the database. Here we are using ZLIB compression, which provides good results but is somewhat slow to execute:

```
import flash.utils.CompressionAlgorithm;

var statement:SQLStatement;

function saveItem():void {
    // compress the bytes
    bytes.position = 0;
    bytes.compress(CompressionAlgorithm.ZLIB);

    var command:String =
        "INSERT INTO mySounds(audio) VALUES (?)";
    statement = new SQLStatement();
    statement.sqlConnection = connection;
    statement.text = command;
    statement.parameters[0] = bytes;

    try {
        statement.execute();
    } catch(error:SQLError) {
        trace(error.message, error.details);
    }
}
```

Retrieve the first audio item from the database, and decompress it to use it:

```
import flash.data.SQLResult;

function getItem(id:Number):ByteArray {
    var command:String = "SELECT * FROM mySounds WHERE id=:id;"
    var statement:SQLStatement = new SQLStatement();
    statement.sqlConnection = connection;
```

```
        statement.text = command;
        statement.parameters[":id"] = id;

        statement.execute(1);
        var result:SQLResult = statement.getResult();
        if (result.data != null) {
            return result.data[0];
        }
        return new ByteArray();
    }

    // to read the data back, decompress it
    bytes = getItem(1).audio;
    bytes.uncompress(CompressionAlgorithm.ZLIB);
    bytes.position = 0;
    // play audio
```

Use the bytes to play the audio in a Sound object, as in the previous example.

WAV files

You can save your recording as a WAV file on your device. Download the Adobe.audio.format.WAVWriter class from the *audio_sampler.zip* file located at *http://www.adobe.com/devnet/air/flex/articles/using_mic_api.html*, and import it to your project.

In this example, we are encoding our previous recording as a WAV file and saving it on the SD card in a directory called *mySounds*. For a review on saving local persistent data, read Chapter 6:

```
import com.adobe.audio.format.WAVWriter;
import flash.filesystem.File;
import flash.filesystem.FileStream;
import flash.filesystem.FileMode;

function saveWav(bytes:ByteArray):void {
    // point to mySounds directory on the SD card.
    var directory:File = File.documentsDirectory.resolvePath("mySounds");
    // if directory does not exist yet, create it
    if (!directory.exists) {
        directory.createDirectory();
    }
    // create name of a new wav file
    var file:File = directory.resolvePath("mySound.wav");

    // create an instance of the WAVWriter class and set properties
    var wav:WAVWriter = new WAVWriter();
    wav.numOfChannels = 1; // mono
    wav.sampleBitRate = 16; // or 8
    wav.samplingRate = 44100; // or 22000

    // rewind to the beginning of the ByteArray
    bytes.position = 0;
```

```
    // create stream as conduit to copy data and write file
    var stream:FileStream = new FileStream();
    stream.open(file, FileMode.WRITE);

    // convert byteArray to WAV format and close stream
    wav.processSamples(stream, bytes, 44100, 1);
    stream.close();
}
```

Open source libraries

The current native libraries cannot load a WAV file dynamically or encode a `ByteAr`
ray as an MP3 file. As an alternative, you can try some of the available open source
libraries.

For instance, Shine, written by Gabriel Bouvigné, is an Alchemy/Flash MP3 encoder
(see *https://github.com/kikko/Shine-MP3-Encoder-on-AS3-Alchemy* and *http://code.goo
gle.com/p/flash-kikko/*):

```
import fr.kikko.lab.ShineMP3Encoder;

encoder = new ShineMP3Encoder(bytes);
encoder.addEventListener(Event.COMPLETE, onEncoding);
encoder.addEventListener(ProgressEvent.PROGRESS, onProgress);

encoder.addEventListener(ErrorEvent.ERRROR, onError);
encoder.start();

file.save(mp3Encoder.mp3Data, "recording.mp3");
```

In addition, the following WAV decoders are also available:

*   AS3WavSound (*http://www.ohloh.net/p/as3wavsound*)
*   standingwave3 (*http://maxl0rd.github.com/standingwave3/*)
*   Ogg/Vorbis (*http://vorbis.com/software/*)
*   Tonfall (*http://code.google.com/p/tonfall/*; this is also an encoder)

Saving to a remote server

If you have access to a streaming media server such as Flash Media Server, you can save
and stream audio to the device. The microphone can be attached to a `NetStream` for
uploading. Audio data can also be streamed from the server and played back using a
`Video` object.

Two compression codecs are available:

```
import flash.media.soundCodec;

mic.codec = SoundCodec.NELLYMOSER; // default
mic.coder = SoundCodec.SPEEX;
```

If you are using this technology, urge your audience to use a WiFi connection over 3G unless they have a flat-fee data plan.

Audio Assets

As with visual assets, there are different methods for using audio assets in your application. We will go over the available options next.

Embedding Files

You can embed sounds in your application by adding them to your Flash library or your Flash Builder project. Embedded files should be small, like the ones used for sound effects or user interface audio feedback.

Your application will not display until all of its assets are loaded. Test it. If it sits on a black screen for too long, you may want to group the sounds in an external *.swf* file that you load as a separate process.

Using Flash Professional

Unless you place audio on the timeline, you need to give it a linkage name. Go to Library→Properties→Linkage and click on Export for ActionScript. Change the name so that it doesn't include an extension, and add a capital letter to conform to class naming conventions. For instance, "mySound.mp3" should be "MySound". Note that the Base class becomes flash.media.Sound:

```
var mySound:MySound = new MySound();
mySound.play();
```

Using Flash Builder

Place your audio file in your project folder. Embed it and assign it to a class so that you can create an instance of it:

```
import flash.media.Sound;

[Embed(source="mySound.mp3")]
public var Simple:Class;

var mySound:Sound = new Simple as Sound;
mySound.play();
```

Using External Files

Using external files is best for long sounds or if you want the flexibility to replace the files without recompiling your application. Please review Chapter 4 on how to package external files with your application:

```
import flash.media.Sound;
import flash.net.URLRequest;

var urlRequest:URLRequest = new URLRequest("mySound.mp3");
var sound:Sound = new Sound();
sound.load(urlRequest);
sound.play();
```

This example works for a small file, which loads quickly. We will cover how to handle larger files in the section "Loading Sounds" on page 147.

 At the time of this writing, there is a bug when playing a sound file. The file plays correctly the first time, but with a small delay every time thereafter. Let's hope that this is fixed in a future release.

Settings and the Audio Codec

The Flash Authoring tool offers the option to modify audio files directly in the library. You can change compression, convert from stereo to mono, and choose a sample rate without requiring an external audio tool. Settings are set globally in the Publish Settings panel and can be overwritten for individual files in the library.

If you own Soundbooth, or another external audio application, you can launch it for an individual sound from within the development tools and make changes, which will be applied to the sound in your project. You can, for instance, change the track from stereo to mono or adjust the volume.

In Flash Professional, select the track in the library, click the top pull-down menu, and select "Edit with" to launch the audio editing application. In Flash Builder, single-click the asset, right-click, and select "Open with" to launch the sound application.

The most professional approach, of course, is to work in an audio application directly, as you have more control over your sound design: all files can be opened together and you can set uniform settings such as volume. Prepare your audio carefully beforehand to remove any unnecessary bytes. For background music, write a small file which loops, rather than a long track.

Compression

Supported compressed formats are MP3 (MPEG-1 Audio Layer 3), AAC (Advanced Audio Coding), WAV (Waveform Audio File Format), and AIFF (Audio Interchange File Format).

MP3 can be imported dynamically using the Sound object. MP3 adds a problematic small silence at the beginning of the track. MP3 encodes incoming audio data in blocks. If the data does not fill up a complete block, the encoder adds padding at the beginning and the end of the track. Read André Michelle's blog on the issue, and a potential solution, at *http://blog.andre-michelle.com/2010/playback-mp3-loop-gapless/*.

AAC audio can also be loaded dynamically using the `NetStream` class. AAC is considered the successor of the MP3 format. It is particularly interesting to us because it is hardware-decoded in AIR for Android:

```
import flash.net.NetConnection;
import flash.net.NetStream;

var connection:NetConnection = new NetConnection();
connection.connect(null);
var stream:NetStream = new NetStream(connection);

var client:Object = new Object();
client.onMetaData = onMetaData;
stream.client = client;

stream.play("someAudio.m4a");
```

To control or manipulate an AAC file, refer to the section "Playing Sounds" on page 149. Here is some sample code:

```
var mySound:SoundTransform;
stream.play("someAudio.m4a");
mySound = stream.soundTransform;

// change volume
mySound.volume = 0.75;
stream.soundTransform = mySound;
```

 AAC or HE-AAC (High Efficiency AAC) is a lossless form of compression. It can support up to 96 kHz and 48 channels, and is high-efficiency (HE), high-fidelity (HiFi), and low-bandwidth. It uses Spectral Band Replication (SBR) and Parametric Stereo (PS) to increase coding efficiency and low use of bandwidth, in particular for streaming.

You can embed WAV or AIFF files in your project or library. Or you can use one of the third-party tools mentioned earlier.

Supported uncompressed settings are Adaptive Differential Pulse Code Modulation (ADPCM), and Raw, which uses no compression at all. Uncompressed formats must be embedded.

Bit rate

The bit rate represents the amount of data encoded for one second of a sound file. The higher the bit rate, the better the audio fidelity, but the bigger the file size. For mobile applications, consider reducing the bit rate that you would normally choose for desktop applications.

Bit rate is represented in kilobits per second (kbps), and ranges from 8 to 160 kbps. The default audio publish setting in Flash Professional is 16 kbps Mono.

Sampling rate

The sampling rate is the number of samples taken from an analog audio signal to make a digital signal—44.1 kHz represents 44,100 samples per second. The most common rates are 11.025, 22.05, and 44.1; 44.1 kHz/16-bit is referred to as CD-Quality and is the sampling rate Flash Player always assumes is used.

Stereo or mono

The external speaker on Android devices is monophonic. The headphones are usually stereo, although the output may not be true stereo.

Working with Sounds

Now that your sound files are ready, let's see how we can use them. All sound-related classes belong to the *flash.media* package and will be introduced throughout this chapter.

Loading Sounds

The Sound class gets access to the audio information to load the sound file. It is a subclass of the EventDispatcher class.

As discussed before, your sound can be embedded, it can be loaded as an external file from your application *assets* directory, or it can be downloaded from a remote server. For the latter, advise your audience to use WiFi over 3G for a better experience.

If you try to play a sound that is not loaded, you will get a runtime error. Create a listener to be notified when the loading is complete, and then play your file:

```
import flash.media.Sound;
import flash.net.URLRequest;
import flash.events.Event;

var sound:Sound = new Sound();
sound.addEventListener(Event.COMPLETE, onLoaded);
var request:URLRequest = new URLRequest("mySound.mp3");
sound.load(request);

// sound fully loaded
function onLoaded(event:Event):void {
    sound.removeEventListener(Event.COMPLETE, onLoaded);
    sound.play();
}
```

You can inform the user that the file has started to load:

```
sound.addEventListener(Event.OPEN, onOpen);

function onOpen(event:Event):void {
```

```
        trace("sound loading");
    }
```

If it is a large file, create a listener to display the progress:

```
import flash.events.ProgressEvent;

sound.addEventListener(ProgressEvent.PROGRESS, onLoading);

function onLoading(event:ProgressEvent):void {
    // display the percentage loaded
    trace(event.bytesLoaded/event.bytesTotal)*100);
}
```

On Android devices, it is important to check for errors, particularly if the file is served from a remote server. Inform your user if there is a network issue:

```
import flash.events.IOErrorEvent;

sound.addEventListener(IOErrorEvent.IO_ERROR, onError);

function onError(event:IOErrorEvent):void {
    trace("sound cannot be loaded", event.text);
}
```

Streaming

Streaming is the process of playing part of a sound file while other parts are loading in the background. The advantage is that you don't need to wait for the whole file to download before playing. In addition, you can play very long tracks without memory constraints.

The audio files must be located on a streaming server. The quality of the server is an important factor to a good experience: 128 kbps is sufficient for audio, but a musician can detect artifacts in high frequency for MP3 encoding. Encoding your audio at 192 kbps is a good compromise.

Requesting the file is the same process as before.

You can start playing the audio as soon as there is enough data in the buffer. Buffering is the process of receiving and storing audio data before it is played. The default buffer time is 1,000 milliseconds. You can overwrite the default using the SoundLoaderCon text class.

In this example, the buffer time is changed to five seconds:

```
import flash.media.SoundLoaderContext;

var sound:Sound = new Sound();
var request:URLRequest = new URLRequest("myStreamingSound.mp3");
var context:SoundLoaderContext = new SoundLoaderContext(5000, true);
sound.load(request, context);
sound.play();
```

The SoundLoaderContext class is also used for security checks when loading sounds, but it may not be required in AIR.

 Streaming MP3 files is buggy when it comes to midstream bit rate changes, a method often used by streaming services such as Internet radios. The audio sounds like it speeds up or is broken in chunks because it uses the bit rate declared at the start of the stream, even after a change.

Playing Sounds

In the earlier example, we used the play method. You can add some optional parameters to have more control over playback. The first parameter represents the starting position, the second parameter the number of times to loop the sound.

In this example, the sound starts at the three-second position and loops five times:

```
sound.play(3000, 5);
```

When it loops again, it starts at the same position, here the third second.

The Sound class does not dispatch an event when it is done playing. The SoundChannel class is used for that purpose, as well as for controlling sound properties such as volume and to stop playback. Create it when a Sound object starts playing. Each sound has its own channel:

```
import flash.media.SoundChannel;

var sound = new Sound();
sound.addEventListener(Event.COMPLETE, onLoaded);
sound.load(new URLRequest("mySound.mp3"));

function onLoaded(event:Event):void {
    sound.removeEventListener(Event.COMPLETE, onLoaded);
    var channel:SoundChannel = sound.play();
    channel.addEventListener(Event.SOUND_COMPLETE, playComplete);
}

function playComplete(event:Event):void {
    event.target.removeEventListener(Event.SOUND_COMPLETE, playComplete);
    trace("sound done playing");
}
```

Displaying Progress

There is no direct way to see playback progress, but you can build a timer to regularly display the channel position in relation to the length of the sound. The sound needs to be fully loaded to acquire its length:

```
import flash.utils.Timer;
import flash.events.TimerEvent;
```

```
var channel:SoundChannel;
var sound:Sound;

// load sound


// on sound loaded
var timer:Timer = new Timer(1000);
timer.addEventListener(TimerEvent.TIMER, showProgress);
channel = sound.play();
channel.addEventListener(Event.SOUND_COMPLETE, playComplete);
timer.start();

function showProgress(event:TimerEvent):void {
    // show progress as a percentage
    var progress:int = Math.round(channel.position/sound.length*100);
}
```

Do not forget to stop the timer when the sound has finished playing:

```
function playComplete(event:Event):void {
    channel.removeEventListener(Event.SOUND_COMPLETE, playComplete);
    timer.removeEventListener(TimerEvent.TIMER, showProgress);
}
```

You do not know the length of a streaming audio file until it is fully loaded. You can, however, estimate the length and adjust it as it progresses:

```
function showProgress(event:TimerEvent):void {
    var percentage:int = sound.bytesLoaded/sound.bytesTotal;
    var estimate:int = Math.ceil(sound.length/percentage);

    // show progress as a percentage
    var progress:int = (channel.position/estimate)*100;
    trace(progress);
}
```

Stopping Sounds

To stop a sound from playing, simply call the stop function on its channel:

```
channel.stop();
```

To stop streaming audio, calling the stop function works once, but the sound starts playing again from the beginning. This is because the stream is still downloading. You also need to stop the downloading process:

```
channel.stop();
sound.close();
```

If you have several sounds playing at the same time, you can stop the sounds of all the channels one at a time.

The best approach is to use the static `SoundMixer` class, which controls embedded and dynamic sounds and the mixed output from multiple sound channels. You can use this class to stop as well as control the volume of all the sounds currently playing:

```
SoundMixer.stopAll();
```

Resuming Sounds

There is no direct way to pause a sound and then resume playing, but you can easily create the same effect by storing the position of the channel where you stop, and start from that same position when playing again:

```
var lastPosition:int = channel.position;
channel.stop();

// to resume from the same position
sound.play(lastPosition);
```

Accessing Metadata

When playing AAC files, you have access to metadata information that can be useful for your application. In this example, we are tracing the duration and the codec:

```
import flash.net.NetConnection;
import flash.net.NetStream;

var connection:NetConnection;

connection = new NetConnection();
connection.connect(null);

var stream:NetStream = new NetStream(connection);

// define the stream client property
var metaObject:Object = new Object();
metaObject.onMetaData = onGetMetaData;
stream.client = metaObject;
stream.play("someAudio.m4a");

function onGetMetaData(data:Object):void {
    // audio duration
    trace(data.duration*1000, "milliseconds");
    // codec
    trace(data.audiocodecid);
    for (var prop:String in data) {
        trace(prop, data[prop]);
    }
}
```

Audio Example Using Multitouch

You can develop a musical instrument or device to trigger audio and music. Android devices only support two simultaneous touches; however, they support a range of gestures. Review Chapter 7 for more information.

You can, for instance, use a left-to-right swipe gesture to turn the volume up and a right-to-left swipe gesture to turn the volume down.

ID3 Tags

ID3 is an audio file tagging format used in software and hardware around the world. The tag is a metadata container stored within MP3 audio files in a predictable format. The ID3Info class stores its properties.

To check that your file has an ID3 region, set a listener for the Event.ID3 event:

```
var sound:Sound = new Sound();
sound.addEventListener(Event.ID3, onMetaData);

function onMetaData(event:Event):void {
    var metaData:ID3Info = Sound(event.target).id3;
    // var metaData:ID3Info = event.target.id3;

    for (var property in metaData) {
        trace(property, metatData[property]);
    }
}
```

Some of the information stored in the ID3 region is the name of the artist, the name of the album, the song title, and the year it was recorded. This is particularly useful if you want to build an audio catalog.

You can read more about ID3 at *http://www.id3.org/*.

Modifying Sound

The SoundTransform class is used to control volume and panning for the SoundChannel and the SoundMixer.

Controlling Volume

The SoundTransform object can be applied to the SoundChannel in two ways.

In this example, it is passed as a parameter when the channel is first created:

```
var sound:Sound = new Sound();
var volume:Number = 0.75;
var soundTransform:SoundTransform = new SoundTransform(volume);
var soundChannel:SoundChannel = sound.play(0, 0, soundTransform);
```

If you change the volume property, the SoundTransform object needs to be reapplied:

```
transform.volume = 0.50;
soundChannel.soundTransform = transform;
```

If you want to change the volume over time, use a Timer or an Enter Frame event. In this example, we bring the volume from silence to full volume, and then back to silence, and so forth. The volume gets reset on the upper and lower bounds because, due to float errors, it may not end up exactly on zero or one:

```
import flash.media.SoundTransform;
import flash.net.URLRequest;
import flash.media.SoundChannel;
import flash.events.Event;

var volume:Number = 0;
var direction:int = 1;
var transform:SoundTransform;

transform = new SoundTransform();
var sound:Sound = new Sound();
sound.load(new URLRequest("mySound.mp3"));
var soundChannel:SoundChannel = sound.play();

stage.addEventListener(Event.ENTER_FRAME, changeVolume);

function changeVolume(event:Event):void {
    volume += 0.01*direction;

    // when reaching upper volume bounds, change direction
    if (volume > 1) {
        volume = 1.0;
        direction *= -1;
    // when reaching lower volume bounds, change direction
    } else if (volume < 0) {
        volume = 0;
        direction *= -1;
    }

    transform.volume = volume;
    soundChannel.soundTransform = transform;
}
```

To change volume globally, use the SoundMixer. In the following example, we mute all the channels at once. Make sure not to confuse the syntax of the SoundTransform class and the soundTransform property which has a lowercase s:

```
var globalTransform:SoundTransform = new SoundTransform();
globalTransform.volume = 0;
SoundMixer.soundTransform = globalTransform;
```

Panning

Panning is the position of the audio signal between the right and left channels in a stereo sound field. Pan has a value from –1 all the way to the left channel to 1 all the way to the right channel.

The external speaker on Android devices is mono. Make sure to inform your users to use their headphones, which are stereo, if you are using this technique.

The pan value is passed as a second parameter when creating a SoundTransform object:

```
var soundTransform:SoundTransform = new SoundTransform(1, -1);
```

The object can be applied to one sound alone via SoundChannel:

```
var channel:SoundChannel = sound.play(0, 1, soundTransform);
```

You can also pan all the sounds via SoundMixer:

```
import flash.media.SoundMixer;
SoundMixer.soundTransform = new SoundTransform(1, -1);
```

A common technique to pan back and forth between channels is to use a Math.sin function, which returns a value between –1 and 1:

```
var panPhase:Number = 0;
var transformObject:SoundTransform;
var channel:SoundChannel

transformObject = new SoundTransform();

function onEnterFrame(event:Event):void {
    transformObject.pan = Math.sin(panPhase);
    channel.soundTransform = transformObject;
    panPhase += 0.05;
}
```

Raw Data and the Sound Spectrum

With the arrival of digital sound, a new art form quickly followed: the visualization of sound.

A sound waveform is the shape of the graph representing the amplitude of a sound over time. The amplitude is the distance of a point on the waveform from the equilibrium line, also called the time-domain. The peak is the highest point in a waveform.

You can read a digital signal to represent sound in real time using amplitude values.

Making Pictures of Music is a project run by mathematics and music academics that analyses and visualizes music pieces. It uses Unsquare Dance, a complex multi-instrumental piece created by Dave Brubeck. For more information, go to *http://www.uwec.edu/walkerjs/PicturesOf Music/MultiInstrumental%20Complex%20Rhythm.htm*.

In AIR, you can draw a sound waveform using the `computeSpectrum` method of the `SoundMixer` class. This method takes a snapshot of the current sound wave and stores the data in a `ByteArray`:

```
SoundMixer.computeSpectrum(bytes, false, 0);
```

The method takes three parameters. The first is the container `ByteArray`. The second optional parameter is `FFTMode` (the fast Fourier transform); `false`, the default, returns a waveform, and `true` returns a frequency spectrum. The third optional parameter is the stretch factor; 0 is the default and represents 44.1 kHz. Resampling at a lower rate results in a smoother waveform and a less detailed frequency. Figure 11-1 shows the drawing generated from this data.

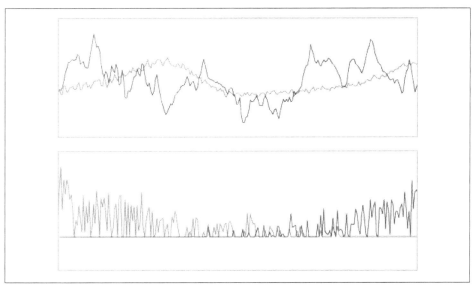

Figure 11-1. A waveform (top) and a frequency spectrum (bottom), both generated from the same piece of audio but setting the fast Fourier transform value to false and then to true

A waveform spectrum contains 512 bytes of data: 256 values for the left channel and 256 values for the right channel. Each byte contains a floating-point value between –1 and 1, which represents the amplitude of the points in the sound waveform.

If you trace the length of the `ByteArray`, it returns a value of 2,048. This is because a floating-point value is made of four bytes: 512 * 4 = 2,048.

Our first approach is to use the drawing API. Drawing a vector is appropriate for a relatively simple sound like a microphone audio recording. For a longer, more complex track, we will look at a different approach after this example.

We are using two loops to read the bytes, one at a time. The loop for the left channel goes from 0 to 256. The loop for the right channel starts at 256 and goes back down to 0. The value of each byte, between –1 and 1, is multiplied by a constant to obtain a value large enough to see. Finally, we draw a line using the loop counter for the x coordinate and we subtract the byte value from the vertical position of the equilibrium line for the y coordinate.

The same process is repeated every Enter_Frame event until the music stops. Don't forget to remove the listener to stop calling the drawMusic function:

```
const CHANNEL_LENGTH:int = 256; // channel division
// equilibrium line y position and byte value multiplier
var PEAK:int = 100;
var bytes:ByteArray;
var sprite:Sprite;
var soundChannel:SoundChannel;

bytes = new ByteArray();
sprite = new Sprite();

var sound:Sound = new Sound();
sound.addEventListener(Event.COMPLETE, onLoaded);
sound.load(new URLRequest("mySound.mp3"));
addChild(sprite);

function onLoaded(event:Event):void {
    soundChannel = new SoundChannel();
    soundChannel = event.target.play();
    soundChannel.addEventListener(Event.SOUND_COMPLETE, onPlayComplete);
    sprite.addEventListener(event.ENTER_FRAME, drawMusic);
}

function drawMusic(event:Event):void {
    var value:Number;
    var i:int;

    SoundMixer.computeSpectrum(bytes, false, 0);

    // erase the previous drawing
    sprite.graphics.clear();

    // move to the far left
    sprite.graphics.moveTo(0, PEAK);
    // left channel in red
    sprite.graphics.lineStyle(0, 0xFF0000);
    for (i = 0; i < CHANNEL_LENGTH; i++) {
        value = bytes.readFloat()*PEAK;
        // increase the x position by 2 pixels
        sprite.graphics.lineTo(i*2, PEAK - value);
    }
```

```
        // move to the far right
        sprite.graphics.lineTo(CHANNEL_LENGTH*2, PEAK);
        // right channel in blue
        sprite.graphics.lineStyle(0, 0x0000FF);
        for (i = CHANNEL_LENGTH; i > 0; i--) {
            sprite.graphics.lineTo(i*2, PEAK - bytes.readFloat()*PEAK);
        }
    }
}

function onPlayComplete(event:Event):void {
    soundChannel. removeEventListener(Event.SOUND_COMPLETE, onPlayComplete);
    sprite.removeEventListener(Event.ENTER_FRAME, drawMusic);
}
```

On most Android phones, which have a width of 480 pixels, the waveform will draw off-screen on the right to pixel 512 (256 * 2). Consider presenting your application in landscape mode and positioning the sprite container centered on the screen.

For better performance, let's draw the vector into a bitmap. As a general rule, on mobile devices, you should avoid the drawingAPI, which is redrawn every frame and degrades performance.

The Sprite is not added to the display list, and therefore is not rendered to the screen. Instead, we create a BitmapData and draw the sprite inside its rectangle:

```
import flash.display.Bitmap;
import flash.display.BitmapData;

var sprite:Sprite;
var bitmap:Bitmap;

sprite = new Sprite();
// draw a BitmapData to draw the waveform
var bitmapData = new BitmapData(480, PEAK*2, true, 0x000000);
// store it in a Bitmap
bitmap = new Bitmap(bitmapData);
// position and add Bitmap to displayList
bitmap.y = 200;
addChild(bitmap);

function drawMusic(event:Event):void {
    var value:Number;
    var i:int;

    SoundMixer.computeSpectrum(bytes, false, 0);

    // use the sprite.graphics as before
    // but does not render it to the screen
    sprite.graphics.clear();
    sprite.graphics.moveTo(0, PEAK);
    sprite.graphics.lineStyle(0, 0xFF0000);
    for (i = 0; i < CHANNEL_LENGTH; i++) {
        value = bytes.readFloat()*PEAK;
        sprite.graphics.lineTo(i*2, PEAK - value);
```

```
    }

    sprite.graphics.lineTo(CHANNEL_LENGTH*2, PEAK);
    sprite.graphics.lineStyle(0, 0x0000FF);
    for (var i:int = CHANNEL_LENGTH; i > 0; i--) {
        value = bytes.readFloat()*PEAK;
        sprite.graphics.lineTo(i*2, PEAK - value);
    }

    // instead draw it into a bitmap
    // empty bitmap
    bitmap.fillRect(bitmap.rect(sprite), 0);
    // draw the sprite onto the bitmap image
    bitmap.draw(sprite);
}
```

Audio and Application Activity

The Android Activity Manager controls applications moving to the foreground or the background based on the user's decision, but doesn't terminate them.

When your application goes to the background, most processes are paused, but audio and timers continue to run. Unless you want your audio to keep playing, you need to listen to two events to monitor a play and pause scenario:

```
import flash.desktop.NativeApplication;
import flash.events.Event;

NativeApplication.nativeApplication.addEventListener
    (Event.ACTIVATE, onActivate);

NativeApplication.nativeApplication.addEventListener
    (Event.DEACTIVATE, onDeactivate);

function onDeactivate(event:Event):void {
    // pause or stop audio
}

function onActivate(event:Event):void {
    // play audio
}
```

Please refer to Chapter 6 for more information.

Conclusion

Audio and music applications are as diverse as the imagination of their creators. Here are a few examples, ranging from applications for creating music with a visual component to saving audio notes:

- Audiotool (*http://www.audiotool.com*) is an online music production studio that enables people worldwide to partake in a shared adventure of creating, sharing, and listening to music.
- SoundCloud (*http://soundcloud.com/*) is a community site for creating, recording, and sharing sounds.
- Isle of Tune (*http://isleoftune.com/*) is a musical sequencer. You build roads with houses and trees. Cars make music based on the landscape through which they are passing.
- RUNXT LIFE (*http://www.runxt.be/#/life/*) is a generative music application based on the cellular automation theory Game of Life. The musical game evolves without human input.
- Voice Notes (*http://coenraets.org/blog/air-for-android-samples/voice-notes-for-an droid/*) is an application for recording voice messages.

CHAPTER 12

Video

If it can be written, or thought, it can be filmed.

—Stanley Kubrick

Watching quality video has become common on the Internet, thanks to the Adobe Flash Player 9, which introduced high-definition video and full-screen support in 2007. Since then, we have seen the evolution of a new type of user who does not watch, or own, a television and relies on the Internet for her viewing.

Mobile devices—and tablets in particular—are expected to offer the same service and convenience. Device manufacturers and software engineers are hard at work to meet this expectation.

Until then, video developers, more than any others, need to gauge limitations and test options for the best user experience. In this chapter, we will go over the different areas to consider for the best video delivery and experience.

Preparing Video

A codec is software used to encode and decode a digital video signal. Engineers try various solutions to maintain video quality while reducing the amount of data, using state-of-the-art compression algorithm design.

A large portion of your work will comprise preparing and testing various configurations.

Codecs

At the time of this writing, AIR for Android supports codecs for On2 VP6, H.263 (Sorenson Spark), and H.264.

H.264, also called MPEG-4 Part 10 or AVC for Advanced Video Coding, delivers high-quality video at lower bit rates than H.263 and On2. It is more complicated to decode, however, and requires native GPU playback or a fast compressor to ensure smooth playback.

H.264 supports the following profiles: Baseline, Extended, Main, and various flavors of High. Test the profiles, as not all of them work with hardware-accelerated media decoding. It appears that only Baseline is using this at the time of this writing.

AAC (Advanced Audio Coding) is the audio codec generally paired with H.264. Nellymoser and Speex are supported, but do not utilize hardware decoding. Review Chapter 11 to learn more about this.

MPEG-4 (Moving Picture Experts Group) H.264 is an industry-standard video compression format. It refers to the container format, which can contain several tracks. The file synchronizes and interleaves the data. In addition to video and audio, the container includes metadata that can store information such as subtitles. It is possible to contain more than one video track, but AIR only recognizes one.

Encoding

You can use Adobe Media Encoder CS5 or a third-party tool such as Sorenson Squeeze or On2 Flix to encode your video.

It is difficult to encode video for every device capacity and display size. Adobe recommends grouping devices into low-end, medium-end, and high-end groups.

If your video is embedded or attached to your application, prepare and provide only one file and use a medium-quality solution to serve all your users. If your video is served over a network, prepare multiple streams.

Gather as much information as possible from the user before selecting the video to play. The criteria are the speed of the network connection and the performance of the device. To determine if the application is running over WiFi or 3G, please refer to "How to Know if GPS or WiFi Is Active" on page 120 in Chapter 10. To get information on the device used, please refer to the section titled "Capabilities" on page 48 in Chapter 5.

We will discuss encoding settings later in this chapter.

Decoding

Containers are wrappers around video and audio tracks holding metadata. MP4 is a common wrapper for the MPEG-4 format and is widely compatible. F4V is Adobe's own format, which builds on the open MPEG-4 standard media file format and supports H.264/AAC-based content. FLV, Adobe's original video container file format, supports codecs such as Sorenson Spark and On2 VP6, and can include an alpha channel and additional metadata such as cue points.

Video decoding is a multithreaded operation. H.264 and AAC are decoded using hardware acceleration on mobile devices to improve frame rate and reduce battery consumption. Rendering is still done in the CPU.

Bit Rate

Bit rate is the number of bits dedicated to the video in one second (measured in kilobits per second or kbps). During the encoding process, the encoder varies the number of bits given in various portions of the video based on how complicated they are, while keeping the average as close to the bit rate you set as possible.

Because the average is calculated on the fly and is not always accurate, it is best to select the two-pass mode even though it takes longer. The first pass analyzes the video and records a statistics log; the second pass encodes the video using the log to stay as close to the desired average bit rate as possible.

Use the network connection speed as a guide for your encoding. The recommendation is to use 80% to 90% of the available bandwidth for video/audio combined, and keep the rest for network fluctuations. Try the following H.264/AAC rates as a starting point:

- WiFi: 500 to 1,000 kbps, audio up to 160 kbps
- 3G: 350 to 450 kbps, audio up to 128 kbps
- 2.5G: 100 kbps, audio up to 32 kbps

Frame Rate

Reduce high frame rates whenever possible. Downsampling by an even factor guarantees a better result. For instance, a film at 30 fps can be downsampled to 15 fps; a film at 24 fps can be downsampled to 12 or 18 fps.

Do not use content encoded at a high frame rate and assume that a lower frame rate in AIR will adjust it. It will not.

If your footage was captured at a frame rate greater than 24 fps and you want to keep the existing frame rate, look at reducing other settings such as the bit rate.

 If your video is the only moving content in your application, you can use a frame rate as low as 12 fps because the video plays at its native frame rate regardless of the application's frame rate. A low frame rate reduces drain on the battery.

Resolution

The pixel resolution is simply the width and height of your video. Never use a video that is larger than the intended display size. Prepare the video at the dimension you need.

High resolution has a greater impact on mobile video playback performance than bit rate. A conservative resolution of 480×360 plays very well; 640×480 is still good. A higher resolution will be challenging on most devices and will result in a poor viewing experience on devices that are not using the GPU for decoding or on devices with a 500 MHz CPU. Resolution recommendations are:

- WiFi or 3G: 480×320
- 2.5G: 320×240

In fact, you can often encode smaller and scale up without a noticeable decrease in picture quality. The high PPI on most devices will still display a high-quality video.

Decrease your video size by even divisors of 16. MPEG video encoders work by dividing the video frames into blocks of 16 by 16, called *macroblocks*. If the dimension does not divide into 16 or close to it, the encoder must do extra work and this may impact the overall encoding target. As an alternate solution, resort to multiples of eight, not four. It is an important practice to achieve maximum compression efficiency.

As for all mobile content, get rid of superfluous content. If necessary, crop the video to a smaller dimension or edit its content, such as trimming a long introduction.

For more information on mobile encoding guidelines, read Adobe's white paper at *http://download.macromedia.com/flashmediaserver/mobile-encoding-android-v2_7.pdf*.

Performance

Hardware is improving quickly, but each device's architecture is a little different. If you want to target the high end of the market, you can add such comments when submitting your applications to the Android Market.

In addition to your encoding settings, there are some best practices to obey for optimal video playback. They are all simple to apply:

- Do not put anything on top of or behind the video, even if it is transparent. This would need to be calculated in the rendering process and would negatively affect video playback.
- Make sure your video window is placed on a full pixel (no half-pixel boundaries).
- Do not use bitmap caching on the video or any other objects on the stage. Do not use filters such as drop shadows or pixel benders. Do not skew or rotate the video. Do not use color transformation or objects with alpha.
- Do not show more than one video at the same time.
- Stop all other processes unless they are absolutely necessary. If you use a progress bar, only call for progress update using a timer every second, not on the enter frame event.

Playing Video

You can play videos running from your device or loaded remotely.

Embedded Video

You can embed a video in your application using Flash Professional. Embedded video will appear in the library as a symbol. Create a `MovieClip` and add the video content to it. You can then control its playback by calling the standard `MovieClip` navigation methods.

Using this approach is simple, but it has disadvantages. The video is compiled into the application and adds to its size. Also, it is always loaded in memory and cannot be removed.

As an alternative, you can embed the video in an external *.swf* file which you load using the `Loader` class.

External Video

You can package the video with your application. It is placed in the *application* directory. The application will not display until all of the assets are loaded. You can also serve the video from a remote web server. The code is identical in both cases.

For the latter, add some buffering logic. We will come back to this topic later in this chapter.

Progressive Video

To load video locally, you need to know the path of the file in your *application* directory.

`NetConnection` creates a connection with the local filesystem when calling its `connect` method. Pass a null parameter in its construction to indicate that it is not streaming.

Within the connection, `NetStream` opens the channel between AIR and the local filesystem. Pass the `connection` object as a parameter in its construction, and use its `play` method to receive video data. Note that this object needs its `client` property defined as well as the `onMetaData` method to prevent a runtime error.

The `Video` object displays the video data.

In this example, the `Video` object dimensions are hardcoded:

```
import flash.net.NetConnection;
import flash.net.NetStream;
import flash.media.Video;
import flash.events.NetStatusEvent;

var connection:NetConnection;
var video:Video;

video = new Video();
video.width = 480;
video.height = 320;
```

```
connection = new NetConnection();
connection.addEventListener(NetStatusEvent.NET_STATUS, netConnectionEvent);
connection.connect(null);

function netConnectionEvent(event:NetStatusEvent):void {
    event.target.removeEventListener(NetStatusEvent.NET_STATUS,
netConnectionEvent);

    if (event.info.code == "NetConnection.Connect.Success") {
        var stream:NetStream = new NetStream(connection);
        stream.addEventListener(NetStatusEvent.NET_STATUS, netStreamEvent);

        var client:Object = new Object();
        client.onMetaData = onMetaData;
        stream.client = client;

        // attach the stream to the video to display
        video.attachNetStream(stream);
        stream.play("someVideo.flv");
        addChild(video);


    }
}

function onMetaData(info:Object):void {}
```

 At the time of this writing, `video.smoothing` is always `false`. This is consistent with AIR runtime default settings, but does not provide the best video experience. Setting `video.smoothing` to `true` does not change it.

SD card

You can play videos from the SD card. Playback is nearly as fast as playing back from the device.

You need to resolve the path to where the video is located before playing it. In this example, there is a directory called *myVideos* on the SD card and a video called *myVideo* inside it:

```
var videosPath:File = File.documentsDirectory.resolvePath("myVideos");
var videoName:String = "myVideo.mp4";

stream.play(videosPath + "/" + videoName);
```

For more information on accessing the filesystem, refer to Chapter 6.

Browsing for video

You cannot use `CameraRoll` to browse for videos, but you can use the filesystem.

You could create a custom video player for the user to play videos installed on the device or on the SD card. The browseForOpen method triggers the filesystem to search for videos:

```
import flash.filesystem.File;
import flash.net.FileFilter;
import flash.media.Video;

var video:Video;

var filter:FileFilter = new FileFilter("video", "*.mp4;*.flv;*.mov;*.f4v");
var file:File = new File();
file.addEventListener(Event.SELECT, fileSelected);
file.browseForOpen("open", [filter]);
```

 At the time of this writing, it seems that only the FLV format is recognized when browsing the filesystem using AIR.

A list of the video files found appears. The following code is executed when the user selects one of the files. The video file is passed in the Event.SELECT event as file.target and is played using its url property. Note how the video is sized and displayed in the onMetaData function. We will cover this technique next:

```
import flash.net.NetConnection;
import flash.net.NetStream;

function fileSelected(event:Event):void {
    video = new Video();

    var connection:NetConnection = new NetConnection();
    connection.connect(null);

    var stream:NetStream = new NetStream(connection);
    var client:Object = new Object();
    client.onMetaData = onMetaData;
    stream.client = client;

    video.attachNetStream(stream);
    stream.play(event.target.url);
}

function onMetaData(info:Object):void {
    video.width = info.width;
    video.height = info.height;
    addChild(video);
}
```

Metadata

The `client` property of `NetStream` is used to listen to `onMetaData`. In this example, we use the video stream width and height, received in the metadata, to scale the `Video` object. Other useful information is the duration, the frame rate, and the codec:

```
// define the Stream client to receive callbacks
var client:Object = new Object();
client.onMetaData = onMetaData;
stream.client = client;

// attach the stream to the video
video.attachNetStream(stream);
stream.play("someVideo.flv");

// size the video object based on the metadata information
function onMetaData(info:Object):void {
    video.width = info.width;
    video.height = info.height;
    addChild(video);

    trace(info.duration);
    trace(info.framerate);
    trace(info.codec);
    for (var prop:String in info) {
        trace(prop, data[prop]);
    }
}
```

Cue points

The `FLVPlaybackComponent` gives us the ability to add cue points to a video. The component listens to the current time code and compares it to a dictionary of cue points. When it finds a match, it dispatches an event with the cue point information.

The cue points come in two forms. Navigation cue points are used as markers for chapters or time-specific commentary. Event cue points are used to trigger events such as calling an ActionScript function. The cue point object looks like this:

```
var cuePoint:Object = {time:5, name:"cue1", type:"actionscript",
parameters:{prop:value}};
```

This component is not available in AIR for Android. If you want to use something similar, you need to write the functionality yourself. It can be a nice addition to bridge your video to your AIR content if you keep your cue points to a minimum. Use them sparsely, as they have an impact on performance.

Cue points can be embedded dynamically server-side if you are recording the file on Flash Media Server.

Buffering

The *moov atom*, video metadata that holds index information, needs to be placed at the beginning of the file for a progressive file. Otherwise, the whole file needs to be completely loaded in memory before playing. This is not an issue for streaming. Look at Renaun Erickson's wrapper to fix the problem, at *http://renaun.com/blog/code/qtin dexswapper/*.

By default, the application uses an input buffer. To modify the default buffering time, use the following:

```
var stream:NetStream = new NetStream(connection);
stream.bufferTime = 5; // value in seconds
```

When using a streaming server, managing bandwidth fluctuation is a good strategy:

```
var stream:NetStream = new NetStream(connection);
stream.addEventListener(NetStatusEvent.NET_STATUS, netStreamEvent);

function netStreamEvent(event:NetStatusEvent):void {
    var buffTime:int;
    swith(event.info.code) {
        case "NetStream.Buffer.Full" :
        buffTime = 15.0;
        break;
        case "NetStream.Buffer.empty" :
        buffTime = 2.0;
        break;
    }
    stream.bufferTime = buffTime;
}
```

Read Fabio Sonnati's article on using dual-threshold buffering, at *http://www.adobe .com/devnet/flashmediaserver/articles/fms_dual_buffering.html*.

RTMP Streaming

Real Time Messaging Protocol (RTMP) is a protocol using a streaming server such as Flash Media Server or a streaming service such as Influxis or Flash Media Server for Amazon Web Services.

Streaming uses a lot of data. Inform your users to use WiFi so that it is not too costly and guarantees the best possible quality experience.

RTMP server

Let's use our RTMP server to stream an on-demand video. As in progressive downloading, streaming uses a `Video`, a `NetConnection`, and a `NetStream` object.

`NetConnection` connects to the streaming server. The protocol used is `rtmp`. Note the `streamClient` variable. You need it for callbacks; otherwise, you will get a runtime error:

```
static const SERVER:String = "rtmp://SERVER_URI/vod/;
static const VIDEO_PATH:String = "/myVideo";

video = new Video();
video.width = 480;
video.height = 320;

connection.addEventListener(NetStatusEvent.NET_STATUS, onNetEvent);
connection.connect(SERVER);

function netConnectionEvent(event:NetStatusEvent):void {
    if (event.info.code == "NetConnection.Connect.Success") {
        var stream:NetStream = new NetStream(connection);
        stream.addEventListener(NetStatusEvent.NET_STATUS, onStreamEvent);

        var streamClient:Object = new Object();
        streamClient.onMetaData = onMetaData;
        stream.client = streamClient;

        video.attachNetStream(stream);
        stream.play(VIDEO_PATH);
        addChild(video);
        break;
    }
}

function onStreamEvent(event:NetStatusEvent):void {}
function onMetaData(info:Object):void {}
function onBWDone():void {}
```

It is a good idea to add listeners for connection errors while debugging and to inform your audience in case of an issue:

```
connection.addEventListener(IOErrorEvent.IO_ERROR, onIOError);
connection.addEventListener
    (SecurityErrorEvent.SECURITY_ERROR, onSecurityError);
connection.addEventListener(AsyncErrorEvent.ASYNC_ERROR, onAsyncError);

function onIOError(event:IOErrorEvent):void {}
function onSecurityError(event:SecurityErrorEvent):void {}
function onASyncError(event:AsyncErrorEvent):void {}
```

Local Flash Media Server

You can install a local Flash Media Server to run and test your applications. Change the path to your local server. To ensure the video plays, turn off *.swf* verifications on the server:

```
static const SERVER:String = "rtmp://localhost/vod/";
```

Flash Media Server offers features to examine and monitor your video streams. The Quality of Service API, for instance, returns the user's current bandwidth. You can extend the functionality of your video management by writing additional server code.

HTTP Dynamic Streaming

Adobe's adaptive streaming delivery method, called HTTP Dynamic Streaming, is another option for live or on-demand video playback. This method is similar to Apple's Adaptive Streaming and Microsoft's Smooth Streaming.

Because HTTP Dynamic Streaming plays back video files in chunks, additional complex logic needs to be built in to put the segments together in the right order and play them back. Therefore, it is recommended that an Open Source Media Framework-based player be used for HTTP Dynamic Streaming.

You can build one from scratch using OSMF, or use a prebuilt solution such as Flash Media Playback or Strobe Media Playback. Video content needs to be prepared for HTTP Dynamic Streaming in a simple post-processing step that creates the segments along with a manifest file that describes the video and its segments. Adobe provides free command-line tools for preparing both on-demand and live streams.

More information on HTTP Dynamic Streaming is available online at *http://www.adobe .com/products/httpdynamicstreaming/* and *http://www.flashstreamworks.com/archive .php?post_id=1278132166*.

Peer-to-Peer Communication

Real Time Media Flow Protocol (RTMFP) is an Adobe proprietary protocol that enables peer-to-peer communication in Flash Player and the AIR runtime. It opens up possibilities for your applications using video.

We will go over a video example in Chapter 15.

Controls

The methods for controlling the stream are `play`, `pause`, `resume`, `seek`, and `close`. You cannot stop the stream because it is still downloading. You need to close it completely.

You can check the progress of the stream by checking its `time` property. Use that value and increment it to seek ahead in the video. You can also seek to a specific time, of course. With progressive download, you can only seek ahead to points in the video file that have been downloaded. With embedded video and RTMP, you can seek anywhere within the video file at any time.

To monitor these events, register for `NetStatusEvent` and its `info.code` object:

```
function onNetEvent(event:NetStatusEvent):void {
    switch (event.info.code) {
        case "NetStream.Play.Start" :
            break;
        case "NetStream.Play.Stop":
            break;
        case " NetStream.Pause.Notify" :
            break;
```

```
        case " NetStream.Unpause.Notify":
            break;
        case "NetStream.Buffer.Full":
            break;
        case "NetStream.Seek.Notify":
            break;
        }
    }
}
```

You cannot use the Sound object to control the audio part on the video. Use the Sound Transform property instead. Here we are setting the volume to silent:

```
var transform:SoundTransform = new SoundTransform();
stream.soundTransform = new SoundTransform(0);
```

YouTube

It is almost impossible to talk about videos without mentioning YouTube. As you most certainly know, YouTube is a file-sharing video site that has changed the propagation of information via video, whether is it pop culture or current events.

YouTube videos can be played on Android devices if they are encoded with the H.264 video codec. Like Google Maps, discussed in Chapter 10, the user is presented with the option to choose between the YouTube local application, if it is installed on his device, and the browser version.

In both cases, you use a URLRequest:

```
<uses-permission android:name="android.permission.INTERNET" />

import flash.net.navigateToURL;
import flash.net.URLRequest;

var youTubePath:String = "http://www.youtube.com/watch?v=";
var videoID:String = someID;

navigateToURL(new URLRequest(youTubePath + videoID);
```

To display the video at full screen, use a different path:

```
var youTubePath:String = "http://www.youtube.com/watch/v/";
```

Capturing Video

The native video camera can be used to capture video within AIR.

Video and the CameraUI Class

You can use the native camera within AIR to capture video. Your application needs to have permission. In Flash Professional, select File→AIR Android settings→Permissions→Camera. In Flash Builder, add the following permission:

```
<uses-permission android:name="android.permission.CAMERA"/>
```

The `flash.media.CameraUI` class is an addition to the ActionScript language to support the device's native camera application. It is a subclass of the `EventDispatcher` class and is only supported on AIR for mobile.

This object allows you to launch the native camera application to shoot a video while your AIR application moves to the background.

 When you use the native camera, it comes to the foreground, your AIR application moves to the background, and `NativeApplication` `Event.DEACTIVATE` is fired. Make sure you don't have any logic that could interfere with the proper running of your application, such as exiting. Likewise, when the native camera application quits and your AIR comes back to the foreground, `Event.ACTIVATE` is called.

The first step is to verify that your device supports access to the camera by checking the `CameraUI.isSupported` property. Note that, as of this writing, Android does not support the front camera natively, and therefore neither does AIR:

```
import flash.media.CameraUI;

if (CameraUI.isSupported == false) {
    trace("no camera accessible");
    return;
}
```

If it is supported, create an instance of the `CameraUI` class.

Register your application to receive camera events. A `MediaEvent.COMPLETE` is dispatched after a picture is taken, an `Event.CANCEL` if no media is selected, and an `ErrorEvent` if there is an error in the process:

```
import flash.events.MediaEvent;
import flash.events.ErrorEvent;
import flash.media.CameraUI;

var cameraUI:CameraUI = new CameraUI();
cameraUI.addEventListener(MediaEvent.COMPLETE, onComplete);
cameraUI.addEventListener(Event.CANCEL, onCancel);
cameraUI.addEventListener(ErrorEvent.ERROR, onError);
```

Call the `launch` function and pass the type `MediaType.VIDEO` as a parameter. This will launch the camera in video mode automatically:

```
import flash.media.MediaType;

var cameraUI:CameraUI = new CameraUI();
cameraUI.launch(MediaType.VIDEO);

function onError(event:ErrorEvent):void {
    trace(event.text);
}
```

The camera application is now active and in the foreground. The AIR application moves to the background and waits.

Once the event is received, the camera application automatically closes and the AIR application moves back to the foreground.

Video capture on Android requires a lot of memory. To avoid having the Activity Manager terminate the application, the capture setting is restricted to low resolution by default, which requires a smaller memory buffer.

 MPEG-4 Visual, Android low-resolution video, is not supported by AIR. Therefore, captured videos cannot be played back in AIR. The native application can be used to play back the recorded videos.

Currently, this functionality should only be used for capturing and not viewing unless you use the native application in the Gallery. The video is saved in a 3GP format that AIR does not support. Trying to play it back will just display a white screen.

In the following example, I provide the code for playback in AIR in case this is resolved in the future.

On select, a `MediaEvent` object is returned:

```
import flash.media.Video;
import flash.net.netConnection;
import flash.net.netStream;

var videoURL:String;
var connection:NetConnection;

function onComplete(event:MediaEvent):void {
    videoURL = event.data.file.url;
    connection = new NetConnection();
    connection.addEventListener(NetStatusEvent.NET_STATUS, onStatus);
}

function onStatus(event:NetStatusEvent):void {
    switch(event.info.code) {
        case "NetConnection.Connect.Success" :
            connectStream();
            break;
        case "NetStream.Play.StreamNotFound" :
            trace("video not found " + videoURL);
            break;
    }
}


function connectStream():void {
    stream = new NetStream(connection);
    stream.addEventListener(NetStatusEvent.NET_STATUS, onStatus);
    stream.addEventListener(AsyncErrorEvent.ASYNC_ERROR, onAsyncError);
```

```
        var video:Video = new Video();
        video.attachNetStream(stream);
        stream.play(videoURL);
        addChild(video);
    }

    function onAsyncError(event:AsyncErrorEvent):void {
        trace("ignore errors");
    }
```

The Camera Class

The device's camera, using the `flash.media.Camera` class, can be attached to a `Video` object in the AIR application. You can use this approach to simulate a web cam or for an Augmented Reality project.

The hardware orientation of the camera is landscape, so try to make your application's orientation landscape too by changing the `aspectRatio` tag in your application descriptor:

```
<aspectRatio>landscape</aspectRatio>
```

The `setMode` function is used to determine the video's resolution:

```
import flash.media.Camera;
import flash.media.Video;

var camera:Camera = Camera.getCamera();
if (camera != null) {
    camera.setMode(stage.stageWidth, stage.stageHeight, 15, true);

    var video:Video = new Video(camera.width, camera.height);
    video.x = 100;
    video.y = 100;
    video.attachCamera(camera);
    addChild(video);
}
```

Note that frames are only captured when the application is in the foreground. If the application moves to the background, capturing is paused but will resume automatically when the application moves to the foreground again.

You can query for the camera properties. Here are a few queries which may be helpful in your development:

```
camera.height;
camera.width;
camera.bandwidth;
camera.fps;
camera.muted
camera.name
```

Documentation and Tutorials

Development around video is constantly evolving. The following two resources are among those that will help you to stay informed:

- The Open Source Media Framework (*http://www.opensourcemediaframework .com/resources.html*) helps developers with video-related products. It is a good place to find code samples, tutorials, and other materials.
- Lisa Larson-Kelly specializes in web video publishing and, more recently, mobile publishing. She offers free tutorials and a newsletter on the latest technology (*http: //learnfromlisa.com/*).

Conclusion

Adobe's effort toward video delivery on mobile devices using AIR has inspired Adobe engineers to revisit Flash Player. We will come back to this point in Chapter 14.

Flash Player 10.2 offers the new `flash.media.StageVideo` class to render video much more quickly. Unlike the traditional `Video` object, which is a `displayObject`, this class is not part of the stage but sits behind it. It relies on video hardware for both decoding and rendering. Instead of having the CPU read back from the GPU to render the video, the GPU now renders the video directly on the display.

For more information, read Thibault Imbert's article at *http://www.adobe.com/devnet/ flashplayer/articles/stage_video.html*.

At the time of this writing, this technology is currently only available in Flash Player, but it should be available in AIR for Android by summer 2011.

CHAPTER 13

StageWebView

> *The Internet is becoming the town square for the*
> *global village of tomorrow.*
>
> —Bill Gates

WebKit is a layout engine that browsers use to render web pages and to support inter-activity and navigation history. Developed by Apple in 2002 and open sourced in 2005, WebKit is the default browser built in for Android.

The AIR runtime for the desktop also includes a version of WebKit built in. However, AIR for Android does not include it, and instead leverages the device's native implementation and gives you access to some of its features via StageWebView.

StageWebView brings the benefits of an Internet browser to your own application. In this chapter, we will briefly discuss accessing the native browser, and then go over what StageWebView has to offer.

The Native Browser

To access the Internet, you need to set the permission for it:

```
<uses-permission android:name="android.permission.INTERNET" />
```

You can launch the Android native browser from an AIR application using the naviga teToURL method. You pass a URL in the same way you do on AIR for the desktop:

```
function onPublicNews():void {
    navigateToURL(new URLRequest("http://www.npr.org"));
}
```

You can also use this method to launch native applications, such as the Android Market, that in turn makes calls to the Internet. The following example opens the Android Market and sets the criteria of applications to display as a URLRequest. Note that the protocol used is *market://* instead of *http://*:

```
function onSearchMarket():void {
    navigateToURL(new URLRequest("market://search?q=food"));
}
```

In both cases, your application moves to the background and the native browser becomes the active application.

We need, instead, a solution whereby HTML content can be embedded inside an AIR for Android application. This is what the StageWebView class does.

The StageWebView Class

The flash.media.StageWebView uclass is a new class for displaying and interacting with rich HTML content in an AIR for Android application. It is a subclass of the EventDis patcher class.

The flash.media.StageWebView class uses the web control as provided by the native system that may vary slightly from one device to another. There is currently very little interaction between AIR and the HTML content.

StageWebView is not a display object, and is therefore not adding to the displayList. Create a StageWebView object and set its stage property to attach it directly to the stage. It always lies on top of your content, so if you want other objects to occupy the same view area, you must remove it first:

```
import flash.media.StageWebView;

var webView:StageWebView = new StageWebView();
webView.stage = this.stage;
```

The size of the area dedicated to web content is defined in the viewPort property as a rectangle. Here it covers the stage width and 75% of the stage height:

```
import flash.geom.Rectangle;

var verticalBounds:int = stage.stageHeight*0.75;
webView.viewPort = new Rectangle(0, 0, stage.stageWidth, verticalBounds);
```

To load content, call the loadURL method and pass the URL of the site. Add a listener so that in case an error occurs you can notify your user. Location is the event property for the site to load:

```
import flash.events.ErrorEvent;

webView.addEventListener(ErrorEvent.ERROR, onError);
webView.loadURL("http://www.npr.org");

function onError(event:ErrorEvent):void {
    trace("not able to reach location: ", event.location);
}
```

Once the website is loaded, you should see it inside your application. It displays and responds as expected.

At the time of this writing, there is a bug when displaying websites with Flash content. Although the content renders and behaves as expected, it is not positioned within the dimensions of the viewport. It bleeds out of the rectangle.

There are several events you can register to monitor activity and collect information.

You can register for the `LocationChangeEvent.LOCATION_CHANGE` event that is fired after a location has been reached:

```
import flash.events.LocationChangeEvent;

var webView:StageWebView = new StageWebView();
webView.stage = this.stage;
webView.addEventListener(LocationChangeEvent.LOCATION_CHANGE, onChange);
webView.loadURL("http://www.npr.org");

function onChange(event:LocationChangeEvent):void {
    trace("you are now at: ", event.location);
    var verticalBounds:int = stage.stageHeight*0.75;
    webView.viewPort = new Rectangle(0, 0, stage.stageWidth, verticalBounds);
}
```

To avoid displaying an empty screen while loading, only display the view when its content is fully loaded and complete by listening to `Event.COMPLETE`.

You can register for the `LocationChangeEvent.LOCATION_CHANGING` event that is fired just before a new web location is requested. You can use this event in three different scenarios. You can prevent navigating to the new location by calling the `preventDefault` function. Most importantly, you need to catch the event to prevent it from opening the native browser and leaving your application. Force the new location to load into Stage WebView and its `viewPort` area:

```
webView.addEventListener(LocationChanged.LOCATION_CHANGING, onChanging);

// prevent going to a new location
function onChanging(event:LocationChanged):void {
    event.preventDefault();
    trace("sorry, you cannot go to: ", event.location);
}

// load new location in the StageWebView
function onChanging(event:LocationChanged):void {
    event.preventDefault();
    webView.load(event.location);
}
```

If your application needs to know when `StageWebView` is in focus, register for the `FOCUS_IN` and `FOCUS_OUT` events. These events get dispatched when clicking inside or outside the rectangle area:

```
import flash.events.FocusEvent;
```

```
webView.addEventListener(FocusEvent.FOCUS_IN, inFocus);
webView.addEventListener(FocusEvent.FOCUS_OUT, outFocus);

function inFocus(event:FocusEvent):void {
    trace("on webview now");
}

function outFocus(event:FocusEvent):void {
    trace("off webview now");
}
```

You can force focus when first launching your application:

```
webView.assignFocus();
```

StageWebView has methods that mirror the functionality of a traditional browser toolbar. In fact, you could re-create a navigation user interface if you wanted to simulate the desktop experience.

The title and location properties return the page information. The stop and reload methods will, as their names indicate, stop the loading of a page or reload it.

The historyBack and historyForward methods load pages that were previously visited. Check that the isHistoryBackEnabled and isHistoryForwardEnabled properties are true to ensure the pages exist in either direction. Currently, the history is not available as a whole. If you want to access it, you must store it yourself as the user navigates through pages.

We will discuss the loadString method in "Local Use" on page 181.

As mentioned before, StageWebView is not added to the display list. To remove it, use the dispose method. Setting the object and its viewPort property to null is meant to aid in the garbage collection process:

```
webView.viewPort = null;
webView.dispose();
webView = null;
```

Design Considerations

You should design your application for the best possible user experience. Toward that end, here are some points you should consider.

First, you have full control of the viewPort dimensions, but not its content. The vast majority of sites are designed only for the desktop. The few that deliver a mobile version take stage dimension into account and offer an adaptive layout and optimized content.

You can reduce the locations to a limited choice using the preventDefault method as previously discussed. If you want to keep the user experience open, prepare your application to accommodate multiple designs as much as possible.

Present your application in landscape mode and full screen. Align your application to the upper-left corner. This will mirror the web experience and users' expectations:

```
import flash.display.StageAlign;
stage.align = StageAlign.TOP_LEFT;
```

If the web page is larger than the `viewPort`, the `StageWebView` displays a scroll bar and zoom controls. There is no option to suppress these controls.

If you choose to keep auto-rotation enabled, you need to set a listener for the stage `Event.RESIZE` event and prevent scaling:

```
import flash.display.StageScaleMode;
stage.scaleMode = StageScaleMode.NO_SCALE;

stage.addEventListener(Event.RESIZE, onStageResized);
```

When the screen rotates, re-create the `viewPort` at the appropriate dimension. It does not resize dynamically:

```
import flash.events.Event;

function onStageResized(event:Event):void {
    webView.viewPort = null;
    var verticalBounds:int = stage.stageHeight*0.75;
    webView.viewPort =
        new Rectangle(0, 0, stage.stageWidth, verticalBounds);
}
```

If you navigate between locations, the native back button takes you back to the previous open application or home. It does not work as a back button for `StageWebView`. This is the expected behavior, of course, because the Internet content is part of your application, not a separate intent.

Either provide an internal back button or override the native back button. Do consider that this is not a recommended Android practice. It is not possible to put elements on top of `StageWebView`, but you can simulate a top navigation above it.

The `drawViewPortToBitmap` function can be used to take a screen capture of the `Stage WebView`. You can take advantage of this feature to temporarily replace `StageWebView` with a bitmap and display other elements on top of it.

Local Use

You can package HTML files with your application and then load them inside `Stage WebView`. You can use this to display a help page for your users, or other HTML content.

Copy the HTML page into a temporary file and load it using its `url`:

```
import flash.filesystem.File;

var file:File = File.applicationDirectory.resolvePath("assets/test.html");
var local:File = File.createTempFile();
file.copyTo(local, true);

webView.loadURL(local.url);
```

Note that it is possible to load a local HTML file to make an Ajax `XMLHttpRequest` on another domain or to make JavaScript calls, as demonstrated in the next paragraph.

The `loadString` method is for displaying HTML formatted text in the `viewPort` area. The text must be fully HTML formatted:

```
// define the string in html format
var myString:String =
        "<html>"
        + "<body bgcolor=\"#FFFF33\">"
        + "<font color=\"#FF0000\">Hello</font color><br>"
        + "<font color=\"#FFFFFF\">Look at me</font color><br><br>"
        + "<a href=\"http://www.google.com\">Click Me</a>"
        + "</body>"
        + "</html>"
webView.loadString(myString, "text/html");

webView.addEventListener(LocationChangeEvent.LOCATION_CHANGING, onChanging);

// load the Google site into the viewport when clicking on the text
function onChanging(event:LocationChangeEvent):void {
    event.preventDefault();
    webView.loadURL(event.location);
}
```

At the time of this writing, this feature is limited and does not provide much more than a `TextField` with `htmlText` would provide. You cannot, for instance, use it to display local assets such as images. It is useful if you want text placed in the `StageWebView` area.

Mobile Ads

Local use in combination with JavaScript is handy when dealing with mobile ads.

At the time of this writing, mobile advertising providers do not offer an AS3 SDK. Rewriting their AS2 code into AS3 to use in AIR does not seem to get ad impressions. Using `StageWebView` to simulate the browser model seems to be the best solution.

Go to *http://developer.admob.com/wiki/Android* or *http://developer.admob.com/wiki/Re quests* for instructions on how to set up an ad request for AdMob before we adapt them for AIR for Android.

You need an embedded HTML page that makes the request to the ad provider with your publisher ID and the `StageWebView` to load the page and monitor the navigation. The HTML page contains a JavaScript script that fetches the ad. It is important to set `manual_mode` to true. Set `test` to `true` during development or to `false` to receive live ads. The parameter in the `getElementById` method must match the name of the `div` in the page. Here we call it `ad_space`. See Figure 13-1 for an example of how the ad is displayed:

```
<html>
<head>
<title>Get Ad</title>
<script type="text/javascript">
```

```
    var admob_vars = {pubid: 'YOUR_ID',
                      bgcolor: 'FFFFFF'
                      text: '000000'
                      test: true,
                      manual_mode: true
                      };

    function displayAd() {
        admob.fetchAd(document.getElementById('ad_space'));
    }
</script>

<script type="text/javascript"
src=http://mm.admob.com/static/iphone/iadmob.js></script>
</head>

<body onload="displayAd()">
<div id="ad_space"></div>
</body>
</html>
```

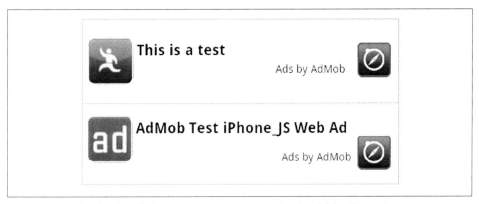

Figure 13-1. AdMob ads with the test property set to true (top) and false (bottom)

The ActionScript looks like this. Put your ad request in a `try catch` block in case the ad provider site is down or it sends back invalid data:

```
import flash.media.StageWebView;
import flash.geom.Rectangle;
import flash.events.LocationChangeEvent;
import flash.events.ErrorEvent;
import flash.filesystem.File;
import flash.filesystem.FileMode;
import flash.filesystem.FileStream;
import flash.media.StageWebView;
import flash.net.navigateToURL;
import flash.net.URLRequest;

var view:StageWebView;
var local:File;
```

```
view = new StageWebView();
view.stage = this.stage;
view.addEventListener(LocationChangeEvent.LOCATION_CHANGE, onChange);
view.addEventListener(LocationChangeEvent.LOCATION_CHANGING, onChanging);
view.addEventListener(ErrorEvent.ERROR, onViewError);
view.viewPort = new Rectangle(0, 0, 480, 60);

var base:File = File.applicationDirectory.resolvePath("adView.html");
local = File.createTempFile();
base.copy(local, true);

try {
    view.loadURL(local.url);
} catch(error:Error) {
}

function onChanging(event:LocationChangeEvent):void {
    event.preventDefault();
    navigateToURL(new URLRequest(event.location));
}

// when the user clicks on the ad
function onChange(event:LocationChangeEvent):void {
    if (event.location != local.url) {
        navigateToURL(new URLRequest(event.location));
        try {
            view.loadURL(local.url);
        } catch(error:Error) {
        }
    }
}

function onViewError(error:ErrorEvent):void {
    trace(error);
}
```

Services and Authentication

Many services, such as Twitter and Facebook, require an authentication token that can only be obtained via an HTML web page. You can use StageWebView to call authentication methods to extract the token. Service data is then available and can be used inside your AIR application.

> A security token is provided by a server and acts as an electronic key. The client application sends a request to a remote service and, upon receipt of the token, uses it to proceed with requesting additional data. It is a way to protect particularly sensitive data. Typically, the token is only valid within a small time frame. It appears that Twitter tokens are persistent, and therefore could be stored on the device for multiple registrations. To guarantee long-term validity, add listeners for Error events and be prepared to request a new token if needed.

OAuth is a robust open standard authorization system. It allows users to hand out tokens instead of usernames and passwords. The token is for a specific site and resources for a defined duration.

Twitter uses OAuth. You can allow users to access their account for authentication and log in to your application so that they can use their account data seamlessly without leaving AIR. You need to register a URL on Twitter to obtain a Consumer key and a Consumer secret, both of which are necessary in your application (see *http://twitter.com/oauth/* for more information).

Sandro Ducceschi offers a library called Tweetr that supports pinless OAuth (see *http://wiki.swfjunkie.com/tweetr*). For a similar application for Facebook, refer to Mark Doherty's example at *http://www.flashmobileblog.com/2010/10/14/facebook-connect-with-air-on-android/*.

Limitations

Despite its benefits, `StageWebView` also has some limitations:

- You cannot layer elements on top of `StageWebView`, although you can simulate it by taking a screen grab as described earlier.
- The interaction between ActionScript and JavaScript is very limited. There is currently no support for `ExternalInterface`, even though you can fake URLs to communicate from HTML to AS.
- You should not use `StageWebView` as a substitute for the native browser. Use it only as a bridge between your application and some needed Internet content. Android devices, for instance, do not support the QuickTime codec.
- There is no direct way in ActionScript to prevent `StageWebView` instances from accepting cookies or to clear cookies.
- The `HTMLLoader` class is supported in AIR for the desktop but not in AIR for Android.

If your application requires more advanced HTML features, consider using other tools. PhoneGap (*http://www.phonegap.com*), for instance, is an open source framework for developing applications for Android, iPhone, iPad, BlackBerry, and Symbian devices.

Conclusion

You can simulate the browser experience further. For instance, you can create bookmarks by storing the locations as local persistent data. You can also simulate the Android native browser window's functionality to display pages in a thumbnail version. To do so, save a bitmap of each page visited and display them at a smaller resolution on request.

CHAPTER 14

Hardware Acceleration

*In this new wave of technology, you can't do it all
yourself, you have to form alliances.*

—Carlos Slim Helu

We tend to forget that the content on our device's display—the high-definition video, the complex animation moving across the screen, the panels that we touch to drag around—none of it is real. We are looking at pixels being updated at a very fast rate to keep us engaged and fooled. It works.

Hardware accelerators use dedicated hardware to perform tasks faster than they would be done in software. They are used to accelerate both video and graphics, to draw changing content on the screen.

This performance technique is relatively new to Flash. NVIDIA, which specializes in the development of GPUs, and Adobe teamed up in 2009 to enable the Flash platform to leverage GPUs on the desktop as well as on smartphones and tablets. The adoption has been easier on mobile devices because each model uses one predictable driver, whereas the desktop has a multitude of scenarios.

In this chapter, we will discuss some of this technology and see how it can best be used for our applications.

Some Definitions

Let's go over some terms that are often used but rarely explained.

The *CPU* (central processing unit) carries out instructions on a computer program. The clock rate on mobile devices varies from 550 MHz to 1.5 GHz.

The *GPU* (graphics processing unit) is a high-performance microprocessor dedicated to manipulating computer graphics. It performs geometric calculations faster than drawing directly to the screen when using the CPU. Its efficiency is measured by how many millions of triangles are processed per second (mt/s). On mobile devices, GPU efficiency ranges from 7 mt/s to more than 28 mt/s. Another important factor is the fill rate, measured in megapixels.

OpenGL ES 2, a subset of the OpenGL standard, is an open source low-level interface between software and graphics acceleration. It was designed for mobile devices, and is supported on the Android platform for Froyo and later versions, the iPhone 3GS and later versions, the iPod, and various Samsung and Nokia devices.

The *buffer* is a region in memory that holds temporary data before it is moved to another location.

Rasterization is the process of taking a vector graphic (primitives or mathematical values such as points, lines, and curves) and converting it to a raster image (a data structure made of pixels). In our context, it just refers to drawing pixels, even if it is just copying them from one place to another.

Scene compositing is the process of creating a scene out of multiple pixel buffers, or textures. The scene is reorganized as elements move around. It is sometimes called *surface compositing*.

A *pixel* is the smallest screen element in a raster image. Vector graphics render with subpixel precision to prevent aliasing.

A *transformation matrix* is a rectangular array of numbers. It is used to store the display object's presentation properties. We will cover this topic in detail in this chapter.

A *display tree* is a data structure that organizes elements in a hierarchical fashion. A display list is a tree structure made of display objects. The stage is the top element. Its children, also called nodes, are different types of display objects, some of which are containers that can also have one or more children. Being aware of the objects' relationship is essential to your success in using hardware acceleration. We will discuss this further in this chapter.

Rendering, or How Things Are Drawn to the Screen

As a developer, you trust that an object is represented as your code intended. From your ActionScript commands to the matching pixels appearing on the screen, a lot is done behind the screens.

To better understand Flash Player and AIR for Android rendering, I recommend watching the MAX 2010 presentations "Deep Dive Into Flash Player Rendering" by Lee Thomason and "Developing Well-Behaved Mobile Applications For Adobe AIR" by David Knight and Renaun Erickson. You can find them at *http://tv.adobe.com*.

Flash is a frame-based system. The code execution happens first, followed by the rendering phase. The concept of the *elastic racetrack* describes this ongoing process whereby one phase must end before the other one begins, and so on.

The current rendering process for Flash Player and the AIR runtime comprises four steps, outlined in the subsections that follow. Annotations regarding *Enhanced Caching/GPU Model* indicate the process, if different, for AIR for Android using `cacheAsBit` `mapMatrix` and GPU rendering.

Computation

Traditional and Enhanced Caching/GPU Model

The renderer, qualified as retained, traverses the display list and keeps a state of all objects. It looks at each object matrix and determines its presentation properties. When a change occurs, it records it and defines the dirty region, areas that have changed, and the objects that need to be redrawn, to narrow down changes to a smaller area. It then concatenates matrices, computes all the transformations, and defines the new state.

Edge and Color Creation

Traditional Model

This step is the most challenging mathematically. It applies to vector objects and bitmaps with blends and filters.

An `SObject` is the `displayObject` equivalent in binary code, and is not accessible via ActionScript. It is made of layers with closed paths, with edges and colors. Edges are defined as quadratic Bezier curves and are used to prevent two closed paths from intersecting. Abutment is used to seam them together. More edges mean more calculation. Color applies to solids and gradients, but also bitmaps, video, and masks (combined color values of all display objects to determine a final color).

Enhanced Caching/GPU Model

No calculation is needed for cached items. They may be rotated, scaled, and skewed using their bitmap representation.

Rasterization

Traditional Model

This step is the most demanding in terms of memory. It uses multithreading for better performance. The screen is divided into dynamically allocated horizontal chunks. Taking one dirty rectangle at a time, lines are scanned from left to right to sort the edges and render a span, which is a horizontal row of pixels. Hidden objects, the alpha channel of a bitmap, and subpixel edges are all part of the calculation.

Enhanced Caching/GPU Model

Transformation cached rendering, also called processing, is used. It converts each vector graphic as a bitmap and keeps it in an off-screen buffer to be reused over time. Once that process it done, scene compositing takes all the bitmaps and re-arranges them as needed.

Presentation

Traditional Model
> Blitting, or pixel *blit*, is the transfer of the back buffer to the screen. Only the dirty rectangles are transferred.

Enhanced Caching/GPU Model
> The process is similar to the traditional model, but the GPU is much faster at moving pixels.

GPU Rendering on Android

The rendering mode used for Android is called *GPU Vector*. Both the creation of individual pixel buffers and scene compositing are done by the GPU. The GPU is particularly useful in this performance-constrained environment.

The GPU rendering technique only benefits vector art. It reduces the time needed to rasterize vector graphics, especially complex ones, to a bitmap. A bitmap is already a pixel buffer, also called a texture. There is no need to duplicate it. In fact, doing so would waste precious memory.

To perform GPU rendering in Android using Flash Professional, go to File→AIR Android settings. Select the General tab, and under Render Mode, select GPU.

In Flash Builder, set the `renderMode` node of the `initialWindow` node of your application descriptor to `gpu`:

```
<initialWindow>
<renderMode>gpu</renderMode>
...
```

If the user has a device that does not perform hardware acceleration, or if it does not work reliably with its drivers, AIR ignores the setting. No message is dispatched.

The cacheAsBitmap Property

The `cacheAsBitmap` property was added in Flash 8 with the Surface Renderer. Its purpose is to optimize the animation of vector graphics along the x- and y-axes, a process called *translation*.

When the `cacheAsBitmap` property is set to `true`, the display object rendered as a bitmap is cached in memory for reuse, as shown in Figure 14-1.

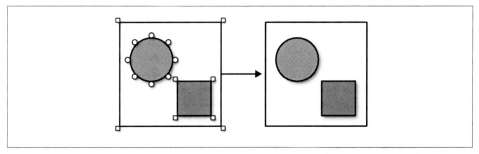

Figure 14-1. Taking vector graphics and rendering them as one bitmap via the cacheAsBitmap property

Because vector graphics use subpixels and bitmaps don't, objects snap to the full pixel and may look different from what you intended. To avoid this, apply the vector image on a full whole-number pixel.

You can set the `cacheAsBitmap` property in Flash Professional under Properties→Cache As Bitmap. You can only apply it to symbols. The art will then be converted to a bitmap at runtime, but it will not be modified in the IDE.

You can also set the property in code:

```
var myVector:Sprite = new Sprite();
myVector.cacheAsBitmap = true;
```

An object is only cached when it has its `visible` property set to `true`. Additionally, if its visibility is turned off, its bitmap representation is discarded.

The following example puts 100 circles on the stage. They animate frantically. Try the code on your device. Click on the stage to toggle the `cacheAsBitmap` property to `true` or `false` and notice the difference in performance. Note that this example is intended to illustrate a point regarding the use of many display objects. If an element always looks the same, as in the example, the best approach would be to create it once and copy it:

```
import flash.display.MovieClip;
import flash.display.Shape;
import flash.events.Event;
import flash.events.MouseEvent;

var container:Vector.<Shape>;
const MAX:int = 100;
var boundsX:int;
var boundsY:int;
var cacheIndicator:Shape;
var toggleCache:Boolean = true;

container = new Vector.<Shape>;
boundsX = stage.stageWidth;
boundsY = stage.stageHeight;

// to keep track of when cacheAsBitmap is on
```

```
cacheIndicator = new Shape();
cacheIndicator.graphics.beginFill(0x999999, 1);
cacheIndicator.graphics.drawRect(5, 5, 50, 50);
cacheIndicator.graphics.endFill();
addChild(cacheIndicator);
```

Create the circles and store them:

```
for (var i:int = 0; i < MAX; i++) {
    var temp:Shape = createCircle();
    container[i] = temp;
    addChild(temp);
}

// to toggle between cacheAsBitmap true or false
stage.addEventListener(MouseEvent.CLICK, toggle);
// animate all circles on EnterFrame
stage.addEventListener(Event.ENTER_FRAME, move);
```

Create individual circles with cacheAsBitmap set to true. Also give them an alpha to make the renderer work harder for testing purposes:

```
function createCircle():Shape {
    var shape:Shape = new Shape();
    shape.graphics.beginFill(Math.random()*0xFFFFFF, Math.random()*1);
    shape.graphics.drawCircle(0, 0, 50);
    shape.graphics.endFill();      shape.x = Math.floor(Math.random()*boundsX);
    shape.y = Math.floor(Math.random()*boundsY);
    shape.cacheAsBitmap = toggleCache;
    return shape;
}

// purposely didn't optimize code to make it work harder
function move(event:Event):void {
    for (var i:int = 0; i < MAX; i++) {
        var mc:Shape = container[i];
        mc.x += (Math.random()-Math.random())*25;
        mc.y += (Math.random()-Math.random())*25;
        if (mc.x < 0 || mc.x > boundsX) {
            mc.x = boundsX/2;
        }
        if (mc.y < 0 || mc.y > boundsY) {
            mc.y = boundsY/2;
        }
    }
}
```

Turn cacheAsBitmap on and off to test performance on the device:

```
function toggle(event:MouseEvent):void {
    toggleCache = !toggleCache;
    cacheIndicator.visible = toggleCache;
    for (var i:int = 0; i < MAX; i++) {
        var mc:Shape = container[i];
        mc.cacheAsBitmap = toggleCache;
    }
}
```

Toggling the cacheAsBitmap property in a live application is not recommended, but it is a good development and debugging technique.

If the display object is scaled, skewed, or rotated, its bitmap copy needs to be updated over and over. You would therefore lose all the benefits of caching.

The cacheAsBitmapMatrix Property

The cacheAsBitmapMatrix property is a new DisplayObject property. It must always be set, along with cacheAsBitmap, equal to true. There is no option to set it manually in the Flash IDE.

You need to create a Matrix and apply it to the object's cacheAsBitmapMatrix property:

```
import flash.geom.Matrix;

myVector.cacheAsBitmap = true;
myVector.cacheAsBitmapMatrix = new Matrix();
```

The added benefit of using cacheAsBitmapMatrix is that you can also change its alpha, scale it, skew it, and rotate it. And it will stay cached, so you can keep the cached element and make more use of it. You do lose some visual quality, but on devices with very high PPI, the quality loss is typically not noticeable.

Another important new feature is the ability to apply the matrix while the display object is not visible so that you have more control over monitoring the initial caching and its performance hit. Furthermore, once your object is cached, you can change its visibility property and it will stay cached. Be careful not to forget invisible objects on the stage:

```
myVector.cacheAsBitmap = true;
myVector.cacheAsBitmapMatrix = new Matrix();
myVector.visible = false;
// object is still cached
```

Let's try another example, but this time, with cacheAsBitmapMatrix, the shapes can rotate and scale without losing the performance benefit of caching. Again, try it on your device:

```
import flash.geom.Matrix;

var container:Vector.<MovieClip>;
var toggleCache:Boolean = true;
const MAX:int = 200;
var boundsX:int;
var boundsY:int;
var myMatrix:Matrix;

container = new Vector.<MovieClip>;
boundsX = stage.stageWidth;
boundsY = stage.stageHeight;
```

Create the Matrix only once and apply it to all the MovieClips:

```
myMatrix = new Matrix();
for (var i:int = 0; i < MAX; i++) {
    var temp:MovieClip = createCircle();
    container[i] = temp;
    addChild(temp);
}
```

Animate all the `MovieClips` on `EnterFrame`:

```
stage.addEventListener(Event.ENTER_FRAME, move);
```

Create a square-shaped `MovieClip`. Give it a random alpha, scale, and direction:

```
function createCircle():MovieClip {
    var mc:MovieClip = new MovieClip();
    mc.graphics.beginFill(Math.random()*0x09FFFF, Math.random()*1);
    mc.graphics.drawRect(-30, -30, 60, 60);
    mc.graphics.endFill();
    mc.x = Math.random()*stage.stageWidth;
    mc.y = Math.random()*stage.stageHeight;
    var scale:Number = Math.random()*1;
    mc.scaleX = mc.scaleY = scale;
    mc.dir = 1;

    // cache it for transformation
    mc.cacheAsBitmap = toggleCache;
    mc.cacheAsBitmapMatrix = myMatrix;
    return mc;
}
```

Scale and rotate individual `MovieClips`:

```
function move(event:Event):void {
    for (var i:int = 0; i < MAX; i++) {
        var mc:MovieClip = container[i];
        mc.scaleX += 0.05*mc.dir;
        mc.scaleY += 0.05*mc.dir;
        mc.rotation += 5*mc.dir;
        if (mc.scaleX < 0.05 || mc.scaleX > 1.0) {
            mc.dir *= -1;
        }
    }
}
```

You should notice a great improvement in tweening animation, even with the large number of objects.

In an effort to preserve memory, all the objects share a single `Matrix` instance. There is no need to create a unique matrix per object because, once assigned, the `Matrix` will not be modified.

 Do not create a new matrix to rotate or scale your object. If you do, it will invalidate your pixel buffer and you will lose the performance benefit. Instead, just modify the display object's scale and rotation properties as in the example.

To use a different initial matrix than the identity matrix, create it and then apply it to your display object. We will discuss matrices later in this chapter.

In our example, the `cacheAsBitmapMatrix` property is applied to objects in a flat display list. Caching becomes a more meticulous exercise when dealing with the display list hierarchy. We will go over this in the next section.

The Display List

The structure of your display list is fundamental in this process for three reasons: memory consumption, tree traversal, and node hierarchy.

Memory Consumption

Memory consumption is the trade-off for better performance in GPU rendering because every off-screen bitmap uses memory. At the same time, mobile development implies less GPU memory caching and RAM.

To get a sense of the memory allocated, you can use the following formula:

```
// 4 bytes are required to store a single 32 bit pixel
// width and height of the tile created
// anti-aliasing defaults to high or 4 in Android
4 * width * height * anti-aliasFactor

A 10 × 10 image represents 1600 bytes
```

Be vigilant about saving memory in other areas.

Favor the `DisplayObject` types that need less memory. If the functionality is sufficient for your application, use a `Shape` or a `Sprite` instead of a `MovieClip`. To determine the size of an object, use the following:

```
import flash.sampler.*;

var shape:Shape = new Shape();
var sprite:Sprite = new Sprite();
var mc:MovieClip = new MovieClip();

trace(getSize(shape), getSize(sprite), getSize(mc));
// 224, 412 and 448 bytes respectively in the AIR runtime
```

The process of creating and removing objects has an impact on performance. For display objects, use object pooling, a method whereby you create a defined number of objects up front and recycle them as needed. Instead of deleting them, make them invisible or remove them from the display list until you need to use them again. I will demonstrate object pooling in Chapter 18.

You should give the same attention to other types of objects. If you need to remove objects, remove listeners and references so that they can be garbage-collected and free up precious memory.

Tree Structure

Keep your display list fairly shallow and narrow.

The renderer needs to traverse the display list and compute the rendering output for every vector-based object. Matrices on the same branch get concatenated. This is the expected management of nested objects: if a Sprite contains another Sprite, the child position is set in relation to its parent.

Node Relationship

This is the most important point for successful use of caching. Caching the wrong objects may result in confusingly slow performance.

The cacheAsBitmapMatrix property must be set on the moving object, not on its container. If you set it on the parent, you create an unnecessarily larger bitmap. Most importantly, if the container has other children that change, the bitmap needs to be redrawn and the caching benefit is lost.

Let's use an example. The parent node, the black box shown in the following figures, has two children, a green circle and a red square. They are all vector graphics as indicated by the points.

In the first scenario (depicted in Figure 14-2), cacheAsBitmapMatrix is set on the parent node. The texture includes its children. A bitmap is created and used for any transformation, like the rotation in the figure, without having to perform expensive vector rasterization. This is a good caching practice:

```
var box:Sprite = new Sprite();
var square:Shape = new Shape();
var circle:Shape = new Shape();

// draw all three items using the drawing API

box.cacheAsBitmap = true;
box.cacheAsBitmapMatrix = new Matrix();
box.rotation = 15;
```

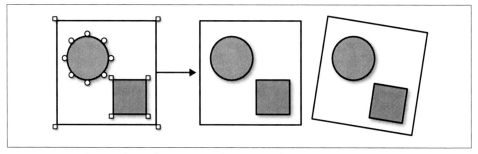

Figure 14-2. Caching and transformation on the parent only

In the second scenario (depicted in Figure 14-3), `cacheAsBitmapMatrix` is still on the parent node. Let's add some interactivity to make the circle larger when clicked. This is a bad use of caching because the circle needs to be rerasterized along with its parent and sibling because they share the same texture:

```
// change datatype so the display object can receive a mouse event
var circle:Sprite = new Sprite();

// draw items using the drawing API
circle.addEventListener(MouseEvent.CLICK, bigMe);

function bigMe(event:MouseEvent):void {
    var leaf:Sprite = event.currentTarget as Sprite;
    leaf.scaleX += .20;
    leaf.scaleY += .20;
}
```

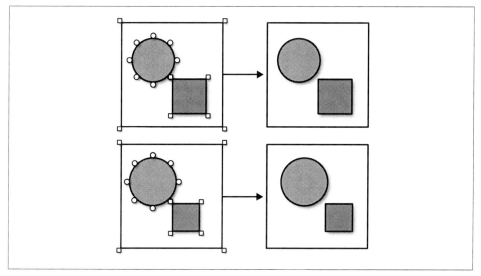

Figure 14-3. Caching on the parent, but transformation on the children

In the third scenario (depicted in Figure 14-4), `cacheAsBitmapMatrix` is set, not on the parent, but on the children. When the circle is rescaled, its bitmap copy can be used instead of rasterization. In fact, both children can be cached for future animation. This is a good use of caching:

```
// change datatype so they can receive mouse events
var square:Sprite = new Sprite();
var circle:Sprite = new Sprite();

// draw items using the drawing API
square.addEventListener(MouseEvent.CLICK, bigMe);
circle.addEventListener(MouseEvent.CLICK, bigMe);

var myMatrix:Matrix = new Matrix();
```

```
square.cacheAsBitmap = true;
square.cacheAsBitmapMatrix = myMatrix;
circle.cacheAsBitmap = true;
circle.cacheAsBitmapMatrix = myMatrix;

function bigMe(event:MouseEvent):void {
    var leaf:Sprite = event.currentTarget as Sprite;
    leaf.scaleX += .20;
    leaf.scaleY += .20;
}
```

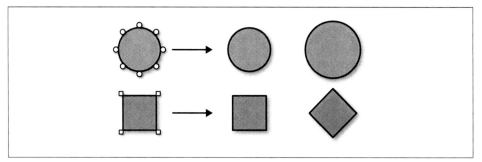

Figure 14-4. Caching and transformation on each individual child

The limitation with using GPU rendering occurs when a parent and its children need to have independent animations as demonstrated earlier. If you cannot break the parent-child structure, stay with vector rendering.

MovieClip with Multiple Frames

Neither cacheAsBitmap nor cacheAsBitmapMatrix works for a MovieClip with multiple frames. If you cache the art on the first frame, as the play head moves, the old bitmap is discarded and the new frame needs to be rasterized again. This is the case even if the animation is a rotation or a position change.

GPU rendering is not the technique for such situations. Instead, load your MovieClip without adding it to the display list. Traverse through its timeline and copy each frame to a bitmap using the BitmapData.draw method. Then display one frame at a time using the BitmapData.copyPixels method.

This technique is developed in detail in Chapter 18.

Interactivity

Setting cacheAsBitmapMatrix to true does not affect the object's interactivity. It still functions as it would in the traditional rendering model both for events and for function calls.

Multiple Rendering Techniques

On Android devices, you could use traditional rendering along with `cacheAsBitmap` and/or `cacheAsBitmapMatrix`. Another technique is to convert your vector assets as bitmaps, in which case no caching is needed. The technique you use may vary from one application to the next.

Remember that caching is meant to be a solution for demanding rendering. It is helpful for games and certain types of animations (not for traditional timeline animation). If there is no display list conflict, as described earlier, caching all assets makes sense. There is no need to use caching for screen-based applications with fairly static UIs.

At the time of this writing, there seems to be a bug using filters on a noncached object while the GPU mode is set in the application descriptor (as in the example below). It should be fixed in a later release:

```
var sprite:Sprite = new Sprite();
sprite.graphics.beginFill(0xFF6600, 1);
sprite.graphics.drawRect(0, 0, 200, 100);
sprite.graphics.endFill();
sprite.filters = [new DropShadowFilter(2, 45, 0x000000, 0.5, 6, 6, 1, 3)];
addChild(sprite);
```

 If you are not using caching, do not leave `renderMode` set to GPU in your application descriptor. Doing so may cause unexpected behavior similar to that described in the text.

Maximum Texture Memory and Texture Size

The maximum texture size supported is 1,024×1,024 (it is 2,048×2,048 for iPhone and iPad). This dimension represents the size after transformation. The maximum memory is not part of the memory consumed by the application, and therefore is not accessible. We will discuss memory consumption in Chapter 19.

2.5D Objects

A 2.5D object is an object with an additional z property that allows for different types of transformation.

If an object has `cacheAsBitmapMatrix` on and a z property is added, the caching is lost.

A 2.5D shape does not need `cacheAsBitmapMatrix` because it is always cached for motion, scaling, and rotation without any additional coding. But if its **visibility** is changed to `false`, it will no longer be cached.

How to Test the Efficiency of GPU Rendering

There are various ways to test application performance beyond the human eye and perception. Testing your frame rate is your best benchmark. Please refer to Chapter 19 for more information.

Matrices

Being familiar with matrices will help you better understand rendering and hardware acceleration. Matrices were first introduced with Flash 8 to give developers more control over manipulation of display objects.

Every display object has an underlying matrix representation, even if it does not have graphics. It is used to determine where, at what scale, and at what orientation an object should be drawn.

A 3×3 matrix is made of rows and columns. Its elements are labeled a, b, c, d, tx, ty, u, v, and w. They are organized as follows:

```
[ a   b   tx ]
[ c   d   ty ]
[ u   v   w  ]
```

Each element represents a specific property. The u, v, and w elements provide extra capabilities that are not used. Their values are constant, and are 0, 0, and 1, respectively:

```
[ x scale    y skew    x position ]
[ x skew     y scale   y position ]
[ 0          0         1          ]
```

There is no property for rotation. Scaling and skewing together can distort coordinates to provide what you see as rotation.

The values are used to calculate and determine a new position based on the transformation. The formula is:

```
x' = x*a + y*c + tx
y' = x*b + y*d + ty
```

where x' and y' (that is, x prime and y prime) represent the new positions based on the transformation.

Identity Matrix

When a matrix without transformation is applied, it is called an identity matrix. This is what we used in our cacheAsBitmapMatrix example earlier:

```
[ 1   0   0 ]
[ 0   1   0 ]
[ 0   0   1 ]
```

Scale is 1 (or full scale) and no skewing is applied. Using the transformation formula, you can see that the new position is identical to the initial position:

```
x' = x*1 + y*0 + 0 = x;
y' = x*0 + y*1 + 0 = y;
```

Transformation Matrix

Let's look at a few transformation matrices in ActionScript and see how they affect the presentation of the object.

You can define a matrix, and pass the value for each property into the constructor:

```
import flash.geom.Matrix;

// Matrix(a, b, c, d, tx, ty)
// size increases by 100% and position moved by 1 pixel on x and y axis
var myMatrix:Matrix = new Matrix(2, 0, 0, 2, 1, 1);
```

You can also define an identity matrix, and then apply transformation using its various methods.

Here is the code for the position transformation (shown in Figure 14-5):

```
var myMatrix:Matrix = new Matrix();
myMatrix.translate(2, 2);
```

```
[ 1  0  2 ]
[ 0  1  2 ]
[ 0  0  1 ]
```

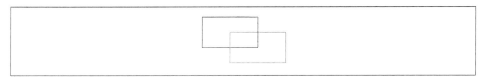

Figure 14-5. Position transformation

Here is the code for the scale transformation (shown in Figure 14-6):

```
myMatrix.scale(a, d);
```

```
[ 1.25  0    0 ]
[ 0     1.25 0 ]
[ 0     0    1 ]
```

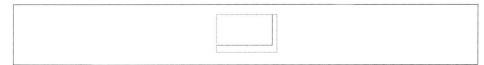

Figure 14-6. Scale transformation

And here is the code for the rotation transformation (shown in Figure 14-7):

```
// 15 represents the angle of rotation
myMatrix.rotate(15)

[ cos(15)  sin(15)  0 ]
[ -sin(15) cos(15)  0 ]
[ 0        0        1 ]
```

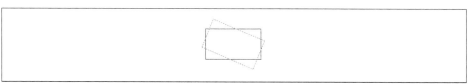

Figure 14-7. Rotation transformation

Skewing does not have a method. You can implement skewing by adjusting the b and c properties of the matrix directly:

```
myMatrix.b = 2;
myMatrix.c = 2;
```

 As mentioned before, do not apply a matrix after your object is cached. You can apply a matrix for the initial transformation in place of the identity matrix, however.

Matrices for Multiscreen Deployment

Defining an initial transformation matrix other than the identity matrix is a good technique for multiscreen deployment and multiple resolutions. Create the art at one size. Detect the device resolution and scale the graphics down to the size you need, using vector graphics scalability. Then cache it:

```
// matrix with object scaled at 25% of its initial size
var myMatrix:Matrix = new Matrix(0.25, 0, 0, 0.25, 0, 0);
myVector.cacheAsBitmapMatrix = myMatrix;
```

Another advantage to using vector art is that there is no anti-alias blur or fuzzy edges. Keep in mind that if you scale up the object again, its edges will be jaggy because you are now enlarging a bitmap.

Matrices Not to Be Used in GPU Mode

Some matrices cannot be used with GPU rendering on Android along with cacheAsBit mapMatrix. These are color transformations, filters, blends, and Pixel Bender.

If you must use filters, do not use GPU mode. Convert your vector art to a bitmap and use the BitmapData.applyFilter() method. Test your application carefully, because filters and blends negatively affect performance for mobile devices.

To learn more about matrices, read Trevor McCauley's "Understanding the Transformation Matrix in Flash 8" at *http://www.senocular.com/flash/tutorials/transformmatrix/*.

Hardware-Accelerated Audio and Video

Hardware acceleration is used on Android devices for other purposes without any setting up or work on your part. As we discussed in Chapter 11 and Chapter 12, hardware acceleration is used to decode AAC audio and some video codecs. Limitations are a function of the device, its driver, and its hardware decoder.

It is not recommended that you play video and use GPU rendering at the same time.

Conclusion

GPU rendering is expected to be available in other platforms as well as in Flash Player in the near future.

This concludes our discussion of APIs. You now have the tools and knowledge to build fantastic applications. The next three chapters cover best practices and building an application that uses many of these APIs.

CHAPTER 15

Your Device and Others

Communication works for those who work at it.

—John Powell

Your Android device, just like your laptop, has network capabilities beyond running self-contained applications or displaying Internet pages. It can communicate in real time with other devices using a local network or a capable remote server.

Developing multiuser applications opens a new dimension to any activity or form of game play. The user is no longer alone with her computer. She shares an activity with others in which the group experience is greater than the sum of its parts.

The application in question can be a remote control for another device, the main application, or the companion application to a larger project. It can also be part of a cluster of devices communicating with one other.

In this chapter, I chose to demonstrate Adobe's Cirrus service in detail because, at the time of this writing, it is free and demonstrates some multiuser possibilities without any server setup. It is well suited for mobile development.

RTMFP UDP

Peer-to-peer (P2P) communication is the real-time transfer of data and media between clients.

Real Time Media Flow Protocol (RTMFP) is an Adobe proprietary protocol. It enables peer-to-peer communication between applications running in Flash Player or the AIR runtime. It is meant to provide a low-latency, secure, peering network experience.

Real Time Messaging Protocol (RTMP) uses Transmission Control Protocol (TCP). RTMFP uses User Datagram Protocol (UDP), which provides better latency, higher security (128-bit AES encryption), and scalability. RTMP is faster than RTMFP, but does not guarantee perfect message ordering and delivery.

RTMP was designed to connect via an RTMFP-capable server, such as the Cirrus service (RTMP uses the Flash Media Server), but it can also be used over a local network using WiFi without the need for a server. Note that Flash Media Server 4.0 speaks RTMFP as well.

P2P Over a Local Network

If your local network supports broadcasting, you can create peer-to-peer direct routing. All the clients need to be on the same subnet, but you do not need to manage them. Verify that your devices have WiFi enabled and are using the same network.

The code to create a peer-to-peer application with RTMFP is quite simple but introduces new concepts. Let's go over all the steps one at a time.

The connection is established using the `flash.net.NetConnection` class. Set a listener to receive a `NetStatusEvent` event. Create the connection by calling the `connect` function and passing `rtmfp` as an argument:

```
import flash.net.NetConnection;
import flash.events.NetStatusEvent;

var connection:NetConnection = new NetConnection();
connection.addEventListener(NetStatusEvent.NET_STATUS, onStatus);
connection.connect("rtmfp:");
```

Wait for the connection to be established. Then several objects need to be created:

```
function onStatus(event:NetStatusEvent):void {
    switch(event.info.code) {
        case "NetConnection.Connect.Success" :
            trace("I am connected");
            // object creation can now happen
            break;
    }
}
```

`NetGroup` is the group of peers. Its capabilities are defined in the `GroupSpecifier`. The `IPMulticastAddress` property stores the IPv4 multicast address. It needs to be in the range 224.0.0.0 through 239.255.255.25. The UDP port should be higher than 1024. A group name is passed in its constructor. Try to make it unique. The `IPMulticast MemberUpdatesEnabled` property must be set to `true` for clients to receive updates from other clients on a LAN. The `postingEnabled` property allows clients to send messages to the group:

```
import flash.net.GroupSpecifier;

var groupName:String = "com.veronique.simple/";
var IPMulticastAddress:String = "230.0.0.1:3000";

var groupSpec:GroupSpecifier = new GroupSpecifier(groupName);
groupSpec.addIPMulticastAddress(IPMulticastAddress);
```

```
groupSpec.ipMulticastMemberUpdatesEnabled = true;
groupSpec.postingEnabled = true;
```

Now create the NetGroup. Pass the connection and the GroupSpecifier in its construction. The latter is passed with an authorization property to define the communication allowed: groupspecWithAuthorizations to post and multicast, or groupspecWithout Authorizations to only receive messages. Note that this setting is only relevant if a posting password is set (as defined by your application):

```
import flash.net.NetGroup;

var netGroup = new NetGroup
        (connection, groupSpec.groupspecWithAuthorizations());
netGroup.addEventListener(NetStatusEvent.NET_STATUS, onStatus);
```

The group is composed of neighbors, you as well as others. Using the same Net StatusEvent event, check for its info.code. Wait to receive the NetGroup.Connect.Suc cess event before using the functionality of NetGroup to avoid getting an error.

When a user joins or leaves the group, the code is as follows:

```
function onStatus(event:NetStatusEvent):void {
    switch(event.info.code) {
        case " NetGroup.Connect.Success" :
            trace("I joined the group");
            break;
        case "NetGroup.Connect.Rejected" :
        case "NetGroup.Connect.Failed" :
            trace("I am not a member");
            break;
    }
}
```

Others in the group receive the following events. Note that if the group is large, only a subset of members is informed that a new peer has joined or left the group:

```
function onStatus(event:NetStatusEvent):void {
    switch(event.info.code) {
        case "NetGroup.Neighbor.Connect" :
            trace("neighbor has arrived", neighborCount);
            break;
        case "NetGroup.Neighbor.Disconnect" :
            trace("neighbor has left");
            break;
    }
}
```

To send a message, use the NetGroup.post method. It takes an Object as an argument. Messages are serialized in AMF (binary format for serialized ActionScript objects), so a variation of data types can be used, such as Object, Number, Integer, and String types:

```
var message:Object = new Object();
message.type = "testing";
message.body = {name:"Véronique", greeting:"Bonjour"};
group.post(message);
```

To receive messages, check for an `info.code` equal to a `NetGroup.Posting.Notify` event. The message is received as `event.info.message`. The message is not distributed to the sender:

```
function onStatus(event:NetStatusEvent):void {
    switch(event.info.code) {
        case "NetGroup.Posting.Notify" :
            trace(event.info.message); // [Object]
            trace(event.info.message.body.greeting); // Bonjour
            break;
    }
}
```

Identical messages are not re-sent. To make each message unique, store the current time as a property of the object:

```
var now:Date = new Date();
message.time = now.getHours() + "_" + now.getMinutes() +
    "_" + now.getSeconds();
group.post(message);
```

If the message only goes in one direction and there will be no overlap between clients, you could use a counter that gets incremented with every new message:

```
message.count = count++;
```

When disconnecting, it is important to remove all objects and their listeners:

```
function onStatus(event:NetStatusEvent):void {
    switch(event.info.code) {
        case "NetConnection.Connect.Rejected" :
        case "Connect.AppShutdown" :
            trace("I am not connected");
            onDisconnect();
            break;
    }
}

function onDisconnect():void {
    group = null;
    netGroup.removeEventListener(NetStatusEvent.NET_STATUS, onStatus);
    netGroup = null;
    connection.removeEventListener(NetStatusEvent.NET_STATUS, onStatus);
    connection = null;
}
```

Color Exchange

Let's create a simple example. The hueMe application starts with a shape of a random color. Each client can send a color value to the other client's application. On the receiving end, the shape changes to the new color (see Figure 15-1).

Figure 15-1. The hueMe application

Draw the initial colored sprite:

```
var sprite:Sprite = new Sprite();
var g:Graphics = sprite.graphics;
g.beginFill(Math.round(Math.random()*0xFFFFFF));
g.drawRect(20, 20, 200, 150);
g.endFill();
```

Create the connection for the P2P communication:

```
var connection:NetConnection = new NetConnection();
connection.addEventListener(NetStatusEvent.NET_STATUS, onStatus);
connection.connect("rtmfp:");
```

Once the connection is established, create the group and check that the user has successfully connected to it:

```
function onStatus(event:NetStatusEvent):void {
    if (event.info.code == "NetConnection.Connect.Success") {
        var groupSpec:GroupSpecifier = new GroupSpecifier("colorGroup");
        groupSpec.addIPMulticastAddress("225.0.0.1:4000");
        groupSepc.postingEnabled = true;
        groupSepc.ipMulticastMemberUpdatesEnabled = true;

        group = new NetGroup(connection,
            groupSpec.groupspecWithAuthorizations());
        group.addEventListener(NetStatusEvent.NET_STATUS, onStatus);

    } else if (event.info.code == "NetGroup.Connect.Success") {
        trace("I am part of the group ");
    }
}
```

Send a random color value to the group when clicking the sprite:

```
g.addEventListener(MouseEvent.CLICK, hueYou);

function hueYou(event:MouseEvent):void {
    var randomHue:int = Math.round(Math.random()*0xFFFFFF);
    var object:Object = {type:"color", hue:randomHue};
    group.post(object);
}
```

Finally, add the functionality to receive the value from other members of the group and color the sprite:

```
import flash.geom.ColorTransform;

function onStatus(event:NetStatusEvent):void {
    ...
```

```
            if (event.info.code == "NetGroup.Posting.Notify") {
                if (event.info.message.type == "color") {
                    applyColor(Number(event.info.message.hue));
                }
            }
        }
    }

    function applyColor(hue:int):void {
        var colorTransform:ColorTransform = new ColorTransform();
        colorTransform.color = hue;
        sprite.transform.colorTransform = colorTransform;
    }
```

Companion AIR Application

To make your application unidirectional, as in a remote control-style application, have one client sending messages and the other receiving messages. Only the networked clients registered for the `NetGroup.Posting.Notify` event receive data.

In Chapter 17, we will build a photo-sharing application between an AIR application on a device and one on the desktop. The two computers complement each other in use and in capabilities.

Mihai Corlan developed an Android remote control for a desktop MP3 player; read about it at *http://corlan.org/2010/07/02/creating-multi-screen-apps-for-android-and -desktop-using-air/*.

Tom Krcha created a remote controller to send accelerometer, speed, and brake information to a car racing game (see *http://www.flashrealtime.com/game-remote-device-con troller/*).

P2P Over a Remote Network

To use networking remotely, you need an RTMFP-capable server, such as Flash Media Server.

If you do not have access to such a server, Adobe provides a beta developer key to use its Cirrus service. Sign up to instantly receive a developer key and a URL, at *http://labs .adobe.com/technologies/cirrus/*.

 If you are behind a firewall, your network needs to be configured to allow outgoing UDP traffic. If it is set to block such traffic, your administrator needs to configure a TURN (Traversal Using Relays around NAT) proxy.

The traditional streaming model requires clients to receive all data from a centralized server cluster. Scaling is achieved by adding more servers. Figure 15-2 shows traditional streaming/communication with the Unicast model and RTMFP in Flash Player/Cirrus.

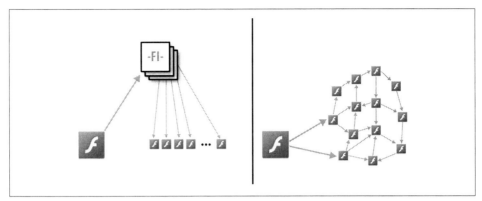

Figure 15-2. Traditional streaming/communication with the Unicast model (left) and RTMFP in Flash Player 10.1/Cirrus 2 (right)

RTMFP, now in its second generation, supports application-level multicast. Multicasting is the process of sending messages as a single transmission from one source to the group where each peer acts as a relay to dispatch the data to the next peer. It reduces the load on the server and there is no need for a streaming server.

The Cirrus service is only for clients communicating directly. It has low latency and good security. It does not support shared objects or custom server-side programming. You could still use shared objects with Flash Media Server, but via the traditional client-server conduit.

The NetGroup uses ring topology. Its neighborCount property stores the number of peers. Each peer is assigned a peerID, which can be mapped to a group address using Group.convertPeerIDToGroupAddress(connection.nearID). An algorithm is run every few seconds to update ring positions for the group.

When the group is connected, you can obtain statistics such as Quality of Service in bytes per second from NetGroup's info property:

```
function onStatus(event:NetStatusEvent):void {
    if (event.info.code == NetGroup.Connect.Success") {
        trace(event.info.group);
        // NetGroupInfo object with Quality of Service statistics
    }
}
```

The NetStream object is now equipped with new multicast properties. For instance, multicastWindowDuration specifies the duration in seconds of the peer-to-peer multicast reassembly window. A short value reduces latency but also quality.

NetGroup is best used for an application with a many-to-many spectrum. NetStream is for a one-to-many or few-to-many spectrum.

Communication can be done in different ways:

- *Posting* is for lots of peers sending small messages.
- *Multicasting* is for any size group, but with a small number of the peers being senders, and for continuous/live data which is large over time.
- *Direct routing* is for sending messages to specific peers in the group using methods such as sendToAllNeighbors, sendToNeighbor, and sendToNearest.
- *Object replication* is for more reliable data delivery whereby information is sent in packets between clients and reassembled.

Matthew Kaufman explains this technology in depth in his MAX 2009 presentation, at *http://tv.adobe.com/watch/max-2009-develop/p2p-on-the-flash-platform-with-rtmfp*.

Simple Text Chat

This example is very similar to the one we created for P2P over a local network, except for a few minor, yet important, changes.

The connection is made to a remote server using the NetConnection object and RTMFP. If you have the Adobe URL and developer key, use them as demonstrated in the following code:

```
const SERVER:String = "rtmfp://" + YOUR_SERVER_ADDRESS;
const KEY:STRING = YOUR_DEVELOPER_KEY;

var connection:NetConnection = new NetConnection();
connection.addEventListener(NetStatusEvent.NET_STATUS, onStatus);
connection.connect(SERVER, KEY);
```

 You may find some examples that use different syntax for connecting as: SERVER + KEY. The new syntax was added in January 2011. It is more secure because your key is no longer appended to the connect URI, but is handled as a separate parameter.

Connecting to a traditional streaming server would still use the URI construct as "rtmfp://server/application/instance" and additional optional parameters to connect, such as a login and password.

The GroupSpecifier now needs serverChannelEnabled set to true to use the Cirrus server, and helps in peer discovery. PostingEnabled is still on to send messages. The IPMulticastAddress property is optional but can help optimize the group topology if the group is large:

```
function onStatus(event:NetStatusEvent):void {
    if (event.info.code == "NetConnection.Connect.Success") {
        var groupSpec:GroupSpecifier = new GroupSpecifier("chatGroup");
        groupSpec.postingEnabled = true;
        groupSpec.serverChannelEnabled = true;

        group = new NetGroup(connection,
```

```
                groupSpec.groupspecWithAuthorizations());
            group.addEventListener(NetStatusEvent.NET_STATUS, onStatus);
        }
    }
```

The exchange of messages is very similar to the local example. Note that a post method is well suited for many peers sending small messages, as in a chat application that is not time-critical:

```
function sendMessage():void {
    var object:Object = new Object();
    object.user = "Véronique";
    object.message = "This is a chat message";
    object.time = new Date().time;
    group.post(object);
}

function onStatus(event:NetStatusEvent):void {
    if (event.info.code == "NetGroup.Posting.Notify") {
        trace(event.info.message);
    }
}
```

Multicast Streaming

This example demonstrates a video chat between one publisher and many receivers who help redistribute the stream to other receivers.

The application connects in the same way as in the previous example, but instead of a NetGroup, we create a NetStream to transfer video, audio, and messages.

Publisher

This is the code for the publisher sending the stream.

To access the camera, add the permission in your descriptor file:

```
<uses-permission android:name="android.permission.CAMERA"/>
```

Set the GroupSpecifier and the NetStream. The GroupSpecifier needs to have multicastEnabled set to true to support streaming:

```
import flash.net.NetStream;
var outStream:NetStream;

function onStatus(event:NetStatusEvent):void {
    if (event.info.code == "NetConnection.Connect.Success") {
        var groupSpec:GroupSpecifier = new GroupSpecifier("videoGroup");
        groupSpec.serverChannelEnabled = true;
        groupSpec.multicastEnabled = true;

        outStream = new NetStream(connection,
                    groupSpec.groupspecWithAuthorizations());
        outStream.addEventListener(NetStatusEvent.NET_STATUS, onStatus);
```

```
        }
    }
```

Once the `NetStream` is connected, add a reference to the camera and the microphone and attach them to the stream. A `Video` object displays the camera feed. Finally, call the `publish` method and pass the name of your choice for the video session:

```
function onStatus(event:NetStatusEvent):void {
    if (event.info.code == "NetStream.Connect.Success") {
        var camera:Camera = Camera.getCamera();
        var video:Video = new Video();
        video.attachCamera(camera);
        addChild(video);

        outStream.attachAudio(Microphone.getMicrophone());
        outStream.attachCamera(camera);
        outStream.publish("remote video");
    }
}
```

Recipients

The code for the peers receiving the video is similar, except for the few changes described next.

The incoming `NetStream`, used for the peers receiving the stream, must be the same `GroupSpecifier` as the publisher's stream. The same stream cannot be used for sending and receiving:

```
var inStream:NetStream = new NetStream(connection,
groupSpec.groupspecWithAuthorizations());
inStream.addEventListener(NetStatusEvent.NET_STATUS, onStatus);
```

The recipient needs a `Video` object but no reference to the microphone and the camera. The `play` method is used to stream the video in:

```
var video:Video = new Video();
addChild(video);
inStream.play("remote video");
```

Sending and receiving data

Along with streams, `NetStream` can be used to send data. It is only an option for the publisher:

```
var object:Object = new Object();
object.type = "chat";
object.message = "hello";
outStream.send("onReceiveData", object);
```

To receive data, the incoming stream must assign a `NetStream.client` for callbacks. Note that the `onReceiveData` function matches the first parameter passed in the publisher `send` call:

```
inStream.client = this;

function onReceiveData(object:Object):void {
    trace(object.type, object.message); // chat, hello
}
```

Closing a stream

Do not forget to remove the stream and its listener after it closes:

```
function onStatus(event:NetStatusEvent):void {
    switch(event.info.code) {
        case "NetStream.Connect.Closed" :
        case "NetStream.Connect.Failed" :
            onDisconnect();
            break;
    }
}

function onDisconnect():void {
    stream.removeEventListener(NetStatusEvent.NET_STATUS, onStatus);
    stream = null;
}
group.peerToPeerDisabled = false;
group.objectReplicationEnabled = true;
```

> Streaming does not pause when the application goes to the background.
> You need to monitor its pause and play functionality. This is important
> to avoid distracting audio playing over other applications and to save
> memory and battery life. Review `Event.DEACTIVATE` and `Event.ACTI
> VATE`, covered in Chapter 6.

End-to-End Stream

Another approach is for the publisher to send a separate stream to each receiver. This
limits the number of users, but is the most efficient transmission with the lowest latency.
No `GroupSpecifier` is needed for this mode of communication. In fact, this is no longer
a group, but a one-to-one transfer or unidirectional `NetStream` channel.

Sending a peer-assisted stream

Set the connection parameter to `NetStream.DIRECT_CONNECTIONS`; the stream now has its
`bufferTime` property set to 0 for maximum speed:

```
var outStream:NetStream =
    new NetStream(connection, NetStream.DIRECT_CONNECTIONS);
outStream.bufferTime = 0;
outStream.addEventListener(NetStatusEvent.NET_STATUS, onStatus);

var video:Video = new Video();
var camera:Camera = Camera.getCamera();
video.attachCamera(camera);
```

```
addChild(video);

outStream.attachAudio(Microphone.getMicrophone());
outStream.attachCamera(camera);
outStream.publish("privateVideo");
```

When first connected, every peer is assigned a unique 256-bit peerID. Cirrus uses it to match it to your IP address and port number when other peers want to communicate with you, as in this example. nearID represents you:

```
var myPeerID:String

function onStatus(event:NetStatusEvent):void {
    if (event.info.code == "NetConnection.Connect.Success) {
        myPeerID = connection.nearID;
        trace(myPeerID);
        // 02024ab55a7284ad9d9d4586dd2dc8d2fa1b207e53118d93a34abc946836fa4
    }
}
```

The receivers need the peerID of the publisher to subscribe. The publisher needs a way to communicate the ID to others. In a professional application, you would use a web service or a remote sharedObject, but for web development, or if you know the people you want to communicate with, you can send your peerID in the body of an email:

```
var myPeerID:String

function onStatus(event:NetStatusEvent):void {
    if (event.info.code == "NetConnection.Connect.Success") {
        myPeerID = connection.nearID;
        navigateToURL(new URLRequest('mailto:FRIEND_EMAIL?subject=id&body='+
myPeerID));
    }
}
```

The streams are not sent until another endpoint subscribes to the publisher's stream.

Receiving a stream

In this example, the subscribers get the ID via email and copy its content into the system clipboard. Then they press the giveMe button:

```
var giveMe:Sprite = new Sprite();
giveMe.y = 100;
var g:Graphics = giveMe.graphics;
g.beginFill(0x0000FF);
g.drawRect(20, 20, 100, 75);
g.endFill();

giveMe.addEventListener(MouseEvent.CLICK, startStream);
```

The startStream method gets the content of the clipboard and uses it to create the stream. The ID needs to be passed as the second parameter in the stream constructor:

```
function startStream():void {
    var id:String =

Clipboard.generalClipboard.getData(ClipboardFormats.TEXT_FORMAT) as String;

    var inStream:NetStream = new NetStream(connection, id);
    inStream.addEventListener(NetStatusEvent.NET_STATUS, onStatus);

    var video:Video = new Video();
    addChild(video);
    inStream.play("privateVideo");

    video.attachNetStream(inStream);
}
```

The publisher has control, if needed, over accepting or rejecting subscribers. When a subscriber attempts to receive the stream, the onPeerConnect method is invoked. Create an object to capture the call. The way to monitor whom to accept (or not) is completely a function of your application:

```
var farPeerID:String;

var outClient:Object = new Object();
outClient.onPeerConnect = onConnect;
outStream.client = outClient;

function onConnect(stream:NetStream):Boolean {
    farPeerID = stream.farID;
    return true; // accept
    OR
    return false; // reject
}
```

The publisher stream has a peerStreams property that holds all the subscribers for the publishing stream. Use NetStream.send() to send messages to all the recipients or Net Stream.peerStreams[0].send() for an individual user, here the first one in the list.

NetConnection.maxPeerConnections returns the limit of peer streams, typically set to a maximum of eight.

Directed Routing

Directed routing is for sending data to a specific peer in a group. Peers can send each other messages if they know their counterpart PeerID. This feature only works in a group via NetGroup. It is not available via NetStream.

Sending a message

Individual messages can be sent from one neighbor to another using the NetGroup.send ToNeighbor method:

```
var groupSpec:GroupSpecifier = new GroupSpecifier("videoGroup");
groupSpec.postingEnabled = true;
```

```
groupSpec.serverChannelEnabled = true;
groupSpec.routingEnabled = true;

var netGroup = new NetGroup(connection,
    groupSpec.groupspecWithAuthorizations());
netGroup.addEventListener(NetStatusEvent.NET_STATUS, onStatus);
```

The message is an Object. It needs a destination which is the peer receiving the message. Here, PeerID is converted to a group address. It also needs the message itself. Here, we added the time to make each message unique and a type to filter the conversation:

```
var message:Object = new Object();
var now:Date = new Date();
message.time = now.getHours() + "" + now.getMinutes()+ "" + now.getSeconds();
message.destination = group.convertPeerIDToGroupAddress(peerID);
message.value = "south";
message.type = "direction";
group.sendToNearest(message, message.destination);
```

Receiving a message

The recipient must be in the same group. The message is received at an event with an info.code value of NetGroup.SendTo.Notify. The recipient checks to see if the message is for her by checking if event.info.fromLocal is true, and if it is not, sends it to the next neighbor until its destination is reached:

```
function onStatus(event:NetStatusEvent):void {
    switch(event.info.code) {
        case "NetGroup.SendTo.Notify" :
            trace(event.info.fromLocal);
            // if true, recipient is the intended destination
            var message:Object = event.info.message;
            (if message.type == "direction") {
                trace(message.value); // south
            }
            break;
    }
}
```

Relay

A simple message relay service was introduced in January 2011. It is not intended for ongoing communication, but rather for a few introductory messages, and is a feature for the Cirrus service only. It requires that the sender knows the PeerID of the recipient.

The sender requests a relay:

```
connection.call("relay", null, "RECIPIENT_ID", "hello");
```

The recipient receives and responds to the relay:

```
connection.client = this;

function onRelay(senderID:String, message):void {
```

```
        trace(senderID); // ID of the sender
        trace(message); // "hello"
}
```

Treasure Hunt

This treasure hunt game illustrates various aspects of this technology.

Referring to Figure 15-3, imagine the first user on the left walking outdoors looking for a treasure without knowing where it is. She streams a live video as she walks to indicate her progress. The second user from the left knows where the treasure is but is off-site. She guides the first user by pressing keys, representing the cardinal points, to send directions. Other peers (in the two screens toward the right) can watch the live stream and chat among themselves.

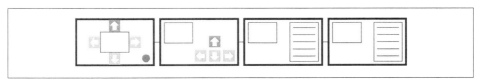

Figure 15-3. The Treasure Hunt activity; the panels shown here are (left to right) for the hunter walking, for the guide, and for users viewing the video and chatting over text

Review the sample code provided in this chapter to build such an application. We covered a one-to-many streaming example. We discussed chat in an earlier example. And we just went over sending direct messages.

As a final exercise, you can put all the pieces together to build a treasure hunt application. Good luck, and please post your results.

Other Multiuser Services

If you want to expand your application beyond what this service offers, several other options are available to set up communication between parties remotely, such the Adobe Media Server, Electrotank's ElectroServer, and gotoAndPlay()'s SmartFox. All of them require server setup and some financing.

ElectroServer was developed for multiplayer games and tools to build a multiplayer lobby system. One installation scales up to tens of thousands of connected game players with message rates of more than 100,000 messages per second. You can try a free 25-user license (see *http://www.electrotank.com/*). Server-side code requires Java or ActionScript 1. It supports AIR and Android.

SmartFox is a platform for developing massive multiuser games and was designed with simplicity in mind. It is fast and reliable and can handle tens of thousands of concurrent clients with low CPU and memory usage. It is well documented. You can try a full version with a free 100-user license (see *http://www.smartfoxserver.com/*). Server-side code requires Java. It supports AIR and Android.

Arduino and Physical Computing

Arduino is an open source electronics platform comprising easy-to-use hardware and software. The microcontroller can receive input from a range of sensors and can send signals to control other devices. It is an environment for bridging computers and the physical world, also called physical computing.

Purchase an Arduino board and a USB cable, and download the software and drivers. Note that you can build your own board and circuitry, but Arduino offers the ease of use of already custom-made boards, especially if this is a new area for you.

Arduino can communicate with ActionScript and AIR via TinkerProxy or Serproxy, which are local proxies between the serial port and AIR via a socket server.

Read Mike Chambers's blog on how to get started, at *http://www.mikechambers.com/ blog/2010/08/04/getting-started-with-flash-and-arduino/*.

Mike also developed a speed detector project for gear cars. It uses AIR 2.5 for Android. Two photo resistors are connected to the board that monitors when their values change. Two laser pointers beam on them at all times. When the car breaks one light and then the next, the times are sent to the AIR application that determines the speed. For more information, go to *http://www.mikechambers.com/blog/2010/08/11/accelerate-flash-ar duino-based-speedometer/*.

Get acquainted with sensors to get ideas. You can detect a variety of things such as light, humidity, temperature, pressure, electric current, sound, and time (for more information, see *http://www.arduino.cc/playground/Main/InterfacingWithHardware*).

Use of this technology is not limited to mobile devices, but such devices offer freedom of movement and open up new possibilities.

Conclusion

This is just the beginning of what you can do with networking devices. Expanding for chat and video, you can add some of the other APIs covered in this book, such as those for geolocation and displaying maps. You can also access Facebook or Twitter data to connect to your network.

CHAPTER 16

ViewManager

If the user can't use it, it doesn't work.

—Susan Dray

Unlike desktop applications, mobile applications only display one screen, or view, at a time. Each screen should be designed for a single task with clear and focused content. Intuitive single-click navigation to move to previous and next steps is key.

We will explore two approaches in this chapter. The first is a navigation system I wrote for my mobile applications using pure ActionScript. The second approach takes advantage of the `ViewNavigator` in the Flex Hero framework for mobile applications. It includes a few additional features such as transitions and a global `ActionBar`.

Navigation

You want your audience to be able to move forward between screens without re-creating the same steps over and over. You may need to provide the logic to navigate back to previous screens.

Google discourages the use of the physical back button for anything but going back to the previous application. However, the functionality exists, and some applications, as well as Flash Builder Mobile, use it to go through the stack of views. In my example, I create a back button within the application instead.

ViewManager

I originally developed this code for a conference scheduler application.

Attendees can carry the scheduler in their pocket and organize and save their own schedules. The application's business logic is fairly simple, but all the screens are interconnected and can be accessed from several different points. For instance, from the session view, the user can access the session's speaker(s), and from the speaker view, the user can access one of the sessions he is speaking at.

We will refer to each screen as a view.

 The source code for this example is provided on this book's website, *http://oreilly.com/catalog/9781449394820*. For the sake of simplicity, the partial code in this chapter only demonstrates three views: the menu, sessions, and session views.

Creating views

The `ViewManager` creates the different views and manages them during the life of the application.

The document class creates an instance of the `ViewManager`. It calls its `init` function and passes a reference of the timeline:

```
import view.ViewManager;

// member variable
private var viewManager:ViewManager;

viewManager = new ViewManager();
viewManager.init(this);
```

The `ViewManager` class stores a reference to the timeline to add and remove views from the display list:

```
private var timeline:MovieClip;

public function init(timeline:MovieClip):void {
    this.timeline = timeline;
}
```

The `ViewManager` creates an instance of each view and stores them in a `viewList` object. The following code assumes the `MenuView`, `SessionsView`, and `SessionView` classes exist.

The initialization process for each view, creation of the view's member variables and references to other objects, only needs to happen once. The process is triggered in the constructor as demonstrated in the section "Individual Views" on page 225. Note that the views are of data type `BaseView`. We will cover this in more detail later in the chapter:

```
private var currentView:BaseView;
private viewList:Object = {};

public function init(timeline:MovieClip):void {
    this.timeline = timeline;

    createView("menu", new MenuView());
    createView("sessions", new SessionsView());
    createView("session", new SessionView());
}

private function createView(name:String, instance:BaseView):void {
```

```
        viewList[name] = instance;
    }
```

The initial view display

When the application first starts, the document class loads an XML document that contains all the data regarding the conference, such as the list of sessions and speakers. While this is taking place, the ViewManager displays an introductory view without any interactivity. Let's modify the init method to add this functionality. The setCurrent View method will be discussed in the next paragraph:

```
public function init(timeline:MovieClip):void {
    this.timeline = timeline;

    createView("intro", new IntroView());
    createView("menu", new MenuView());
    createView("sessions", new SessionsView());
    createView("session", new SessionView());

    setCurrentView({view:"intro"});
}
```

The current view display

Once the data is loaded, parsed, and stored in the model part of the application, the document class calls the onDataReady method on the ViewManager:

```
// set up application, model and get data from external xml
viewManager.onDataReady();
```

In turn, the ViewManager defines the new view by calling the setCurrentView method and passes an object with the property view to define the view to display:

```
public function onDataReady():void {
    setCurrentView({view:"menu"});
}
```

The setCurrentView method removes the previous view if there is one. It then stores the view in the currentView variable and adds it to the display list. Two methods, onHide and onShow, are called via the IView interface, discussed next. Each view uses the methods to clear or add from the display list and destroy objects.

The method also registers the view for a custom ClickEvent.NAV_EVENT with the setCur rentView method of the ViewManager as the callback function. We will review the use of this custom event in the section "Creating a custom event" on page 224:

```
import view.ClickEvent;

private var currentView:BaseView;

private function setCurrentView(object:Object):void {
    // remove current view
    if (currentView) {
        currentView.removeEventListener(ClickEvent.NAV_EVENT, goTo);
```

```
        IView(currentView).onHide();
        timeline.removeChild(currentView);
        currentView = null;
    }

    // add new view
    currentView = viewList[object.view];
    if (object.id != undefined) {
        currentView.setID(object.id);
    }
    currentView.addEventListener(ClickEvent.NAV_EVENT, goTo, false, 0, true);
    IView(currentView).onShow();
    timeline.addChild(currentView);
}

// pass event data object
private function goTo(event:ClickEvent):void {
    setCurrentView(event.data);
}
```

The IView interface

It is imperative that all views have the two methods, onHide and onShow, so we use an
IView interface. Each view also needs a method—here it is clickAway—to navigate to
the next view. In our application, this always occurs upon user interaction. We will
therefore use a MouseEvent:

```
package view {
    import flash.events.MouseEvent;

    public interface IView
    {
        function onShow():void
        function onHide():void
        function clickAway(event:MouseEvent):void
    }
}
```

Creating a custom event

A custom event is used to pass the destination view and additional data, if needed, from
the current view. For example, if the user is looking at the screen displaying all the
conference sessions and clicks on a specific session, we use the event object to pass the
session ID to the Session view, as illustrated in Figure 16-1:

```
{view:"session", id:5}
```

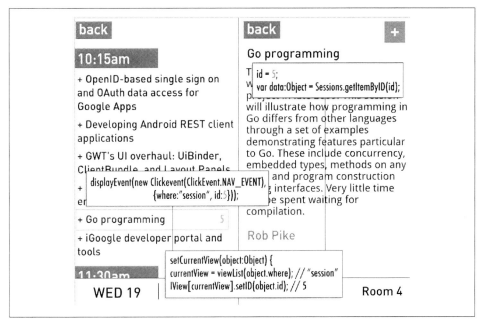

Figure 16-1. *The mechanism to send destination and data from the current view to the destination view via the ViewManager*

The custom class is as follows. Its `data` property is an object, so we can add additional parameters as needed:

```
import flash.events.Event;
import events.ClickEvent;

final public calls ClickEvent extends Event {
    public static const NAV_EVENT:String = "NavEvent";
    public var data:Object;

    public function ClickEvent(type:String, data:Object = null) {
        super(type, true, true);
        this.data = data;
    }

    public override function clone():Event {
        return new ClickEvent(this.type, this.data);
    }
}
```

Individual Views

Let's examine some of the views.

Inheritance

Some functionality is identical for all views. For this reason, they all inherit from the same super class, called `BaseView`. Here we declare two member variables, id and con tainer, and a function, setID. It is a simple class initially. We will develop it further in this chapter to add a button and interactivity to navigate in reverse:

```
package view {
    import flash.display.Sprite;
    import flash.events.Event;
    import flash.events.MouseEvent;

    public class BaseView extends Sprite
    {
        protected var id:int;
        protected var container:Sprite;

        protected function SeID(id:int):void {
            this.id = id;
        }
    }
}
```

The following code is for the `MenuView` class. It adds three buttons—for sessions, speakers, and a custom schedule—and their listeners on onShow. It clears listeners and empties the display list on onHide. Figure 16-2 shows the Menu view of the AIR scheduler application for the 2010 GoogleIO conference:

```
package view {
    import flash.events.MouseEvent;
    import view.ClickEvent;

    final public class MenuView extends BaseView implements IView() {

        public function MenuView(){}

        public function onShow():void {
            var sessions:sessionsBut = new sessionsBut();
            sessions.view = "sessions";
            sessions.addEventListener(MouseEvent.CLICK, onClickAway);

            var speakers:speakersBut = new speakersBut();
            speakers.view = "speakers";
            speakers.addEventListener(MouseEvent.CLICK, onClickAway);

            var schedule:scheduleBut = new scheduleBut();
            schedule.view = "schedule";
            schedule.addEventListener(MouseEvent.CLICK, onClickAway);

            addChild(sessions);
            addChild(speakers);
            addChild(schedule);
        }

        public function onHide():void {
```

```
        while(numChildren > 0) {
            getChildAt(0).
            removeEventListener(MouseEvent.CLICK, onClickAway);
            removeChildAt(0);
        }
    }

    public function onClickAway(event:MouseEvent):void {
        dispatchEvent(new ClickEvent(ClickEvent.NAV_EVENT,
                            {view:event.currentTarget.view});
    }
  }
}
```

Figure 16-2. The Menu view of the AIR scheduler application for the 2010 GoogleIO conference

The next example shows the SessionsView code. Note that the code is minimal to keep the focus on navigation. For instance, the scrolling mechanism was left out. The full application is provided in the code depository, and I will cover scrolling in Chapter 17, in the Album example.

As mentioned before, the initialization process for each view only needs to happen once for the life of the application. Here the SessionsView class acquires the data for the sessions just once if its list variable is null.

The sessions data is stored in a Vector object called sessionList of the static class Sessions (not covered here) and is populated with objects of data type Session. It is already sorted and organized by day and time:

```
package view {
    import events.ClickEvent;
```

```
import flash.events.MouseEvent;
import model.Sessions; // static class holds list of all Sessions
import model.Session; // class holds individual session data

final public class SessionsView extends BaseView implements IView() {
    private var list:Vector.<Session>;

    public function SessionsView (){}
]

public function onShow():void {
    container = new Sprite();

    // request list of sessions if not acquired yet
    if (list == null) {
        list = Sessions.sessionList;
    }
    // display sessions
    showSessions();
  }
}
```

We traverse the list of sessions and display all the sessions with the hardcoded date of 19. Again, this is to keep this example simple. The conference took place over two days and would, in a full example, require a UI to choose between one of the two dates:

```
private showSessions():void {
    var timeKeeper:String = "0";

    var bounds:int = list.length;
    var ypos:int = 50;
    for (var i:int = 0; i < bounds; i++) {
        var session:Session = list[i];

        // display a blue time indicator if it is a new time
        if (session.time > timeKeeper) {
            timeKeeper = session.time;
            ypos += 15;

            // TimeBar is a movieclip
            var bar:TimeBar = new TimeBar();
            bar.y = ypos;
            bar.timeInfo.text = timeKeeper;
            container.addChild(bar);
            ypos += 60;
        }

        // load the individual session
        // it returns its height to position the next element below it
        var newPos = loadSession(session, ypos);
        ypos =+ (newPos + 10);
    }
    addChild(container);
}
```

```
private loadSession(session:Session, ypos:int):int {

    // SessionSmall is a movieclip
    var mc:SessionSmall = new SessionSmall();
    mc.y = ypos;
    mc.id = session.id;
    mc.what.autoSize = TextFieldAutoSize.LEFT;
    mc.what.text = "+ " + session.title;
    mc.back.height = mc.what.height;
    mc.addEventListener(MouseEvent.CLICK, clickAway, false, 0, true);
    container.addChild(mc);

    // return the session movie clip height
    return mc.what.height;
}
```

When the user chooses a session, its ID is passed along with the destination view:

```
public function clickAway(event:MouseEvent):void {
    dispatchEvent(new ClickEvent(ClickEvent.NAV_EVENT,
                 {view:"session", id:event.currentTarget.id}));
}
```

In the onHide method, all the children of the Sprite container are removed as well as their listeners if they have one. Then the container itself is removed. Figure 16-3 shows the sessions broken down by day and time:

```
public function onHide():void {
    while (container.numChildren > 0) {
        var child:MovieClip = container.getChildAt(0) as MovieClip;
        if (child.id != null) {
            child.removeEventListener(MouseEvent.CLICK, clickAway);
        }
        container.removeChild(child);
    }
    removeChild(container);
    container = null;
}
```

Here is the SessionView code. The method displays all the data related to a session. This includes the session title, a description, the speakers involved, and the room, category, and rank:

```
package view {
    import events.ClickEvent;
    import flash.events.MouseEvent;
    import model.Sessions;
    import model.Speakers; // static class that holds Speakers data

    final public class SessionView extends BaseView implements IView() {

        public function SessionView(){}

        public function onShow():void {
            // search Sessions by id
            var data:Object = Sessions.getItemByID(id);
```

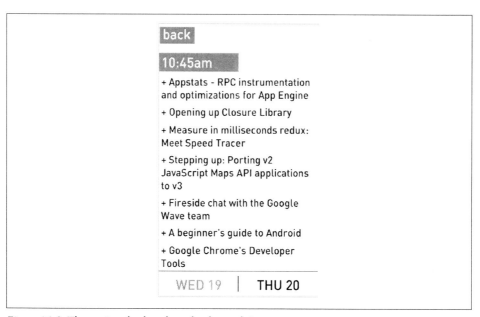

Figure 16-3. The sessions broken down by day and time

```
container = new Sprite();
addChild(container);

// display title and description
// SessionMovie is a movieclip
var session:SessionMovie = new SessionMovie();
session.title.autoSize = TextFieldAutoSize.LEFT;
session.title.text = data.title;
session.body.text  = data.description;
container.addChild(session);

// display list of speakers
for (var i:int; i < data.speakers.length; i++) {
    var bio:Bio = new Bio();
    bio.id = data.speakers[i];
    // search list of speakers by id
    var bioData:Object = Speakers.getItemByID(bio.id);
    bio.speaker.text = bioData.first + " " + bioData.last;
    bio.addEventListener(MouseEvent.CLICK,
    clickAway, false, 0, true);
}

// display category, level, rank and room number
// Border is a movieClip
var border:Border = new Border();
// categories is a movieclip with frame labels matching category
border.categories.gotoAndStop(data.tag);
// rank is a movieclip with a text field
border.rank.text = String(data.type);
```

```
        // room is a movieclip with a text field
        border.room.text = String(data.room);
        container.addChild(border);
    }
```

Clicking on one of the speakers takes the user to a new speaker destination view defined by an ID:

```
public function clickAway(event:MouseEvent):void {
    dispatchEvent(new ClickEvent(ClickEvent.NAV_EVENT,
            {view:"speaker", id:event.currentTarget.id}));
    }
}
```

In the onHide method, all the children of the Sprite container are removed as well as their listeners if they have one. Then the container itself is removed:

```
public function onHide():void {
    while(container.numChildren > 0) {
        var child:container.getChildAt(0);
        if (child.id != null) {
            child removeEventListener(MouseEvent.CLICK, clickAway);
        }
        container.removeChild(child);
    }
    removeChild(container);
    container = null;
}
```

Figure 16-4 shows a subset of information for a session.

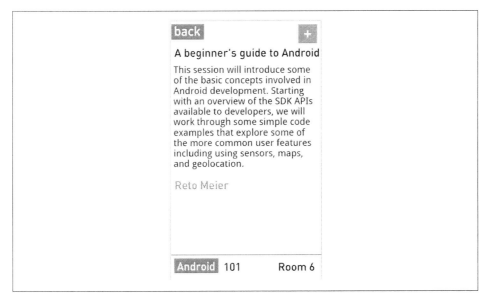

Figure 16-4. A subset of information for a session, including the speaker(s) name, category, level of expertise, and room number

Breadcrumb Navigation

You can use different approaches for the user to navigate between screens.

AIR does not have access to the Options menu triggered by pressing the Menu key. If you want to create a native-like look and feel, you can design a similar-looking menu in your application for the application's key views. The advantage of this approach is that the navigation menu does not take real estate away from your application. It is made visible when pressing the Menu key and collapses after a selection is made.

Another approach is to use *breadcrumb navigation*. This is a common and intuitive type of interface. It registers the user's selection as he goes from screen to screen and stores his history. A persistent button gives the user the option to go back. Figure 16-5 shows a breadcrumb navigation flow and view stack.

We only need to make a few changes to add this functionality.

Let's add the functionality to the `BaseView` class to include a back button to the `displayList` and a callback function to dispatch a `goBack` event when the back button is pressed. In the `onShow` function, the `onBack` method of the super class is called last so that the back button is always at the top level of the display list.

This is the `BaseView` class:

```
import flash.events.Event;

protected function onBack():void {
    var backButton:BackButton = new BackButton();
    backButton.addEventListener(MouseEvent.CLICK, onGoBack);
    addChild(backButton);
}

private function onGoBack(event:MouseEvent):void {
    event.stopPropagation();
    event.currentTarget.removeEventListener(MouseEvent.CLICK, onGoBack);

    removeChild(event.currentTarget as MovieClip);
    dispatchEvent(new Event("goBack"));
}
```

This is the `SessionsView` class modified to call the `onBack` method of the `BaseView` class:

```
public function onShow():void {
    container = new Sprite();

    // request list of sessions if not acquired yet
    if (list == null) {
        list = Sessions.sessionList;
    }
    // display sessions
    showSessions();

    // add back button
```

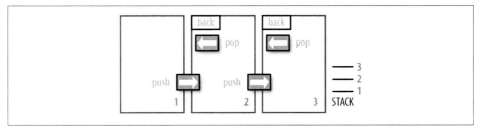

Figure 16-5. Breadcrumb navigation flow and view stack

```
        super.onBack();
    }
```

The ViewManager class also needs to be edited. The visited views are stored in a Vec
tor. In the setCurrentView function, the new view is pushed to the stack:

```
private currentView:BaseView;
private var viewStack:Vector.<BaseView>;

private function goTo(event:ClickEvent):void {
    viewStack.push(event.data);
    setCurrentView(event.data);
}


private function setCurrentView(object:Object):void {

    if (currentView) {
        currentView.removeEventListener(ViewEvent.CLICK, goTo);
        IView(currentView).onHide();
        currentView.removeEventListener("goBack", goBack);
        timeline.removeChild(currentView);
    }

    currentView = viewList[object.view];
    if (object.id != undefined) {
        currentView.setID(object.id);
    }
    timeline.addChild(currentView);
    currentView.addEventListener(ClickEvent.NAV_EVENT, goTo, false, 0, true);
    currentView.addEventListener("goBack", goBack, false, 0, true);
    IView(currentView).onShow();
}
```

When the back button is pressed, the current view is removed from the stack first. The
setCurrentView method is then called and the last view stored is passed as an argument:

```
private function goBack(e:Event):void {
    viewStack.pop();
    setCurrentView(viewStack[viewStack.length - 1]);
}
```

You can now easily add views to your application. If you want to add a transition between views, the simplest solution is to take a screen grab of the current view and tween it on a top layer while you are revealing the destination view.

Once this navigation functionality is in place, you can now focus on other aspects, perhaps more abstract or challenging, of your project.

Flash Builder ViewNavigator

Flash Builder and its Hero APIs provide functionality to handle view management.

Create a new project under File→New→Flex Mobile project. On the Mobile Settings panel, choose Application template→Mobile Application, then select Finish. Look at the main default application file. A `firstView` tag was added to the `MobileApplica` `tion` tag. It points to an MXML file inside a *views* directory:

```
<s:MobileApplication
    xmlns:fx="http://ns.adobe.com/mxml/2009"
    xmlns:s="library://ns.adboec.com/flex/spark"
    firstView="views.OpeningView"
    }
}
```

Notice a new directory called *views* inside your default application file. It contains the MXML file which was named after your project, as well as *HomeView.mxml*, and was given a title of *HomeView*. This is the default first view which appears when the application starts:

```
<s:View
    xmlns:fx="http://ns.adobe.com/mxml/2009"
    xmlns:s="library://ns.adboec.com/flex/spark"
    title="HomeView">
    <fx:Declarations> </fx:Declarations>
</s:View>
```

 The concept of a splash screen, or a *default.png* file, does not exist in Android as it does in iOS. The user sees a black screen until the application is loaded. Flex provides an option to display an image first while it initializes the application to reduce the sense of delay. The image is automatically replaced by the default view when ready.

A few new components were created especially for mobile development. The `spark.components.ViewNavigatorApplication` container automatically creates a `ViewNavigator` object. It is a container that consists of a collection of views, and is used to control the navigation between views, their addition or removal, and the navigation history.

The View is also a container. It extends from the Group component. Note its `naviga` `tor` attribute which references the ViewNavigator container and its `data` attribute which is used to store an Object, whether the view is currently visible or was previously visited.

The View dispatches three events of type FlexEvent. `FlexEvent.VIEW_ACTIVATE` and `Flex` `Event.VIEW_DEACTIVATE` are self-explanatory. `FlexEvent.REMOVING` is dispatched when the view is about to be deactivated.

Views are destroyed to keep a small footprint. If a particular view is complicated and may take some time to display, you can keep it in memory and set its `destructionPo` `licy` attribute to `none`.

Let's add two buttons to our default view to navigate to another view:

```
<s:View
    xmlns:fx="http://ns.adobe.com/mxml/2009"
    xmlns:s="library://ns.adboec.com/flex/spark"
    title="HomeView">
    <fx:Declarations> </fx:Declarations>

    <fx:Script>
        private function onClick(event:MouseEvent):void {
            navigator.pushView(ContextView);
        }
    </fx:Script>

    <s:Button id="Apples" click="onClick(event)" y="100" />
    <s:Button id="Oranges" click="onClick(event)" y="200" />
</s:View>
```

Clicking on the buttons calls the onClick function which, in turn, calls the navigator's pushView method. This method navigates to a view we will call ContextView. The push View method takes three arguments: the name of the view, a data object, and a transition animation of type ViewTransition. Only the first parameter is required.

Other navigation methods are popView to go back to the previous view, popToFirst View to jump to the default first view, and the self-explanatory popAll and replace View. navigator.activeView returns the current view.

Change the onClick function to pass the button ID as an argument:

```
private function onClick(event:MouseEvent):void {
    navigator.pushView(ContextView, {fruit:event.currentTarget.id});
}
```

Now create the second view to navigate to. Right-click on the *views* folder, create a new project under New→MXML Component, and enter **ContextView** in the Name field. Note that the file is based on `spark.components.View`.

Add one text field to populate the view with the data received and one button to navigate back to the first view. Note the add tag which is dispatched when a view is added to the container:

```
<s:View
    xmlns:fx="http://ns.adobe.com/mxml/2009"
    xmlns:s="library://ns.adboec.com/flex/spark"
    title="ContextView">
    <fx:Declarations> </fx:Declarations>


    <s:add>
        context.text = data.fruit;
    </s:add>

    <fx:Script>
        private function onClick(event:MouseEvent):void {
            navigator.pushView(HomeView);
        }
    </fx:Script>

    <s:Button click="onClick(event)" />
    <s:TextArea id="context" />
</s:View>
```

Run this example and test the navigation. The context text area is populated with the data passed.

By default, a ViewTransition animates between screens, where one view slides out and the other slides in, defined as SlideViewTransition. You can change it for one of the following transitions: CrossFadeViewTransition, FlipViewTransition, or ZoomViewTransition.

The default transition can be changed in navigator.defaultPopTransition and navigator.defaultPushTransition:

```
import spark.transitions.CrossFadeViewTransition;
import spark.transitions.FlipViewTransition;

var pushTransition = new FlipViewTransition();
navigator.defaultPushTransition = pushTransition;

var popTransition = new CrossFadeViewTransition();
navigator.defaultPopTransition = popTransition;

// OR

private function onClick(event:MouseEvent):void {
    navigator.pushView(HomeView, {}, FlipViewTransition);
}
```

To suppress the transition altogether, enter the following in the *Default Application* file:

```
navigator.transitionEnabled = false;
// OR
ViewNavigator.defaultPushTransition = null;
ViewNavigator.defaultPopTransition = null;
```

A default `ActionBar` control is placed at the top of the screen. It functions as a control and navigation menu and provides contextual information, such as the current active view. It has a navigation area, a control area, and an action area. To modify it, use the `navigationContent`, `titleContent`, and `actionContent` tags.

By default, the name of the active view shows in the `titleContent`. To add a button to the `navigationContent` tag to go back home, use:

```
private function goHome():void {
    navigator.popToFirstView();
}

<s:navigationContent>
    <s:Button label="Home" click="goHome()"/>
</s:navigationContent>
```

If you use it, move all navigation functionality from the views to it. Alternatively, you can choose not to use it at all. To hide it at the view level, use the following:

```
<s:creationComplete>
    actionBarVisible = false;
</s:creationComplete>
```

To hide it at the application level, use this code:

```
navigator.actionBar.visible = false;
navigator.actionBar.includeInLayout = false;
```

Pressing the back button automatically goes back to the previous view. To overwrite this functionality, set a null `navigationContent` as follows:

```
<s:navigationContent/>
```

If the user leaves the application on a specific view, you can start the application again on the same view with the same data by using the `sessionCachingEnabled` tag:

```
<s:MobileApplication
    xmlns:fx="http://ns.adobe.com/mxml/2009"
    xmlns:s="library://ns.adboec.com/flex/spark"
    sessionCachingEnabled="true"
    firstView="views.OpeningView"
    }
}
```

Conclusion

You now have the fundamentals to create the view and navigation components of your application, whether you choose to write pure ActionScript or develop a Flex mobile application. Once your views are in place, you can dive into the workings of your application functionality.

In the next chapter, we will develop a complete application using many of the APIs we covered previously.

CHAPTER 17

Case Study

You live and learn. At any rate, you live.

—Douglas Noel Adams

The Album is a project composed of two AIR applications, one for mobile and one for the desktop. It covers many of the APIs we have discussed in other chapters, and it is meant to be an overview of the book so that you can see how much you have learned.

The Album Application

In the mobile version of the AIR application, the user takes a picture or pulls one from the camera roll. She can save it to a dedicated database, along with an audio caption and geolocation information. The group of saved images is viewable in a scrollable menu. Images can be sent from the device to the desktop via a wireless network.

In the desktop version, the user can see an image at full resolution on a large screen. It can be saved to the desktop, and it can also be edited and uploaded to a photo service.

 Thanks to Mihai Corlan for his original idea which I expanded for this case study: *http://corlan.org/2010/07/08/androidpictures-or-how-to-share-phone-pictures-with-desktops/*.

Please download the two applications from this book's website at *http://oreilly.com/catalog/9781449394820*.

This chapter does not discuss all the code for this project. Instead, it highlights some specific points of interest. Every API used in this application was covered in the book and should be easy to follow. Refer to the code comments for additional information.

The Album application does not exist in the Android Market, nor is it meant for public consumption. It was developed for the sole purpose of demonstration and is not of production quality.

Design

The design is simple, using primary colors and crisp type. The project was not developed for flexible layout. It was created at 800×480 resolution with auto-orientation turned off; you can use it as a base from which to experiment developing for other resolutions. The art is provided in a Flash movie to use in Flash Professional or as an *.swc* file to import into Flash Builder by selecting Properties→ActionScript Build Path→Library Path and clicking on "Add swc."

Architecture

The source code consists of the `Main` document class and the *model*, *view*, and *events* packages (see Figure 17-1).

The *model* package contains the `AudioManager`, the `SQLManager`, the `GeoService`, and the `PeerService`. The *view* package contains the `NavigationManager` and the various views. The *events* package contains the various custom events.

The `SQLManager` class is static, so it can be accessed from anywhere in the application without instantiation. The other model classes are passed by reference.

Flow

The flow of the application is straightforward. The user goes through a series of simple tasks, one step at a time. In the opening screen, the `OpeningView`, the user can select a new picture or go to the group menu of images, as shown in Figure 17-2.

From the `AddView` page, the user can open the Media Gallery or launch the camera, as shown in Figure 17-3. Both choices go to the same `CameraView` view. An `id` parameter is passed to the new view to determine the mode.

The image data received from either of the sources is resized to fit the dimensions of the stage. The user can take another picture or accept the current photograph if satisfied. The image `url` is sent to the `SQLManager` to store in its `class` variable `current Photo` of type `Object`, and the application goes to the `CaptionView`.

In the `CaptionView`, the user can skip the caption-recording step or launch the `Audio Manager`. The recording is limited to four seconds and automatically plays the caption sound back. The user can record again or choose to keep the audio. The `AudioMan ager` compresses the recording as a WAV file and saves it on the SD card. Its `url` is saved in the `SQLManager`'s `currentPhoto` object. The next step is to add geographic information.

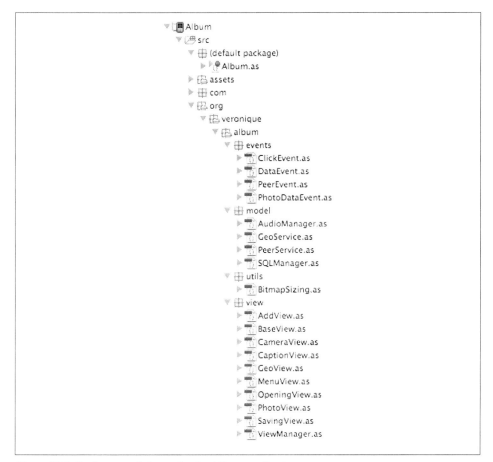

Figure 17-1. Packages and classes for the Album application

Figure 17-2. The OpeningView

In the GeoView, the user can skip or launch the GeoService. This service creates an instance of the GeoLocation, fetches coordinates, and then requests the corresponding city and country from the Yahoo! API. As in the previous steps, the geodata is saved in the SQLManager's currentPhoto object. These three steps are shown in Figure 17-4.

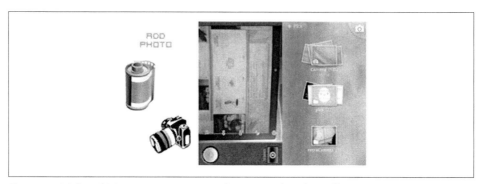

Figure 17-3. The AddView, native camera application, and Media Gallery

Figure 17-4. The CameraView, CaptionView, and GeoView

In the `SavingView` mode, data saving can be skipped or the data can be saved. For the latter, the `SQLManager` opens an SQL connection and saves the data, then closes the connection. The application goes back to the `OpeningView`.

Back at our starting point, another navigation choice is the Group menu. The `Menu View` page requests the number of images saved for the `SQLManager` and displays it as a list of items. If the list height is taller than the screen, it becomes scrollable. Selecting one of the items takes the user to the `PhotoView` screen. The `SavingView` page and `MenuView` page are shown in Figure 17-5.

The `PhotoView` displays the image selected in the `MenuView`. Choosing to connect calls the `PeerService` to set up a P2P connection using the WiFi network. Once it is established, the data is requested from the `SQLManager` using the item ID. The data is then sent. It includes the `byteArray` from the image, a WAV file for the audio, and the city and country as text. These steps are displayed in Figure 17-6.

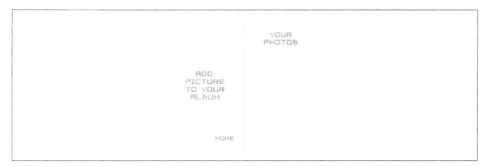

Figure 17-5. The SavingView and MenuView

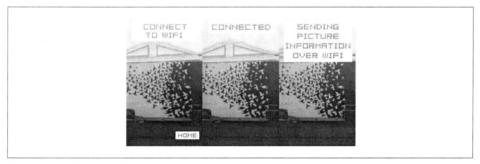

Figure 17-6. The PhotoView and the steps to send the picture information using a P2P connection

Permissions

This application needs the following permissions to access the Internet, write to the SD card, and access GPS sensors, the camera, and the microphone:

```
<android>
<manifestAdditions>
<![CDATA[
    <manifest>
        <uses-permission
         android:name="android.permission.INTERNET"/>
        <uses-permission
         android:name="android.permission.WRITE_EXTERNAL_STORAGE"/>
        <uses-permission
         android:name="android.permission.ACCESS_FINE_LOCATION"/>
        <uses-permission
         android:name="android.permission.ACCESS_COARSE_LOCATION"/>
        <uses-permission
         android:name="android.permission.CAMERA"/>
        <uses-permission
         android:name="android.permission.RECORD_AUDIO"/>
    </manifest>
]]>
</manifestAdditions>
</android>
```

Navigation

The `ViewManager` class discussed here is almost identical to the one discussed in Chapter 16, except that we do not need a back button and breadcrumb navigation. The flow is a step-by-step process whereby the user can choose to skip the steps that are optional.

Images

The `CameraView` is used to get an image, either by using the media library or by taking one using the camera. The choice is based on a parameter passed from the previous screen. The process of receiving the bytes, scaling, and displaying the image is the same regardless of the image source. It is done by a utility class called `BitmapDataSizing` and is based on the dimensions of the screen.

To improve this application, check if an image is already saved when the user selects it again to avoid duplicates.

Audio

The audio caption is a novel way to save a comment along with the image. There is no image service that provides the ability to package an audio commentary, but you could build such an application.

As we discussed in Chapter 11, bytes can be saved as WAV files using the Adobe class `WAVReader` and then extracted using a third-party library. Here, we create an *Album* directory on the SD card and a *mySounds* directory inside it to store the WAV files.

Reverse Geolocation

As we covered in Chapter 10, reverse geolocation is the process of using geographical coordinates to get an address location such as a city and a street address.

In this application, we are only interested in the city name and country. Therefore, coarse data is sufficient. We do not need to wait for the GPS data to stabilize. As soon as we get a response for the Yahoo! service, we move on to the next step.

SQLite

`SQLManager` is a static class, so it can be accessed from anywhere in the application. The `Main` class holds an object which stores information related to a photo until it is complete and ready to be saved:

```
var currentPhoto:Object = {photo:"", audio:"", geo:""};
```

The `photo` property stores the path to where the image is saved in the Gallery. The `audio` property stores the path to where the WAV file is located and the `geo` property stores a string with city and country information.

From the `SavingView` view, the object is saved in the *myAlbum.db* file on the SD card.

P2P Connection

The peer-to-peer connection is used to send the image, audio caption, and location over a LAN. This example is to demonstrate the potential of what you can do more than a proper use case because the transfer is slow, unless the information is sent in packets and reassembled. This technology is feasible for fairly small amounts of data and has a lot of potential for gaming and social applications.

Once the user has selected an image, she can transfer it to a companion desktop application from the `SavingView` view. The `PeerService` class handles the communication to the LAN and the posting of data.

We cover a lot of this functionality in Chapter 15.

Scrolling Navigation

The `MenuView` that displays the images saved in the database has scrolling capability if the content is larger than the height of the screen.

There are two challenges to address. The first is the performance of a potentially large list to scroll. The second is the overlapping interactive objects. The scrollable list contains elements that also respond to a mouse event. Both functionalities need to work without conflicting.

We only need to scroll the view if the container is larger than the device height, so there is no need to add unnecessary code. Let's check its dimensions in the `onShow` method:

```
function onShow():void {
    deviceHeight = stage.stageHeight;

    container = new Sprite();
    addChild(container);
    // populate container

    if (container.height > deviceHeight) {
        trace("we need to add scrolling functionality");
    }
}
```

If the `container` sprite is taller than the screen, let's add the functionality to scroll. Touch events do not perform as well as mouse events. Because we only need one touch point, we will use a mouse event to detect the user interaction. Note that we set `cacheAsBit` map to `true` on the container to improve rendering:

```
function onShow():void {
    if (container.height > deviceHeight) {
        container.cacheAsBitmap = true;
        stage.addEventListener(MouseEvent.MOUSE_DOWN,
                          touchBegin, false, 0, true);
```

```
        stage.addEventListener(MouseEvent.MOUSE_UP,
                                touchEnd, false, 0, true);
    }
}
```

To determine if the mode is to scroll or to click an element that is part of the container, we start a timeout. We will see later why we need this timer in relation to the elements:

```
import flash.utils.setTimeout;

var oldY:Number = 0.0;
var newY:Number = 0.0;
var timeout:int;

function touchBegin(event:MouseEvent):void {
    oldY = event.stageY;
    newY = event.stageY;
    timeout = setTimeOut(startMove, 400);
}
```

When the time expires, we set the mode to scrollable by calling the startMove method. We want to capture the position change on MOUSE_MOVE but only need to render the change to the screen on ENTER_FRAME. This guarantees a smoother and more consistent motion. UpdateAfterEvent should never be used in mobile development because it is too demanding for devices:

```
function startMove(event:MouseEvent):void {
    stage.addEventListener(MouseEvent.MOUSE_MOVE,
                            touchMove, false, 0, true);
    stage.addEventListener(Event.ENTER_FRAME, frameEvent, false, 0, true);
}
```

When the finger moves, we update the value of the newY coordinate:

```
function touchMove(event:MouseEvent):void {
    newY = event.stageY;
}
```

On the enterFrame event, we render the screen using the new position. The container is moved according to the new position. To improve performance, we show and hide the elements that are not in view using predefined bounds:

```
var totalChildren:int = container.numChildren;
var topBounds:int = -30;

function frameEvent(event:Event):void {
    if (newY != oldY) {
        var newPos = newY - oldY;
        oldY = newY;

        container.y += newPos;
        for (var i:int = 0; i < totalChildren; i++) {
            var mc:MovieClip = container.getChildAt(i) as MovieClip;
            var pos:Number = container.y + mc.y;
            mc.visible = (pos > topBounds && pos < deviceHeight);
        }
```

On touchEnd, the listeners are removed:

```
function touchEnd(event:MouseEvent):void {
    stage.removeEventListener(MouseEvent.MOUSE_MOVE, touchMove);
    stage.removeEventListener(Event.ENTER_FRAME, frameEvent);
}
```

As mentioned before, elements in the container have their own mouse event listeners:

```
element.addEventListener(MouseEvent.MOUSE_DOWN, timeMe, false, 0, true);
element.addEventListener(MouseEvent.MOUSE_UP, clickAway, false, 0, true);
```

On mouse down, the boolean variable isMoving is set to false and the visual cue indicates that the element was selected:

```
var isMoving:Boolean = false;
var selected:MovieClip;

function timeMe():void {
    isMoving = false;
    selected = event.currentTarget as MovieClip;
    selected.what.textColor = 0x336699;
}
```

On mouse up and within the time allowed, the stage listeners and the timeout are removed. If the boolean isMoving is still set to false and the target is the selected item, the application navigates to the next view:

```
function clickAway(event:MouseEvent):void {
    touchEnd(event);
    clearTimeOut(timeout);
    if (selected == event.currentTarget && isMoving == false) {
        dispatchEvent(new ClickEvent(ClickEvent.NAV_EVENT,
                            {view:"speaker", id:selected.id}));
    }
}
```

Now let's add to the frameEvent code to handle deactivating the element when scrolling. Check that an element was pressed, and check that the selected variable holds a value and that the motion is more than two pixels. This is to account for screens that are very responsive. If both conditions are met, change the boolean value, reset the look of the element, and set the selected variable to null:

```
function frameEvent(event:Event):void {
    if (newY != oldY) {
        var newPos = newY - oldY;
        oldY = newY;

        container.y += newPos;
        for (var i:int = 0; i < totalChildren; i++) {
            var mc:MovieClip = container.getChildAt(i) as MovieClip;
            var pos:Number = container.y + mc.y;
            mc.visible = (pos > topBounds && pos < deviceHeight);
        }
```

```
            if (selected != null && Math.abs(newPos) > 2) {
                isMoving = true;
                selected.what.textColor = 0x000000;
                selected = null;
            }
        }
    }
```

There are various approaches to handle scrolling. For a large number of elements, the optimal way is to only create as many element containers as are visible on the screen and populate their content on the fly. Instead of moving a large list, move the containers as in a carousel animation and update their content by pulling the data from a `Vector` or other form of data content.

If you are using Flash Builder and components, look at the Adobe lighthouse package (*http://www.adobe.com/devnet/devices/fpmobile.html*). It contains `DraggableVertical Container` for display objects and `DraggableVerticalList` for items.

Desktop Functionality

The AIR desktop application, as shown in Figure 17-7, is set to receive the data and display it. Seeing a high resolution on a large screen demonstrates how good the camera quality of some devices can be. The image can be saved on the desktop as a JPEG.

Figure 17-7. AIR desktop companion application to display images received from the device

Another technology, not demonstrated here, is Pixel Bender, used for image manipulation. It is not available for AIR for Android but is for AIR on the desktop. So this would be another good use case where devices and the desktop can complete one another.

Conclusion

The application we discussed in this chapter has a simple purpose, but it covers many aspects of what you can do with AIR for Android. Feel free to expand on it and publish your own application.

CHAPTER 18

Asset Management

Good design is obvious. Great design is transparent.

—Joe Sparano

Preparing and managing art in mobile development requires a close collaboration between the designer and the developer.

In addition to planning ahead for multiple screens, good design needs to conform to acceptable performance. Some of the work takes place in the preparation, but a lot needs to happen during development.

In this chapter, we will cover some aspects of design, from preparation to management at runtime.

Text

Text should be a particular concern. The absence of a physical keyboard introduces a new interface and user experience. Embedding and rendering fonts affects size and performance.

The Virtual Keyboard

On most devices, pressing on an input text field brings up the virtual keyboard. AIR for Android only uses the Android default alphabet keyboard.

Be aware of the space the keyboard occupies. The stage position is automatically adjusted to keep the text field visible. If the text field is toward the bottom, the application moves the stage up. To dismiss the virtual keyboard, the user usually needs to tap on the stage. Make sure you leave a noninteractive area for the user to tap on.

If you want to overwrite the default behavior, set the `softKeyboardBehavior` tag of the application descriptor to none.

```
<softKeyboardBehavior>none</softKeyboardBehavior>
```

To control how the application moves, set a listener on the softKeyboardActivating event, which is dispatched when the keyboard opens. Use the softKeyboardRect property of the stage, which contains the dimensions of the area covered by the keyboard:

```
import flash.events.SoftKeyboardEvent;
import flash.text.TextField;
import flash.text.TextFieldType;

var textField:TextField = new TextField();
textField.type = TextFieldType.INPUT;
textField.width = 400;
textField.height = 200;
addChild(textField);

textField.addEventListener
    (SoftKeyboardEvent.SOFT_KEYBOARD_ACTIVATE, onKeyboard);
textField.addEventListener
    (SoftKeyboardEvent.SOFT_KEYBOARD_DEACTIVATE, onKeyboard);

function onKeyboard(event:SoftKeyboardEvent):void {
trace(stage.softKeybardRect.y);
trace(stage.softKeybardRect);
}
```

For fullscreen mode, use the keyboard dimensions as an approximation. The values returned may not be perfectly exact.

Fonts

Try to use device fonts for input text fields, as they render faster than embedded fonts. The Font Embedding dialog box monitor in Flash Professional CS5 and later monitors font usage in your application. You can also generate a size report that lists all the assets, including fonts. Only include the font families you use.

The choice of Android font families is limited but well targeted to the Android style. Figure 18-1 shows the Droid Serif font, created by Steve Matteson of Ascender Corporation.

With AIR 2.6 and up, support is provided for scrolling text; text selection for cut, copy, and paste; and context menus.

Consider using an alternative to input text fields, such as already populated fields or plus and minus buttons for digits. The recommended font size is at least 14 pixels, so that text is readable on high-density devices.

The Flash Text Engine

An application with impeccable typography stands out. The Text Layout Framework (TLF) provides the tooling for text quality but is heavy and not yet ready for mobile.

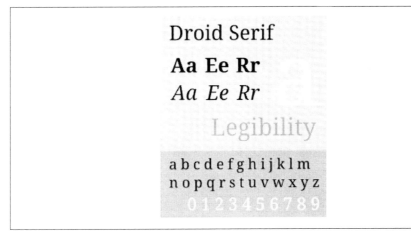

Figure 18-1. The Droid Serif font

The Flash Text Engine (FTE) is the low-level API below the TLF. It is light and renders exquisite script with great precision. It is not as immediately accessible as other tools, however. For simplicity, use it for read-only text and keep the classic `TextField` object for input text if needed.

Here is a "Hello world" example:

```
import flash.text.engine.*;

var fd:FontDescription = new FontDescription();
var ef:ElementFormat = new ElementFormat(fd);
var te:TextElement = new TextElement("Hello world", ef);
var tb:TextBlock = new TextBlock();
tb.content = te;
var tl:TextLine = tb.createTextLine(null, 200);
addChild(tl);
```

`FontDescription` is for the font family. `ElementFormat` is for styling and layout. `TextElement` is for the content as text and inline graphic. `TextBlock` is the *Factory* to create one block of text. Finally, `TextLine` is the display object for a single line of text. Figure 18-2 depicts the classes needed to create text using the Flash Text Engine.

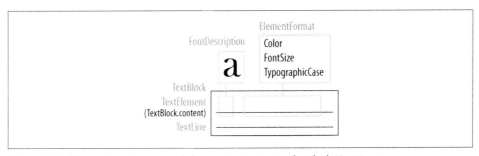

Figure 18-2. The various classes needed to create text using the Flash Text Engine

This is a lot of classes for such a simple example, but it introduces the benefit of using this engine. It gives you access to a vast range of typographic settings, bidirectional layout, and support for most scripts. Please refer to the article I wrote on FTE to learn more (see *http://www.developria.com/2009/03/flash-text-engine.html*).

Optimizing Art

If you or your designer uses Flash Professional as a paint tool, optimize the shapes under Modify→Shape→Optimize. Then, convert strokes to fill.

Use a utility to optimize PNG and JPEG formats. Both PNG Optimizer (*http://www .pngoptimizer.com/*) and ImageOptim (*http://imageoptim.pornel.net/*) are free and will reduce the file size of your images.

If you have several vectors that are not moving, are grouped, or are on top of each other, convert them to a single bitmap. Crop the alpha channel of your bitmap carefully. Remove the alpha channel completely on PNGs if you don't need it. In Photoshop, use the File→Save for Web & Devices option instead of File→Save As. Save your image as PNG-8.

Never put an image on top of a video, especially if it has an alpha channel. As noted in Chapter 14 in "Rendering, or How Things Are Drawn to the Screen" on page 188, alpha information needs to be computed along with other elements on the fly.

To monitor the rendering process, make the redraw regions visible. They are the dirty regions that are processed and rendered. In AIR, you do not have access to the context menu, but you can show the regions in code and choose the color:

```
flash.profiler.showRedrawRegions(true, 0xFF0000);
```

Bitmap Size and Mip Mapping

The dimension of your bitmap does matter for *downscaling* bitmaps. Downscaling is the process of creating smaller and larger dimensions of a bitmap in place of the original art to improve scaling images. This process is done directly from the original to the desired size. It was precomputed in previous versions of Flash Player.

Both width and height values must be an even number. A perfect bitmap is one with dimensions that are a power of two, but it is enough if the dimensions are divisible by eight. The following numbers demonstrate downscaling a bitmap for the resolution of a Nexus One and a Samsung Galaxy Tab. The mip levels, scaling values reduced in half, work out perfectly:

```
800x480 > 400x240 > 200x120 > 100x60
1024x600 > 512x300 > 256x150 > 128x75
```

A bitmap at 1,000 by 200 would reduce to three mip levels, but a bitmap at 998 by 200 only reduces to one level.

The point to take away from this is that you should create assets that fit within these dimensions.

Vector Graphics at Runtime

Vector graphics scale well, and are therefore reusable and reduce production time, but they render slowly.

Scaling

Create your vector art at medium size and resize it on the fly as needed. This is a great technique for multiple-screen deployment. Let's assume your original art was created for an 800×480 device and the application is detecting a tablet at 1,024×600, resulting in a scale difference of about 30%. Let's scale up the art:

```
var dpi:int = Capabilities.screenDPI;
var screenX:int = Capabilities.screenResolutionX;
var screenY:int = Capabilities.screenResolutionY;
var diagonal:Number = Math.sqrt((screenX*screenX)+(screenY*screenY))/dpi;

// if diagonal is higher than 6, we will assume it is a tablet
if (diagonal >= 6) {
    myVector.scaleX = myVector.scaleY = 1.30;
}
```

cacheAsBitmap

If the object's only transformation is along the axes, use `cacheAsBitmap`:

```
myVector.cacheAsBitmap = true;

this.addEventListener(Event.ENTER_FRAME, moveArt);
function moveArt(event:Event):void {
    myVector.x += 1;
}
```

cacheAsBitmapMatrix

To rotate, scale, or alpha the object, use `cacheAsBitmapMatrix` along with `cacheAsBit map`: Both are required for the caching to work.

```
import flash.geom.Matrix;

myVector.cacheAsBitmap();
myVector.cacheAsBitmapMatrix = new Matrix();
this.addEventListener(Event.ENTER_FRAME, onMoveArt);

function onMoveArt(event:Event):void {
    myVector.x += 1;
```

```
    myVector.rotation += 1;
}
```

Vector to Bitmap

If the object is animated with filters or if multiple vector assets need to be composited, draw them into a bitmap. Here, if the device is a tablet (as determined by the diagonal size), we scale the art and apply a drop shadow filter. We then draw the vector art into a bitmap.

```
import flash.display.Bitmap;
import flash.display.BitmapData;
import flash.filters.DropShadowFilter;

if (diagonal >= 6) {
    myVector.scaleX = myVector.scaleY = 1.30;
}

var shadow:DropShadowFilter = new DropShadowFilter();
shadow.distance = 5;
shadow.angle = 35;
myVector.filters = [shadow];

var bitmapData:BitmapData = new BitmapData(myVector.width, myVector.height);
bitmapData.draw(vector);
var bitmap:Bitmap = new Bitmap(bitmapData);
```

Compositing Vector Graphics

A common use case for vector graphics is the creation of a customized avatar in a virtual world. Discrete parts, such as hair, shirt, and shoes, are separate assets. They can be changed and saved at runtime. The avatar, however, animates best as a whole, so once the avatar information is collected and all the discrete parts are loaded, they can be composited as one single object.

Use the `BitmapData.draw` method to render vector graphics into a bitmap. The first parameter, the only one required, is the source, bitmap, or vector. The following parameters are a `Matrix`, a `ColorTransform`, a blend mode, a `Rectangle`, and smoothing (only for the `BitmapData` source).

In this example, we are using the `Matrix` to scale the assets down to half their original size. Define the dimension of the `BitmapData` object used to store the pixels of the assets loaded and a `Matrix`:

```
import flash.display.BitmapData;
import flash.geom.Matrix;

const CELL_WIDTH:int = 50;
const CELL_HEIGHT:int = 100;
var composite:BitmapData = new BitmapData(CELL_WIDTH, CELL_HEIGHT, true, 0);
var matrix:Matrix = new Matrix(0.50, 0, 0, 0.50, 0, 0);
```

Create a Vector to store the path of the assets. The art must be loaded in the order it will be composited, as you would with layers in Flash or Photoshop:

```
var assets:Vector.<String> = new Vector.<String>;
assets[0] = PATH_SKIN_ASSET;
assets[1] = PATH_HAIR_ASSET;
assets[2] = PATH_SHIRT_ASSET;
var counter:int = 0;
```

Load one image at a time using a Loader object. A counter variable is used to traverse the Vector and load all the assets. Every time one is available in AIR, it is converted to a bitmap and added to BitmapData. Note that the draw method has the alpha argument set to true to preserve the area of the vector without pixels so that it remains transparent:

```
import flash.display.Loader;
import flash.net.URLRequest;
import flash.events.Event;

var loader:Loader = new Loader();
loader loader.contentLoaderInfo.addEventListener(Event.COMPLETE, onLoaded);
loading();

function loading():void {
    loader.load(new URLRequest(assets[counter]));
}

function onLoaded(event:Event):void {
    composite.draw(event.target.content, matrix);
    counter++;
    if (counter < assets.length) {
        loading();
    } else {
        loader.contentLoaderInfo.removeEventListener(
            Event.COMPLETE, onLoaded);
        display();
    }
}
```

Once all the assets are loaded and composited, create a Bitmap to render the image to the screen:

```
import flash.display.Bitmap;

function display():void {
    var bitmap:Bitmap = new Bitmap(composite);
    addChild(bitmap);
}
```

MovieClip with Multiple Frames

Art production may require the use of a movie clip with multiple frames. This is a familiar workflow for many designers while also having the flexibility of being resizable.

Converting a `MovieClip` with vector art to a bitmap for better rendering is a good practice, but neither `cacheAsBitmap` nor `cacheAsBitmapMatrix` works for a `MovieClip` with multiple frames. If you cache the art on the first frame, as the play head moves, the old bitmap is discarded and the new frame needs to be rasterized. This is the case even if the animation is just a rotation or a position transformation.

GPU rendering is not the technique to use for such a case. Instead, load your `Movie Clip` without adding it to the display list.

This time, we need to load a single *.swf* file and traverse its timeline to copy each frame. Load the external *.swf* file comprising 10 frames:

```
var loader:Loader = new Loader();
loader.contentLoaderInfo.addEventListener(Event.COMPLETE, onLoadComplete);
loader.load(new URLRequest(PATH_TO_SWF));
```

Create a rectangle for the cell at a predefined size. Traverse the `MovieClip`, and use `draw`, as before, to copy the vector into a bitmap. Then use `copyPixels` to add the new pixels into another `BitmapData` that is the width of the total number of frames:

```
function onLoadComplete(event:Event):void {
    event.target.removeEventListener(Event.COMPLETE, onLoaded);

    var mc:MovieClip = event.target.content as MovieClip;
    var totalWidth:int = mc.totalFrames*CELL_WIDTH;
    var complete:BitmapData =
        new BitmapData(totalWidth, CELL_HEIGHT, true, 0);
    var rectangle:Rectangle = new Rectangle(0, 0, CELL_WIDTH, CELL_HEIGHT);

    var bounds:int = mc.totalFrames;
    for (var i:int = 0; i < bounds; i++) {
        mc.gotoAndStop(i+1);
        var frame:BitmapData =
            new BitmapData(CELL_WIDTH, CELL_HEIGHT, true, 0);
        frame.draw(mc, scaleMatrix);
        complete.copyPixels(image, rectangle, new Point(i*CELL_WIDTH, 0));
    }

    frame.dispose();
    loader.unloadAndStop(mc);
    mc = null;
```

Display the large `BitmapData` into a `Bitmap` to render it to the screen:

```
var bitmap:Bitmap = new Bitmap(complete);
bitmap.smoothing = true;
addChild(bitmap);
```

Use the reverse process to display a single frame. Here we show the third frame:

```
var cellBitmap:BitmapData = new BitmapData(CELL_WIDTH, CELL_HEIGHT, true, 0);
var rectangle:Rectangle =
        new Rectangle(CELL_WIDTH*3, 0, CELL_WIDTH+CELL_WIDTH*3, CELL_HEIGHT);
cellBitmap.copyPixels(complete, rectangle, new Point(0, 0));
```

```
    var bitmap:Bitmap = new Bitmap(cellBitmap);
    addChild(bitmap);
```

Next we will cover creating an animation from a sprite sheet bitmap.

Sprite Sheet and Blitting

Xerox PARC first created the *bit-block* transfer, *Bit BLIT* for short, for the Smalltalk system in 1975. *Blitting* is a computer graphics operation. It takes at least one bitmap and combines it with another. It has been a standard technique used since the beginning of the digital gaming industry.

Let's see how we can use this technology for our purposes.

Blitting

A *sprite sheet*, also called a *tile sheet animation*, is a collection of images arranged into a single image. Traditionally, each sprite represents one frame of an animation.

In AIR, especially on mobile devices, the sprite sheet has benefits beyond animation. It can be used for ease of production and to load a single large image rather than monitoring many small loading processes. Also, bitmap manipulation is very quick. Figure 18-3 shows a sprite sheet for a walk cycle.

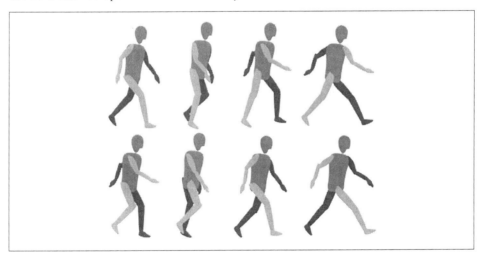

Figure 18-3. A sprite sheet for a walk cycle

The motion is created in code to copy various areas of the image to the screen. All images have the same predictable repetitive width and height, so copying a rectangular region can be automated. Use measurement with integers in powers of two for faster calculation. Verify that the element that is animating is in the same relative position throughout, preferably from the upper left corner or the baseline.

Use the `BitmapData.copyPixels` method to copy a defined area. Required parameters are the source bitmap, a rectangle, and a destination point. The method copies a rectangular area for a source image to a destination area of the same size.

Let's import the graphics of the walking man shown in Figure 18-3 as a PNG image:

```
var complete:BitmapData;
var walkIndex:int = 0;
const TOTAL:int = 8;

var loader:Loader = new Loader();
loader loader.contentLoaderInfo.addEventListener(Event.COMPLETE, onLoaded);
loader.load(new URLRequest("/assets/walkingMan.png"));

function onLoaded(event:Event):void {
    event.target.removeEventListener(Event.COMPLETE, onLoaded);
    complete = event.target.content.bitmapData;
}
```

Add an `ENTER_FRAME` event listener. Change the definition of the rectangle to copy a different segment of the original bitmap, and push these pixels into the `BitmapData` called `cell`. Wrap it into a `Bitmap` to render it to the screen:

```
var cell:BitmapData = new BitmapData(CELL_WIDTH, CELL_HEIGHT, true, 0);
stage.addEventListener(Event.ENTER_FRAME, walk);

function walk(event:Event):void {
    var rectangle:Rectangle = new Rectangle(
                        CELL_WIDTH*walkIndex, 0,
                        CELL_WIDTH+CELL_WIDTH*walkIndex, CELL_HEIGHT);
    cell.copyPixels(complete, rectangle, new Point(0, 0));
    var bitmap:Bitmap = new Bitmap(cellBitmap);
    addChild(bitmap);

    walkIndex++;
    if (walkIndex == TOTAL) {
        walkIndex = 0;
    }
}
```

Some open source AIR applications are available to ease the process of creating sprite sheets. Sprite Sheet Maker, by Mike Jones, lets you import separate PNGs, reorganize them as needed, and export them as the final sprite sheet (see *http://blog.flashgen.com/ 2010/12/21/sprite-sheet-maker-preview/*). SWFSheet, by Keith Peters, imports an *.swf* file and converts it to a sprite sheet (see *http://www.bit-101.com/blog/?p=2939*). Keith takes advantage of Flash as an animation tool and shows the *.swf* running. The number of frames captured can be adjusted, as well as the frame area and the sprite dimension before exporting the final PNG.

Custom Cursor

If appropriate for your application, adding a custom cursor gives an extra professional polish to your UI.

In the past, you needed to hide the mouse and drag around a sprite, which had negative performance effects. Now you have access to native mouse cursors through the operating system cursor mechanism.

Use the new MouseCursorData class and make its data property a Vector of one or several bitmapData objects. For multiple bitmapData objects, the cursor animates at its own frame rate (if you provide it). The maximum dimension is 32×32. Define its hotSpot property if you only want a part of the cursor to be active.

Refer to the documentation for an example, at *http://help.adobe.com/en_US/FlashPlat form/reference/actionscript/3/flash/ui/MouseCursorData.html*.

Asynchronous Bitmap Decoding

An improvement to AIR 2.6 allows the decoding of bitmaps on a separate thread. To take advantage of this, use the LoaderContext class as follows:

```
import flash.system.LoaderContext;
import flash.display.Loader;

var lc:LoaderContext = new LoaderContext();
lc.imageDecodingPolicy = ImageDecodingPolicy.ON_LOAD;
var loader:Loader = new Loader();
loader.load(new URLRequest("image.jpg", lc);
```

This improvement also works with Loader.loadBytes().

The asynchronous decoding allows animations to play smoother. For instance, while you have an animation running, you can now load another graphic in the background without concern that the process will temporary interrupt the animation.

Caching Assets

If your application uses dynamic downloaded assets, similar to a Facebook application displaying your contacts picture, consider caching the assets on your device. Doing so will prevent the overhead of a download every time your application initializes.

Save this technique for small files so that you don't abuse the user's storage capacity.

Here, we are looking at the name of the file as part of a url. Check if the file already exists on the SD card. If it does, load it locally. If it does not, get the file from a remote server and save it to the device:

```
import flash.display.Loader;
import flash.net.URLRequest;
import flash.filesystem.File;


import flash.filesystem.FileStream;
import flash.filesystem.FileMode;
import flash.net.URLLoader;
import flash.net.URLLoaderDataFormat;

var stream:FileStream;
var fileName:String;
var file:File;
var urlLoader:URLLoader;

var url:String = "http://www.v-ro.com/cat.jpeg";
fileName = new String(url).split("/").pop(); // cat.jpeg
file = File.applicationStorageDirectory.resolvePath(fileName);

if (file.exists) {
    var loader:Loader = new Loader();
    loader.contentLoaderInfo.addEventListener(Event.COMPLETE, onLocal);
    loader.load(new URLRequest(file.url));
} else {
    urlLoader = new urlLoader ();
    urlLoader.dataFormat = URLLoaderDataFormat.BINARY;
    loader.addEventListener(Event.COMPLETE, onRemote);
    loader.load(new URLRequest(url));
}

function onLocal(event:Event):void {
    event.currentTarget.removeEventListener(Event.Complete, onLocal);
    addChild(event.currentTarget.content);
}

function onRemote(event:Event):void {
    event.target.removeEventListener(Event.COMPLETE, onRemote);
    var byteArray:ByteArray = event.target.data as ByteArray;
    stream.open(file, FileMode.WRITE);
    stream.writeBytes(data, 0, data.length);
    stream.close();

    var loader:Loader = new Loader();
    loader.loadBytes(byteArray);
    addChild(loader);
}
```

Components

If you use the Flex framework, try the Tour de Flex application (see Figure 18-4). It is a good starting point for examples using components to develop AIR for Android applications. You can get it from the Android Market.

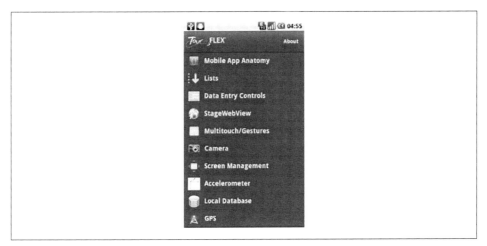

Figure 18-4. The Tour de Flex application

Flash Builder was initially not suited for mobile development. Components, such as the DataGrid or the Chart, were too complex and too large for the memory footprint.

Some work has been done from the ground up to optimize the framework with Flex Hero. Some components were rewritten to be mobile-optimized. The mobile theme, used when the MobileApplication tag is detected, has larger, touch-friendly controls, including for scroll bars.

The ViewNavigator helps in the development and management of screens and offers transition animations. The TabNavigator is used for subnavigation. The ActionBar is used for global navigation and messaging. We will come back to this in more detail in Chapter 19.

Using ActionScript and bitmaps is recommended over MXML and FXG at runtime.

If you like the convenience of components but prefer pure ActionScript development, Keith Peters has created lightweight and easy-to-use components (see *http://www.min imalcomps.com/* and *http://www.bit-101.com/blog/?p=2979*).

Conclusion

These are just some of the areas to look at to best design and develop your application.

Mobile devices have their own form factor and real estate, and are therefore unique. Treat them as special citizens and their applications as a new, upcoming niche. Here are some resources to reference for good graphic and interaction design:

* *http://developer.apple.com/library/ios/#documentation/UserExperience/Concep tual/MobileHIG/Introduction/Introduction.html*
* *http://www.androidpatterns.com*

CHAPTER 19

Best Practices for Development

Make everything as simple as possible,
but not simpler.

—Albert Einstein

Best practices and optimization are popular topics, especially with today's focus on mobile development. Rather than trying to cover everything in this chapter, I will point you to some good resources and limit the text to a few key points and some less frequently discussed topics.

If you are reading this, you are already a committed developer who spends time doing research. Understanding the mechanics of the AIR runtime and the ActionScript APIs will empower you as a coder both in quality and in speed, not to mention in marketability in the workplace and in popularity among your peers.

Resources on Optimization

In a document titled "Application Design Goals," Google provides objectives with three areas of focus: performance, responsiveness, and seamlessness. It also provides a short list of recommendations: don't drop data, don't interrupt the user, design your UI to work with multiple screen resolutions, assume the network is slow, don't assume the touchscreen or keyboard exists (i.e., write logic to detect them), and conserve the device's battery. Even though this document is targeted at Android development, it is insightful to ActionScript developers as well. Read it at *http://developer.android.com/guide/practices/design/index.html*.

Adobe offers a white paper titled "Optimizing Performance for the Flash Platform" with a special focus on mobile. It is a 90-page document with practical topics and code snippets. You can read it as a PDF document or online, at *http://help.adobe.com/en_US/as3/mobile/index.html*.

For ongoing articles and announcements, visit the Adobe AIR Developer Center, at *http://www.adobe.com/devnet/air.html*.

Where to Find Help

You can get help and information from a variety of areas.

Documentation

Launch the language reference help from within your editor for language-specific information. I do not recommend using the search capability at *http://help.adobe.com* directly, as it directs you to the Adobe Support page, which is not specific enough for our purposes.

Type in a class name in the IDE text editor, and then select it. In Flash Professional, click the question mark on the top right. In Flash Builder, press Shift-F2. As shown in Figure 19-1, the information is presented in ASDoc style as HTML frames. The upper left frame lists packages, language elements, and appendixes. The lower left frame lists classes in the package in context. The right frame displays the class you are searching for. The content comprises an introductory paragraph and the list of properties, methods, and events.

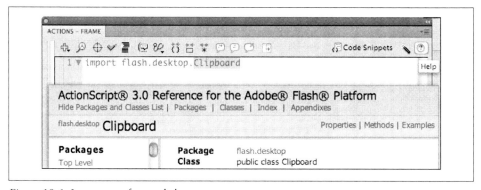

Figure 19-1. Language reference help

The Internet

Use the Google search engine to find undocumented material starting with "as3" or "AIR", especially now that you know the syntax of the class or API you are interested in. The Flash community is vibrant and posts solutions and examples, often before Adobe makes them official.

Read blogs for up-to-date information and code snippets. Visit websites for in-depth articles and application examples.

The Community

Post questions on the Adobe forums. This is a good place to ask beginner- to intermediate-level questions and gain access to the Adobe engineering team.

Attend conferences. Many sessions cover the latest in technology. In fact, it is often the arena chosen by software companies to make announcements and give sneak peeks.

Be active. Share your work. If you demonstrate interest and knowledge, you may be invited to be part of the prerelease lists. This will put you in the privileged position of testing and making suggestions on beta products. Be aware of Adobe bugs so that you can find workarounds for them, and if you witness new bugs, report them at *http://bugs .adobe.com/*.

Find a user group in your area. If one does not exist, create it.

How Does It Run?

Flash is a frame-based system. Knowing how it runs is fundamental to understanding performance issues.

The Concept of Frame

The *concept of frame* refers to a block of time more than traversing a frame on the traditional timeline, especially now that few developers use the timeline or put code on frames.

Code execution happens first, in the form of events and code; then the screen is rendered, and so on. Even if no ActionScript code needs to be executed, nor `displayOb ject` transformed, the process always happens.

The *elastic racetrack termination* encapsulates this notion of a loop process with potential elasticity and irregularity if the process takes longer than expected. The expectation is determined by the frame rate as you defined it. At 24 frames per second, the default rate on mobile devices, a frame has 1/24 of a second to run code and render the screen.

A high frame rate carries out more operations, but this does not imply better performance on mobile devices if they are not able to keep up, and it drains the battery. A lower but consistent frame rate guarantees smoother playback and a better user experience.

The four blocks starting from the left in Figure 19-2 and Figure 19-3 represent the analysis of events first and the execution of your code in response second.

The runtime never attempts to exceed the frame rate, or speed up if it is idle, but it may slow down if one of the two phases takes longer than expected. Some fluctuation is expected. But in the case of a consistently slow frame rate, or an erratic one, look for the bottleneck. In Figure 19-3, rendering slows down the frame rate.

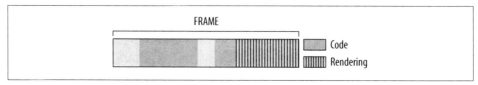

Figure 19-2. One frame in terms of code execution and rendering

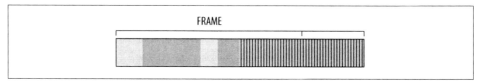

Figure 19-3. A slower frame rate due to rendering

We covered rendering at some length in Chapter 14, so we will now focus on code execution.

Calculating the frame rate

Here is some code you can use to calculate your frame rate. To get a relatively accurate frame rate, interact with your application as you expect your audience to. Test it with other native processes running in the background:

```
import flash.utils.Timer;
import flash.events.Event;

var frames:int = 0;
var time:Number = new Date().time;
var timer:Timer = new Timer(1000);
timer.addEventListener(TimerEvent.TIMER, onTimer);
timer.start();
this.addEventListener(Event.ENTER_FRAME, onEnterFrame);

function onEnterFrame(event:Event):void {
    frames++;
}

function onTimer(event:TimerEvent):void {
    var now:Date = new Date();
    var lapse:int = now.time - time;
    trace("FPS: " + frames*1000/lapse);

    time = now.time;
    frames = 0;
}
```

The section "Diagnostics Tools" on page 277 discusses other methods.

Improving performance

Change your application frame rate if it is idle or goes to the background. Revisit Chapter 6 for more on this topic.

Because the ActionScript Virtual Machine handles code execution and rendering on a single thread, only one thing can happen at a time. This is why a processor-intensive operation blocks the renderer until completion or a complex rendering may delay the next code execution.

Use asynchronous events, which use a different thread, whenever possible. The operation may take a little bit longer but will resolve some of the bottlenecks. We already discussed asynchronous bitmap decoding in Chapter 18.

SQLite operation can be done in synchronous or asynchronous mode. Only one mode can be used at a time:

```
SQLConnection.openAsync();

SQLConnection.open();
```

Operations on the filesystem can also be asynchronous. Use such operations for fairly large files:

```
fileStream.openAsync(file, FileMode.READ);

fileStream.open(file, FileMode.READ);
```

If your code performs long operations, you can restructure it to execute in chunks instead of all at once.

Rendering related to sensors should be done on `EnterFrame`, not when the sensor updates, which can be more frequent than the refresh rate and can be irregular. If you use `EnterFrame`, create a single listener to manage all your objects.

Never use the `updateAfterEvent` function. It forces rendering for faster animation. On mobile devices, it will reduce your frame rate. If you need extremely high-speed animation, AIR is not the right tool for the job.

Setting the stage quality to low, or toggling settings, is a good option for faster rendering:

```
stage.quality = StageQuality.LOW;
stage.quality = StageQuality.HIGH;
```

Memory

Let's say it one more time: the memory on mobile devices is limited. If you exceed it, Android will terminate your application.

Creating Objects

Choose the appropriate object. For instance, use a `Sprite` instead of a `MovieClip` if you don't need multiple frames. Use a `Vector`, which is more efficient than an `Array`, to store objects. Call the `getSize()` function to determine the memory footprint for a particular data type.

Allocating new blocks of memory is costly. Create your objects at an idle time, ideally when your application first initializes, and reuse them throughout your application.

Object pooling creates a pool to store objects and re-use them over time. In this example, we pop an object, or create one if none exists, and then push it back when done until the next use:

```
import flash.display.Sprite;

var pool:Vector.<Sprite>();

// get a new Sprite
var sprite:Sprite = popSprite();
sprite.init(); // set properties as needed
addChild(sprite);

function popSprite():Sprite {
    var sprite:Sprite;
    if (pool.length > 0) {
        sprite = pool.pop();    } else {
        sprite = new Sprite();
    }
    return sprite;
}
```

When the object is no longer needed, return it:

```
removeChild(sprite);
pushSprite(sprite);

function pushSprite(sprite:Sprite):void {
    pool.push(sprite);
}
```

This approach is organic. The application creates objects as needed until it reaches a sufficient quantity to recycle them. Another method is to create all the objects initially, up to a maximum amount.

Removing Objects

Memory is dynamic. As objects are deleted, memory is released via a process called garbage collection.

Only primitive types, such as `String`, `Number`, and `Boolean`, are used directly. All other types are used using a reference, which must be removed to clear them from memory. This includes removing a child from a `displayList`, splicing an `Array` array or a `Vec` tor, stopping and deleting a Timer, removing an EventListener, or nulling a reference from another object.

Once this is all done, set the object to null to help the garbage collector work more quickly.

Use the disposeXML method for an XML object. It traverses the tree and sets all pointers between parents and children to null to make the object available for immediate garbage collection:

```
import flash.system.System;

function onXMLLoaded(event:Event):void {
    var xml:XML = event.target.data;
    // sudo code to parse and store data
    var dataStorage = parseXML(XML);
    System.disposeXML(xml);
    xml = null;
}
```

Use the dispose method for a BitmapData object:

```
var bitmapData:BitmapData = new BitmapData(480, 800);
bitmapData.dispose();
bitmapData = null;
```

One of the principal reasons for memory leaks is lingering event listeners. A common recommendation today is to set weak event listeners as shown in the code below. Weak references are not counted by the garbage collector as references, a topic we will cover next:

```
var sprite:Sprite = new Sprite();

// strongly referenced listeners
sprite.addEventListener(MouseEvent.CLICK, onClick);

// weakly referenced listeners
// eventName, listener, capturePhase, priority, useWeakReference
sprite.addEventListener(MouseEvent.CLICK, onClick, false, 1, true);
```

Use this approach with caution. Too many developers tend to rely on it instead of removing listeners in code. As a responsible coder, you should be diligent about doing the proper housekeeping.

If your code is large, or difficult to maintain, you can create an array to store listeners or a mechanic to automate their removal.

Create a destroy method to use in your classes to remove listeners and objects. To enforce the practice, use an IDestroy interface in which all classes need to have the destroy method but can implement it according to their individual needs:

```
// interface
public interface IDestroy {
    function destroy():void;
}
```

```
// class A
public class ClassA implements IDestroy {
    public function ClassA() {
    }
    public function destroy():void {
        // remove listeners
        // clear display list
        while (numChildren > 0) {
            removeChildAt(0);
        }
    }
}

// class B
public class ClassB implements IDestroy {
    public function ClassB() {
    }
    public function destroy(event:):void {
        // empty arrays
        // set variables to null
        // call garbage collection
        System.gc();
    }
}
```

If one of your classes implements the interface but erroneously does not have a destroy method, you will see the following error:

```
Interface method destroy in namespace com:IDestroy not implemented by class
com.ClassC
```

Garbage Collection

Garbage collection is an automatic mechanism that deallocates the memory used by objects when they are no longer referenced in the application. It is important because it releases memory for future use, and particularly so for mobile devices with limited memory.

The garbage collector is not predictable, but you can sometimes monitor it by watching your memory consumption using the System class. totalMemory refers to the portion of memory allocated to your code. privateMemory is the entire memory consumption of the application. All functions return bytes; divide by 1,024 to obtain kilobytes:

```
import flash.system.System;

System.privateMemory/1024;

System.totalMemory/1024;
System.totalMemoryNumber/1024 // returned as NUMBER for greater precision
System.freeMemory/1024; // memory unused
```

You can call the garbage collector directly in AIR, but it requires significant memory and can result in a noticeable slowdown in the application. For this reason, reuse objects or clean them up quickly and frequently as described earlier:

```
System.gc();
```

The AIR runtime uses two different methods for best results.

Reference count keeps track of the object and marks it for deletion when it has a value of zero if it has no reference:

```
var a:Object = new Object(); count is 1 for a;
var b:Object = a;            2 for b;
a = null;                    1 for a;
b = null;                    0 for b;
```

This method fails when two objects reference each another:

```
var a:Object = new Object();   is 1 for a;
var b:Object = new Object();   is 1 for b;
a.b = b;                       2 for b;
b.a = a;                       2 for a;
a = null;                      1 for a;
b = null;                      1 for b;
```

Mark sweeping handles this issue in a more accurate way but takes longer and does not happen as often. It traverses the entire application tree and marks an object that has a reference, marks its children, and so on, recursively. Objects that are not marked can be assumed to be eligible for collection.

In AIR for Android, the garbage collector is more iterative and objects are collected more frequently because memory is in short supply. For this reason, be attentive to making sensors and objects with listener member variables, not local variables.

Events

EventDispatcher is the base class for all objects that can be a target for events. Many native classes inherit from this class with their own appropriate events:

```
import flash.display.Sprite;
import flash.events.MouseEvent;

// this draws a button listening to a mouse event
var sprite:Sprite = new Sprite();
sprite.addEventListener(MouseEvent.CLICK, onClick);


import flash.utils.Timer;
import flash.events.TimerEvent;

// this creates a timer listening to a timer event
var timer:Timer = new Timer(1000);
timer.addEventListener(TimerEvent.TIMER , onTimer);
timer.start();
```

`event.target` is the object associated with the listening function, or its scope:

```
function onClick(event:MouseEvent):void {
    trace(event.target); // Sprite
}

function onTimer(event:TimerEvent):void {
    trace(event.target); // Timer
}
```

The listener object, also known as the event handler, is called when the event happens (the `onClick` or `onTimer` functions in the preceding example). It takes a single event instance as a parameter.

The dispatcher, the mechanism that monitors the event, saves a reference of the listener to call back when an event occurs, and its target, in a queue.

You must use `removeEventListener` to remove these references from memory. Removing the target will not do it:

```
sprite.removeEventListener(MouseEvent.CLICK, onClick);
timer.removeEventListener(TimerEvent.TIMER , onTimer);
```

Event Propagation

For display objects, an event starts from the root parent, travels down the tree to the object that is registered, and travels back up.

Event propagation has three phases. The *capturing* phase occurs when the propagated event, after being received by the system, starts its search from the root parent. The *targeting* phase occurs when the event reaches the object registered for it. The *bubbling* phase is the event following the path in reverse.

Note that the event only needs to traverse until it finds the object that is registered. Regardless, you can see how keeping your `displayList` shallow would have a significant impact on performance.

If you want to stop the event during its journey, you can use the following methods. The latter method prevents other remaining event listeners from executing. This is a good technique for optimizing your mobile application:

```
function eventVisiting(event:MouseEvent):void {
    if (event.target) {
        event.stopPropagation();
        // OR
        event.stopImmediatePropagation();
    }
}
```

To prevent objects from being targeted, you can use:

```
someObject.mouseEnabled = false;
someParent.mouseChildren = false;
```

Events for objects that are not on the `displayList` flow directly to the target.

One Listener for Many Children

Let's demonstrate the benefit of the event model. Imagine that you have many objects that need to transform in response to a mouse event. In this example, their scale changes upon a click.

Create the objects:

```
import flash.display.Sprite;

var sw:int = stage.stageWidth;
var sh:int = stage.stageHeight;

for (var i:int = 0; i < 20; i++) {
    var temp:Sprite = createSprite();
}

function createSprite():Sprite {
    var temp:Sprite = new Sprite();
    var g:Graphics = temp.graphics;
    g.beginFill(0x3399FF, 1);
    g.drawRect(0, 0, 100, 75);
    g.endFill();
    temp.x = Math.random()*sw;
    temp.y = Math.random()*sh;
}
```

Put them in a container instead of adding them to the stage:

```
var container:Sprite = new Sprite;
addChild(container);

for (var i:int = 0; i < 20; i++) {
    var temp:Sprite = createSprite();
    addChild(temp);
}
```

Add a single listener to the container instead of creating a listener for each object:

```
import flash.events.MouseEvent;

var objectClicked:Sprite;

container.addEventListener(MouseEvent.CLICK, onObjectClick, false);

function onObjectClick(event:MouseEvent):void {
    event.stopPropagation();
    objectClicked = event.target as Sprite;
    objectClicked.scaleX = objectClicked.scaleY = Math.random();
}
```

Generic and Custom Events

In some situations, you may need to send an event that is not built in. In such cases, make your class a subclass of the EventDispatcher or create a member variable as an EventDispatcher.

In this example, we load an external opening animation. When it reaches its last frame, we are notified so that we can unload it and continue with the application.

Add an EventListener and use dispatchEvent to trigger the event:

```
package {

    public class myClass extends EventDispatcher {
        public function myClass() {
            loadOpening();
        }

        function loadOpening():void {
            // load a swf with a timeline animation
            background.addEventListener("OpeningDone", removeBackground);
        }

        function removeBackground(event:Event):void {
            removeChild(background);
        }
    }
}
```

The code on the last frame of the opening *.swf* is:

```
stop();
dispatchEvent(new Event("OpeningDone"));
```

In the current event model, the listener function only receives one parameter: the event. If you want to pass additional parameters, you need to write your own custom class that inherits from the Event class. In the following example, the CustomEvent class has an event of type CONNECTED. It passes a parameter called **parameters** of type Object:

```
package {
    import flash.events.Event;

    final public class CustomEvent extends Event {
        public static const CONNECTED:String = "connected";
        public var parameters:Object;

        public function CustomEvent(type:String, parameters:Object = null) {
            // type, bubbles, cancelable
            super(type, true, true);
            this.parameters = parameters;
        }

        // this is needed if the event is re-dispatched
        public override function clone():Event {
            return new CustomEvent(this.type, this.parameters);
```

```
        }
      }
    }

    addEventListener(CustomEvent.CONNECTED, onConnected);
    dispatchEvent(new CustomEvent(CustomEvent.CONNECTED, {name:"somebody"}));
```

Diagnostics Tools

You can monitor performance and memory using diagnostics tools. Let's look at a few of them.

Hi-Res-Stats

The Hi-Res-Stats class, from mrdoob, calculates the frame rate, the time to render each frame, the amount of memory used per frame, and the maximum frame rate and memory consumption. Import the library and add a new instance of Stats as a displayObject. This is simple and convenient to use (see *https://github.com/bigfish*):

```
    import net.hires.debug.*;
    var myStats:Stats = new Stats();
    addChild(myStats);
```

Because it needs to be added to the displayList and draws its progress visually, as shown in Figure 19-4, this tool may impact rendering slightly, or get in the way of other graphics. A trick I use is to toggle its visibility when pressing the native search key on my device:

```
    import flash.ui.Keyboard;
    import flash.events.KeyboardEvent;

    stage.addEventListener(KeyboardEvent.KEY_DOWN, onKey);

    function onKey(e:KeyboardEvent):void {
        switch (e.keyCode) {
            case Keyboard.SEARCH:
                event.preventDefault();
                myStats.visible = !myStats.visible;
                break;
        }
    }
```

Figure 19-4. Hi-Res-Stats display

Flash Builder Profiler

The premium version of Flash Builder comes with Flash Builder Profiler, which watches live data and samples your application at small, regular intervals and over time. It is well documented. Figure 19-5 shows the Configure Profiler screen.

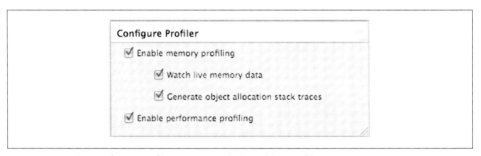

Figure 19-5. The Configure Profiler screen in Flash Builder Profiler

When "Enable memory profiling" is selected, the profiler collects memory data and memory usage. This is helpful for detecting memory leaks or the creation of large objects. It shows how many instances of an object are used.

When "Watch live memory data" is selected, the profiler displays memory usage data for live objects. When "Generate object allocation stack traces" is selected, every new creation of an object is recorded.

When "Enable performance profiling" is selected, the profiler collects stack trace data at time intervals. You can use this information to determine where your application spends its execution time. It shows how much time is spent on a function or a process.

You can also take memory snapshots and performance profiles on demand and compare them to previous ones. When doing so, the garbage collector is first run implicitly. Garbage collection can also be monitored.

Flash Preload Profiler

The Flash Preload Profiler is an open source multipurpose profiler created by Jean-Philippe Auclair. This tool features a simple interface and provides data regarding frame rate history and memory history, both current and maximum.

Other more unusual and helpful features are the overdraw graph, mouse listener graph, internal events graph, `displayObject` life cycle graph, full sampler recording dump, memory allocation/collection dump, function performance dump, and run on debug/release SWFs capability. More information on the Flash Preload Profiler is available at *http://jpauclair.net/2010/12/23/complete-flash-profiler-its-getting-serious/*.

Grant Skinner's PerformanceTest

Grant's `PerformanceTest` class is a tool for doing unit testing and formal test suites. Some of its core features are the ability to track time and memory usage for functions, and the ability to test rendering time for display objects. The class performs multiple iterations to get minimum, maximum, and deviation values, and it runs tests synchronously or queued asynchronously.

The class returns a `MethodTest` report as a text document or XML file. It can perform comparisons between different versions of Flash Player and different versions of the same code base. More information on this class is available at *http://gskinner.com/blog/archives/2010/02/performancetest.html*.

Native Tools

The Android Debug Bridge (ADB) `logcat` command grabs information from the device and dumps it onto a log screen via USB. A lot of information is provided. Some basic knowledge of the Android framework will help you understand it better. Refer to Chapter 3 for more information on native tools.

Conclusion

The ActionScript language is constantly evolving. With mobile development, the emphasis has been on performance, especially with optimization in the JIT, the garbage collection policy, and leveraging hardware.

Keep informed so that you can take advantage of it as it improves, along with (and independent of) the editing tools.

Index

We'd like to hear your suggestions for improving our indexes. Send email to *index@oreilly.com*.

About the Author

Véronique Brossier is Senior Flash Engineer at MTVNetworks and an adjunct professor at ITP/New York University. She has worked on many applications for the world of art and entertainment, including the Google IO 2010 Scheduler for Adobe, The New York Visitor Center and the 9/11 Memorial website for Local Projects, NickLab for R/Greenberg Associates, WebToons for Funny Garbage and Cartoon Network Online, the Hall of Biodiversity at the American Museum of National History, and many more.

Colophon

The animal on the cover of *Developing Android Applications for Adobe AIR* is the Royal Flycatcher (*Onychorhynchus coronatus*). This bird's most distinctive feature is a regal, fan-like crest, which gives the bird its scientific name (from the Latin *corōna*, for garland or crown). This colorful crest is usually tucked down against the bird's head, and only appears when it is courting or agitated. The Royal Flycatcher's habitat ranges from Mexico through Central and South America, and four localized subspecies are recognized.

Measuring 16-16.5 cm long, the Royal Flycatcher has mostly dull brown plumage, though there is slight variation across subspecies in the coloring of the rump and tail, which can range from bright cinnamon to a darker rust color. Its whitish throat is contrasted with a yellow underbelly. When visible, the bird's striking crest is colored scarlet (in the male) or bright yellow (in the female), highlighted with blue- and black-colored tips and spots.

As its name implies, the Royal Flycatcher appears to primarily eat aerial insects, such as dragonflies. Its natural habitat is humid and deciduous lowland forest, and so deforestation in Ecuador and Brazil has resulted in a vulnerable status for some Royal Flycatcher subspecies. While these birds may forage in a wide range of habitats, an intact, moist forest is necessary for survival during the breeding season. There is similarity in voice across subspecies, with each producing a clear *pree-o* call similar to that made by the jacamar and manakin, fellow tropical birds.

The cover image is from Johnson's *Natural History*. The cover font is Adobe ITC Garamond. The text font is Linotype Birka; the heading font is Adobe Myriad Condensed; and the code font is LucasFont's TheSansMonoCondensed.

Get even more for your money.

Join the O'Reilly Community, and register the O'Reilly books you own. It's free, and you'll get:

- $4.99 ebook upgrade offer
- 40% upgrade offer on O'Reilly print books
- Membership discounts on books and events
- Free lifetime updates to ebooks and videos
- Multiple ebook formats, DRM FREE
- Participation in the O'Reilly community
- Newsletters
- Account management
- 100% Satisfaction Guarantee

Signing up is easy:

1. Go to: oreilly.com/go/register
2. Create an O'Reilly login.
3. Provide your address.
4. Register your books.

Note: English-language books only

To order books online:
oreilly.com/store

For questions about products or an order:
orders@oreilly.com

To sign up to get topic-specific email announcements and/or news about upcoming books, conferences, special offers, and new technologies:
elists@oreilly.com

For technical questions about book content:
booktech@oreilly.com

To submit new book proposals to our editors:
proposals@oreilly.com

O'Reilly books are available in multiple DRM-free ebook formats. For more information:
oreilly.com/ebooks

O'REILLY®

Spreading the knowledge of innovators   oreilly.com

Buy this book and get access to the online edition for 45 days—for free!

Developing Android Applications with Adobe® AIR™

By Véronique Brossier
April 2011, $39.99
ISBN 9781449394820

With Safari Books Online, you can:

Access the contents of thousands of technology and business books

- Quickly search over 7000 books and certification guides
- Download whole books or chapters in PDF format, at no extra cost, to print or read on the go
- Copy and paste code
- Save up to 35% on O'Reilly print books
- **New!** Access mobile-friendly books directly from cell phones and mobile devices

Stay up-to-date on emerging topics before the books are published

- Get on-demand access to evolving manuscripts.
- Interact directly with authors of upcoming books

Explore thousands of hours of video on technology and design topics

- Learn from expert video tutorials
- Watch and replay recorded conference sessions

To try out Safari and the online edition of this book FREE for 45 days, go to **www.oreilly.com/go/safarienabled** and enter the coupon code JBLPHAA. To see the complete Safari Library, visit safari.oreilly.com.

O'REILLY®

Spreading the knowledge of innovators   safari.oreilly.com

CPSIA information can be obtained at www.ICGtesting.com
260527BV00001B/95-1500/P

9 781449 394820